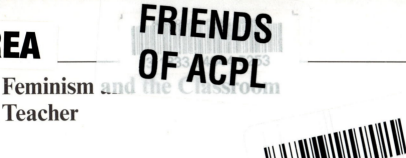

Feminism and the Classroom Teacher

How has feminism influenced contemporary educational practices? Is feminism relevant to today's teachers? *Feminism and the Classroom Teacher* undertakes a feminist analysis of the work and everyday realities of the schoolteacher, providing evidence that feminism is still relevant as a way of thinking about the social world and as a lived reality.

The authors draw on a wide range of material to illustrate the histories, relationships and possible futures of feminism and teaching. The book illustrates the different layers of teachers' work and examines the intellectual and practical contingencies of the classroom context through feminist analysis. The careers of teachers and the teaching career are considered, from initial recruitment through to educational leadership. International perspectives are reflected, providing insight into the development of feminist theory in different countries. Throughout the book there is a focus on the experiences of feminist teachers and the contradictory realities of feminist classrooms. The book concludes by addressing the feminist empirical project on teaching.

Providing a unique contribution to the literature in the area of gender and education, the authors' objective is to articulate the educational discourses of gender – how gender is constructed, performed and sustained through discourse and material practices. The overall aim of the book is to ascertain the extent to which women teachers specifically, and the feminist project more generally, have contributed to theoretical understandings and practical accomplishments of teaching.

Amanda Coffey lectures in Sociology and Research Methods at Cardiff University. Her research interests include gender and education, the sociology of the professions and young people and citizenship. She is the author of several books and has published in a range of journals and edited collections.

Sara Delamont is Reader in Sociology at Cardiff University. She has published extensively on social interaction in schools and classrooms, women's education, women intellectuals, and the anthropology of contemporary Europe.

Feminism and the Classroom Teacher
Research, Praxis, Pedagogy

Amanda Coffey and Sara Delamont

London and New York

First published 2000 by RoutledgeFalmer
11 New Fetter Lane, London EC4P 4EE

Simultaneously published in the USA and Canada
by RoutledgeFalmer, 29 West 35th Street,
New York, NY 10001

RoutledgeFalmer is an imprint of the Taylor & Francis Group

© 2000 Amanda Coffey and Sara Delamont

Typeset in Times by Taylor & Francis Books Ltd
Printed and bound in Great Britain by Biddles Ltd, Guildford and
King's Lynn

British Library Cataloguing in Publication Data
A catalogue record for this book is available from the British Library

Library of Congress Cataloging in Publication Data
Coffey, Amanda, 1967–
    Feminism and the classroom teacher: research, praxis, and pedagogy/ Amanda Coffey
    and Sara Delamont
        p. cm.
    1. Feminism and education. 2. Teaching–Social aspects. 3. Postmodernism and
    education. I. Delamont, Sara, 1947– II. Title

LC197 .C63 2000
371.1'0082–dc21   99-055625

ISBN 0–750–70749–6 (pbk)
ISBN 0–750–70750–X (hbk)

Contents

Acknowledgements

We are grateful to Thomas Good, Ivor Goodson and especially Bruce Biddle for asking us to write about feminism and the teacher's work for the *International Handbook of Teachers and Teaching.* We are also grateful to Malcolm Clarkson for having faith in our proposal to develop our ideas into a book, and to Anna Clarkson for seeing the project through. We acknowledge the services of the arts and social studies, and education libraries at Cardiff University. Lesley Pugsley undertook the initial bibliographic searches, and Karen Chivers wordprocessed the manuscript. We have both benefited from conversations with Sandra Acker on many of the topics in this volume.

Amanda Coffey would like to thank the personnel committee of Cardiff University for granting a period of study leave, and colleagues in the School of Social Sciences for their support in making this possible. Special thanks also to Julian Pitt for unflagging support and good humour, even when the going gets tough.

Sara Delamont would like to thank Paul Atkinson for being there.

Introduction

As anyone who has ever done it knows, confronting patriarchy or critiquing malestream knowledge is not easy: it involves risk and there are consequences. There is so little support for radically feminist work ... [But] As for the idea that feminists should be ragpickers in the bins of male ideas, we are not as naked as that.

(Brodribb 1992: xxiii)

This book explores the consequences and risks of confronting patriarchy and critiquing malestream knowledge in the classroom. Our aim is to undertake an analysis of teachers and their work which takes account of feminist, postfeminist, post-structuralist and postmodern scholarship. Feminist scholarship and empirical work have been fundamental in shaping our understandings of education and teaching over recent decades. Indeed it could easily be argued that feminism, broadly conceived, has been responsible for shaping the theory and practice of teaching over the course of the twentieth century. The feminist educational project has informed research and helped to shape policy.

For the purposes of this book we are using a feminist perspective that draws mainly on liberal and radical feminism rather than Marxist or socialist feminism. More generally we draw on recent calls to post-structuralist feminism. We have focused on imbalances between males and females in teaching (a classic liberal feminist tactic) and critiqued the knowledge base of research on teaching (a classic radical feminist tactic). We also believe in a reality that gender and power are (re)constructed through discursive practices and are subject to shifts and changes. We draw on a definition of feminism articulated by Donna Haraway (1989: 290).

Feminist theory and practice ... seek to explain and change historical systems of sexual difference, whereby 'men' and 'women' are socially constituted and positioned in relations of hierarchy and antagonism.

Our overall aim in this book is to undertake a feminist analysis of the work and everyday realities of the (school)teacher. Inevitably much of our focus is on the life and work of women (and feminist) teachers. However the empirical data and analytic discussions we present have a broader relevance. Over the course of the book we are seeking to ascertain the extent to which women teachers specifically – and the feminist project more generally – have contributed to theoretical understandings and practical accomplishments of teaching. As a contribution to the body of work on gender and education, we are concerned with the educational discourses of gender – that is, how gender is constructed and performed through discursive and material practices.

Structure and Organization

In order to explore the relationships, histories and futures of feminism and teaching we have drawn together a critical mass of literature. There is no established feminist analysis of the teacher's work – in either national or international contexts. There are, of course, well-cited feminist critiques of the literature on teaching as a profession (see, for example, Acker 1983, 1994; Delamont and Atkinson 1990), and we draw upon those as part of our analyses. The research and literature we discuss come from a range of countries, and employ a variety of research modes and theoretical perspectives. We draw most heavily on North American and British work, but also include work from the rest of Europe and Australasia (and from other English-speaking countries where available). We do not claim to provide an exhaustive review of all available literature. We hope we have been successful in drawing together the polemic and the empirical, the cited and the more diverse and scattered bodies of material.

The material and our analyses are arranged into broad themes, which in turn inform the chapter structure and organization. Chapter 1 explains the place of a feminist analysis in a postmodern intellectual climate. Following that are four chapters that concentrate on different aspects of the everyday work of the teacher. Chapter 2 explores the practical contingencies of the school classroom, and Chapter 3 concentrates on the intellectual, 'knowledge' work of the teacher. Chapters 4 and 5 deal with the teaching career path and the day-to-day biographies and experiences of teachers. In both these chapters issues of discrimination, empowerment, coping and success are addressed – at both individual and structural levels. In Chapters 6, 7 and 8 we turn our attention to the situated, historical and professional contexts of the teaching career. Chapter 6 examines the education and training of new recruits to teaching, and seeks to provide a feminist analysis of the policy context, curriculum content and everyday realities. Chapters 7 and 8 draw upon historical and contemporary, sociological and feminist perspectives on the teaching profession, in order to explore feminist contributions and analytical tensions. Our intention here is to recognize the historical legacy of feminism on teaching, and to consider this legacy in the context of theorizing about the profession. In Chapter 9 we return to the feminist project in education and teaching, specifically addressing epistemology and research praxis. We explore feminist analyses of contemporary research methods, indicating how diverse approaches can and have been used to gather data on the teacher's work. In this chapter we also provide our ideas on how the empirical project can be taken forward.

Vignettes

At the end of each chapter we provide a fictional vignette. These serve as introductions to the substantive topics of each following chapter, in what we hope are recognisable and plausible scenarios. They are partially based on experiences that have been told to us, together with a little artistic licence. The vignettes are set in Ledshire, a fictional city and county in England.

Note

We end this introduction with the words of Petra Munro, who has recently published an exemplary text, drawing on the life-history narratives of women teachers. One of her concluding questions remains at the heart of the feminist (educational) project and provides a useful starting point for this volume:

> I do not mean to romanticize the lives of women teachers or to suggest a monolithic view of women teachers as resistors. Yet, in today's post-modern world I walk a fine line. For as women, if we explore our agency or claim our own voices, we are reminded of the potential totalizing tendencies of asserting a stable and coherent identity. Yet, if we abandon our search do we risk complying with patriarchy's aim to name our desires?

> (Munro 1998: 124)

Fighting feminism ...

Ledshire is a cathedral city in Southern England with a famous university. In the graduate centre gym, one cold winter day, Arlette Traherne and Carlotta Comperton are warming up before aerobics. Arlette is doing a Ph.D. in Women's Studies, Carlotta is a teacher doing an Ed.D. part time. They have been friends for five years. Carlotta is complaining about two of her colleagues:

'There's Mr Paradine saying, "Carlotta, there's the unit in the history syllabus on feminism. You'll have to teach that – I've never understood what you feminists were on about," and Bijou Desborough saying, "Oh yes, Carlotta – you are a feminist, aren't you? Of course, my generation are past all that," and she's twenty-four, quite old enough to know better.'

1 Feminisms, Postfeminisms and Postmodernism

The debates among feminist theorists ... sharpen the critical edge of feminist thought by insisting on an ongoing self-reflection in feminist theorizing focussed on the interrelationships of organized demands for authority ... feminist theorising not only treats literary concerns and cultural traditions as a means of provoking and suppressing modes of reading the social; it also redresses the terms by which social science frames theoretical perspectives and research methodologies.

(Clough 1994: 169)

Introduction

This chapter aims to explore the place of a feminist analysis in a post-modern and post-structuralist intellectual climate. Thus we aim to provide a theoretical backdrop to a general feminist analysis of the work and life of the classroom teacher. Feminism, as both an intellectual movement and a practical strategy, has a long history and it would be a grand task to attempt a thoroughgoing review of its developments, theoretical, empirical and practical, in a short introductory piece. It goes without saying that we do not attempt such a feat. Rather our aim is to highlight and illuminate trends and contemporary developments in feminist thought, as a way of framing feminist educational theory and praxis. We do this by beginning with a discussion of the diversity in feminist thought and action, and then progressing to a discussion of the relationships between feminism, postmodernism and post-structuralism.

Feminisms

We have chosen here to talk of *feminisms*, rather than feminism in the singular, as a way of highlighting multiple meanings and realities of contemporary feminism. Indeed, since the early nineteenth century there have been many strands of feminism, so it is not surprising that they still exist, and have further multiplied, today. The feminist movement of the nineteenth century had several different streams of thought within it. Olive Banks

(1981), writing of the British and American scene, separated three groups; the evangelical, the Enlightenment and the communitarian socialist traditions. Each grouping had its roots in the late eighteenth century. The evangelical feminists drew their inspiration from their religious beliefs (Quakers, Unitarians, and other non-conformists) and were focused on the social issues of the day. Their feminism was closely related to campaigns to abolish slavery, introduce temperance, and attack prostitution, pornography and immorality. The second group of feminists identified by Banks (1981) drew inspiration from the Enlightenment which swept intellectual circles in Europe in the late eighteenth century. John Stuart Mill and Mary Wollstonecraft are the central figures in this tradition. They emphasized the importance of rational thought, evidence, and the theoretical ideas of rights, autonomy and individualism. The communitarian socialist tradition grew out of the French Saint-Simonian movement, and then added Marxist ideas in the later part of the century. Among those who were inspired by socialism are those Banks calls Utopians, who wanted communal living, free love and pooled child-rearing. Perhaps the most enduring version of feminism to emerge from the nineteenth and early twentieth centuries is that of a liberal, individualistic feminism. Indeed Gaby Weiner (1994) suggests that this is perhaps the most accepted of all feminisms, grounded in a social democratic, natural justice and equal opportunities tradition, and believing that through democratic social reform women (and men) should be free to determine their political, social, educational and labour market roles and futures.

So-called second-wave feminism is commonly dated from the late 1960s, and like earlier movements incorporates a number of divisions. Most commentators identify three major strands. Liberal feminism (equal opportunities), radical feminism (separatist) and socialist (Marxist) feminism. In addition today, most scholars would also wish to identify black feminism and lesbian feminism, on the grounds that other feminisms fail to incorporate racism and the black experience (see Humm 1992, Mirza 1997, Roman 1992, Weiner 1994) and heterosexism and the lesbian experience (see Jackson 1996, Richardson 1996, Van Every 1996, Wilton 1995).

The different feminist positions that have been articulated since the 1970s have generated different research agendas for education (Weiner 1994). However, both first-wave and second-wave feminisms have been concerned with the education and intellectual development and opportunities for women, along with tackling violence against women and children, raising the status of women's and children's health, and ensuring that female voices and experiences are treated seriously. The relationship between feminist perspectives and feminist action has been central and key to historical and contemporary campaigns. The intellectual continuities between historical feminist education campaigns (of the 1870s, for example) and contemporary feminist educational debates should also not be underemphasized.

One of the differences (or developments perhaps) between first-wave and second-wave feminisms in the English-speaking world is particularly relevant to education, and to the work of the teacher. In general, the first-wave feminists of the United States, Australia, Canada, New Zealand and the United Kingdom were concerned to widen academic secondary education, higher education and professional training to include girls and women. In an era where only males could study algebra, Greek, Hebrew, Latin and the physical sciences, the goal of feminists was to provide these opportunities to girls and women, and prove that they could excel at them. There were a few feminists who queried the epistemological status of the male knowledge base, but this was not a major preoccupation. It did, however, form a particular theme of the second-wave feminist movement, which widened the focus of feminism by challenging the epistemological basis, the methods, and the content of mainstream ('malestream') knowledge. This shows in the academic departments, degree courses and textbooks established in women's studies; in the feminist publishing houses and feminist lists in the established houses; in the social science methods textbooks; and in arts and social science disciplines where there are now feminist journals, women's caucuses in the learned societies, and books on many feminist topics.

A critical review of the established research on teachers and teaching from a feminist perspective is a typical product of second-wave feminism. However, 1999 is a hard time to write a feminist critique of the literature on the work of the teacher because feminism is under attack. Apart from the routine hostility and abuse that feminism has always attracted because it challenges the male-dominated, patriarchal status quo (see the papers in Arnot and Weiler 1993 and in Laslett and Thorne 1997), there are now serious claims that feminism is dead. Clearly we do not believe these claims, but we do have to address them before we can proceed.

Postmodernisms – A Postfeminist Era?

If we date second-wave feminism from the late 1960s, then by the 1980s announcements in popular media began to suggest that it was over, and we were entering a postfeminist era. These proclamations were paralleled among academics and intellectuals by announcements heralding the arrival of the postmodern era, and the current vogue for claiming postmodernism as the intellectual movement of the 1990s. We have not addressed the polemical debates in the media about the 'postfeminist' era in this book. For our purposes feminism is alive as a thought style, a focus and rational for political activity and for research, and a way of life in higher education and in schools, albeit a minority perspective. We are, however, concerned with the intellectual challenge to feminism posed by postmodernism, not least because of its uncanny parallels with the intellectual challenge that Freudianism posed to first-wave feminism.

The intellectual theories underpinning the first-wave feminist movement, which had made its central tenets progressive and modern in the second half of the nineteenth century, came under critical scrutiny after the 1914–18 war. One of the intellectual challenges to first-wave feminism came from the newly popular doctrines of Freudianism. Many intellectuals were attracted to a new set of ideas that were challenging to nineteenth-century sexual mores; the main planks of the first-wave feminists' moral and political credibility were redefined as sinister, unnatural and perverted by the central tenets of Freudianism. The intellectual leaders of the first wave, such as Jane Addams in the USA (Deegan 1988), were quite unable to come to terms with the attack, far less marshal a counter-argument, as Martha Vicinus (1985) has demonstrated. Indeed, it was not until the 1960s that an intellectually viable feminist challenge to Freudianism was produced. (This argument is explored in more detail in Vicinus 1985 and Delamont 1992a.) If postmodernism is going to have the same dominant effect on the intelligentsia and intellectual life in the next few decades that Freudianism did in the English-speaking world after 1918, then feminists are going to need to be aware of its potential for insidious detraction from their intellectual gains.

At its simplest, postmodernism is a challenge to the consensus held among the educated classes in the Western capitalist nations, since the Enlightenment at the end of the eighteenth century, that universal, objective scientific truths can be reached by scientific methods. Such beliefs have never been held by the majority in Western societies, or by anyone in many other cultures. For most of the world, poverty, lack of any education, beliefs about gender, and strong religious faith have stood between the working classes, women, and even whole populations and the scientific revolution of the Enlightenment. Even in advanced industrial societies many of those with access to education rejected the Enlightenment: for example, those many Americans who chose, and continue to choose, a literal reading of the Bible over science (see Barker 1979).

For those who have had the luxury of the two centuries of the Enlightenment, postmodernism is a serious challenge (Lather 1991). Postmodernism argues that there are no universal truths to be discovered, because all human investigators are grounded in human society and can only produce partial, local and historically specific insights. While most scientists are totally untroubled by such claims – if they are even aware of them being advanced – and continue to 'do' science in the traditional way, the impact of postmodernism on the humanities and social sciences has been considerable, profound and, for some, traumatic. Because postmodernism denies that there are any universal truths, it also runs the risk of destroying any scholarly work that tries to produce generalized, universalistic theories (of anything). Patti Lather summarizes postmodernism as follows:

> The essence of the postmodern argument is that the dualisms which continue to dominate Western thought are inadequate for under-

standing a world of multiple causes and effects interacting in complex and non-linear ways, all of which are rooted in a limitless array of historical and cultural specificities.

(Lather 1991: 21)

There are at least two responses to postmodernism's challenge to the feminist academic work of the 1960s and 1970s. Some people argue that the whole idea of 'liberating' women by uncovering evidence about injustice and appealing via rational argument for social change is killed by postmodernism. So, for example, gathering data on violence against women, and campaigning to change the law and set up women's refuges using those data, is 'written off' as an outmoded activity. And developing out of such data new theories of the family that focus on power and patriarchy is an equally outdated response. It is not surprising that many of the scholars who have argued that postmodernism renders such rational research passé are middle-class white men in secure jobs in industrialized countries. Thus Elizabeth Fox-Genovese has commented:

> Surely it is no coincidence that the Western white male elite proclaimed the death of the subject at precisely the moment at which it might have had to share that status with the women and peoples of other races and classes who were beginning to challenge its supremacy.

(Fox-Genovese 1986: 134)

A similar point is made by Somer Brodribb (1992: 7–8) when she states that 'post-modernism is the cultural capital of late patriarchy'. A typically hostile reaction to postmodernism from a feminist scholar comes from the historian Joan Hoff:

> Postmodern theory disadvantages the field of women's history in three ways. First, it is hostile to the basic concept of linear time and of cause and effect assumptions which most professionally trained historians continue to honour in their teaching and writing. Second, postmodern theory's misogynist and very specific historical origins among post World War II Parisian Intellectuals – from Levi-Strauss and Lacan to Foucault and Derrida – require excessive intellectual modification and machinations to include women. Finally, it is politically paralysing.

(Hoff 1994: 151)

If this version of postmodernism is the insightful and powerful one – for of course it is not possible in postmodernism to describe or characterize postmodernism as 'true' (or 'false') because truth (and falsehood) are terms from modernism that have themselves been swept away – the implication for a feminist analysis of teachers' work are twofold. *Either* the intellectual work, and the research base, will not be done at all because the historical moment for it has passed. *Or* such an analysis will be done, but will be seen by many as already old-fashioned and will be redundant as soon as it is produced.

There is, however, a completely different version of postmodernism. For every Hoff, warning that postmodernism is politically paralysing *and* destructive of scholarly activity, there are other feminist intellectuals for whom postmodernism is empowering. Jane Flax, for example, argues that 'Postmodern philosophers seek to throw into radical doubt beliefs ... derived from the Enlightenment' (Flax 1990: 41). Flax lists among the beliefs thrown into doubt: the existence of a stable self, reason, an objective foundation for knowledge, and universalism. As she forcefully expresses: 'The meanings – or even existence – of concepts essential to all forms of Enlightenment metanarrative (reason, history, science, self, knowledge, power, gender, and the inherent superiority of Western culture) have been subjected to increasingly corrosive attacks' (Flax 1993: 450).

For Flax, postmodernism is potentially threatening for feminism because 'Three of the discourses feminists have attempted to adapt to our own purposes, liberal political theory, Marxism, and empirical social science, express some form of this Enlightenment dream' (Flax 1993: 448). However, as she points out, much feminist scholarship has been critical of the contents of the Enlightenment dream, yet simultaneously 'unable to abandon them' (Flax 1993: 47). For Flax this is not a proper feminist response. Because the Enlightenment was a *male* intellectual project, feminists must abandon it in order to create their own intellectual project. Flax is confident that the insights of postmodernism will set women free from a childlike state in which we wait for 'higher authorities' to rescue us, clinging to a naïve myth of 'sisterhood'. Indeed, as Weiner argues, feminism shares some of the goals of postmodernism, and indeed could be viewed as an earlier impetus to it: 'I *do* believe that feminist theory has been immensely important in asking questions about knowledge, power, nature and wish it were more acknowledged that feminists were way ahead of postmodernists in critiquing the structures and universalities of modernity' (Weiner 1994: 24).

Certainly, feminists cannot hide from postmodernism. Feminism must ride all new intellectual currents or be drowned by them, and there are serious scholars who offer us their version of postmodernism which is a feminist version, or a feminist-friendly version. Stephen Ball (1994), for example, bases his postmodernism in Foucault, and remains totally confident that postmodernism is not politically paralysing. Ball's concepts from postmodernism can be deployed to build feminist analyses of teachers' work (in evidence in his own work in contemporary English schools). In the optimistic view, postmodernism is entirely compatible with feminist ideas, because it attacks the intellectual authority of dead white males. Using a postmodernist analysis, Freud, Bowlby, Parsons and Bettelheim have no more basis for their supposedly scientific theories about gender than those nineteenth-century authors who argued that if women learnt Ancient Greek it would use up too much of their blood and they would become sterile (Burstyn 1980, Russett 1990).

When we come to apply those ideas to the large body of empirical evidence on who enters teaching, how teachers are trained, what happens in classrooms, and what makes up the occupational culture of teaching, a useful analytic standpoint can be derived from Sandra Harding (1993), the philosopher of science, who has drawn a distinction between 'strong' and 'weak' meanings of objectivity. The conventional meaning of objectivity, Harding argues, is weak because it has failed to strip out and examine the researchers' taken-for-granted, hidden, unexplicated agendas and cultural assumptions. These assumptions have been central to Western intellectual thought since the Enlightenment and include the assumption that mind and body can be treated separately, or that reason and emotion can be disentangled, or that masculinity and femininity are separable from social relations. 'Strong' objectivity would include an examination of all unexplicated beliefs, and makes all the assumptions the subject of scrutiny.

In Harding's feminist work, published in the 1980s, she concentrated on showing how Anglo-American science rested on unexamined assumptions about rationality being male and subjectivity being female – and of course therefore contaminating. Just as Eve polluted the Garden of Eden, and Pandora opened the box, so, too, do emotion and subjectivity pollute science (see Harding 1986, 1987, 1991 and 1993, Harding and Hintikka 1983). Such arguments may seem far removed from empirical work on teachers and teaching, but in fact the data on classroom processes and teachers' lives are collected with methods that are grounded in epistemologies dating from the Enlightenment. (We provide a detailed discussion of the relationships between feminist epistemology, methodologies and research methods in Chapter 9.)

In common, then, with many feminist scholars, we do not believe that postmodernism heralds the death of feminism as theory, method or intellectual project. We do recognize that the ideas and intellectual climate that derive from postmodernism have impacted upon the meanings, articulations and actions of feminism. These may be critical and challenging, but they can also be exciting and empowering.

Post-structuralist Feminism and Feminist Pluralism

If feminism was ever a certain and boundaried theoretical perspective, then the borders are now dislodged and disrupted:

> Invocations of 'feminism' became marked by the naming of varieties, like naming the genuses of flowers: *Marxist* feminism, *socialist* feminism, *radical* feminism, *liberal* feminism, oh, and *revolutionary*

feminism; and we should not forget that academic careers have been built upon the naming of these varieties and the maintenance of divisions between them. Now there are no longer even these certainties (not that there really ever were, for few of us understood our ideas and praxes for long within such confined and static terms).

(Stanley 1997: 9)

The recognition (and indeed) celebration of a range of feminist epistemologies is in keeping with a postmodern position, and an increasing concern with multiple subjectivities, voices and realities (Weiner 1994). By actively promoting feminist pluralism, Liz Stanley (1990) has argued that we are able to reject forms of feminism that have articulated, albeit in a disguised form, hegemonic claims. This avoids any one form of feminism being set up as a dominant discourse, and recognizes multiple narratives, meanings and realities (Benhabib 1995). Recent articulations of this feminist position draw on the ideas of Foucault and post-structural perspectives to illuminate the importance of discursive practices (see Blackmore 1999, Middleton 1995, Munro 1998, Weiner 1994). This perspective acknowledges the reality of multiple feminisms and identifies the ways in which gender, power, difference, subject and agency are constituted, though not determined, by discourse. Discursive practices hence 'constrain and shape possibilities for action, and therefore have the capacity to be both emancipating and repressive' (Blackmore 1999: 17).

Post-structural feminism creates 'new ways of seeing and knowing' (Weiner 1994: 63), viewing social relations in terms of plurality and diversity, and recognizing that individuals are active in engaging in discourses through which they in turn are shaped. Weiner (1994) identifies discursive spaces, through which women can resist subject positioning and fixed, static identities. Monolithic categories and grand narratives are rejected, and replaced by concepts of identity formation and power that are more complex, multiple, shifting, contradictory and reflexive. Some feminist commentators who utilize this kind of position recognize that there is the potential here for the romanization of the individual. Also that a concentration on discourse and discursive fields may indeed limit the experiences that women can articulate (see Munro 1998, who talks of non-discursive articulations). There is potential inherent in such a position that gender is constantly viewed as 'in trouble' and in a constant state of (re)production and (re)creation. This in itself may make it difficult to develop theories of gender and power, and render praxis and pedagogy based on such theories and understandings problematic. However, the value in post-structuralist feminist perspectives is the way in which they prioritize the discursive and social practices that constitute everyday life, and establish the contradictory nature of how power and authority actually work. For example, by viewing women teachers as constructed and reconstructed, we can begin to view the work of the teachers as part of the discursive practices that enable these processes. And by viewing individuals as powerful and powerless in different discursive spaces (Blackmore 1999), we can begin to develop new feminist understandings of the relationships between gender and power in teaching and the everyday realities of women teachers.

Conclusion

As we indicated in our introduction, this chapter forms the theoretical backdrop to our analysis of the everyday world and work of the teacher. We do not base our analyses that follow on a systematic overview of each form of feminism and how it tackles questions of education and teaching. Rather we draw on the analytic tools of *feminisms* to provide both a critique of school practices and the creative potential for new knowledges and practices. The chapters that follow are thematically rather than theoretically organized. In each we are concerned with utilizing feminist perspectives as mechanisms by which teachers and their work can be understood, challenged and changed. Central to this analysis is our understanding that feminism fuses theory and practice and, in terms of education, yields both praxis and pedagogy (Weiler 1991, Weiner 1994). Hence we are concerned not only with documenting the everyday realities of women teachers. We also seek to discover the discursive, institutional and material spaces through which women teachers are able to shift from powerless to powerful agents of classroom and social change.

> ### *In every school in every town ...*
>
> Ledbury is an industrial town about twenty miles from Ledchester. Carlotta is a history teacher at Ledbury High, one of the comprehensive secondary schools there. It is second lesson of a warm summer afternoon and she is covering the causes of the Second World War with her sixteen-year-olds when a scuffle breaks out in the centre of the room. Davida Lessiter and Aidan Holderness seem to be in dispute about something. On investigation, Davida accuses Aidan of distracting her by telling dirty jokes to his neighbour and trying to 'borrow' her homework to copy. Carlotta moves Aidan to an empty desk at the front of the room, and he slouches forward muttering: 'All you women stick together – Nothing is ever *her* fault – Are you both lesbians? – History is boring – Why don't you move her away from *me*?' Carlotta decides to ignore this and returns to the invasion of Poland, but thinks to herself how tiring such male behaviour is.

2 Classroom Life

The Everyday Work of the Teacher

My science program was pretty much textbook, paper, pencil, filmstrip, video etc. I knew I had to change my teaching style. I wanted student learning to be more interactive, authentic and meaningful .... I learned about project-based science which is curriculum centred around driving questions and engages students in teamwork and discovery learning.

(Dudley 1997: 73)

Introduction

Jacquilyn Dudley is an African-American teacher of 12-year-olds in the Midwest of the USA. Her description of her decision to change the way she organized and delivered her science lessons serves as a good introduction to the subject of this chapter: the everyday work of the teacher. The largest part of the everyday work of the teacher, or of the majority of teachers, takes place in the classroom, and so we have concentrated on providing a feminist perspective of classroom work. Towards the end of the chapter we deal briefly with the work of the teacher in the wider school, and in the community. (Other chapters also deal with the everyday realities of the teacher's work. See, for example, Chapter 3 on knowledge and Chapter 5 on biographies and experiences.) The separation we have made between the classroom and other domains of the teacher's work is made for analytical convenience – in reality we recognize that the wider school regime permeates the classroom. The teacher's work extends beyond the classroom walls (Gibson 1988, Grant 1988, Metz 1978, Proweller 1998, Swidler 1978), and the community is often a brooding presence (see, for example, Darmanin 1995, Foley 1989, Peshkin 1978, 1985, Walford and Miller 1991).

In the context of the classroom, the everyday work of the teacher can be conceptualized in a number of ways. In this chapter we have chosen to concentrate on three sets of issues – immediacy and autonomy; talk and the control of talk; and discipline and control – and to provide a feminist analysis of these. We recognize that a major task of the teacher in their everyday work is the control, organization, transmission and reproduction of knowledge, and so we devote the whole of Chapter 3 to an exploration of the curriculum and school knowledge.

Immediate Work, Autonomous Teachers

Philip W. Jackson's *Life in Classrooms* (1968) highlighted that classroom teachers must operate under conditions that require a sense of immediacy and 'front-stage' work. The front of the classroom is the teacher's stage (Tartwijk et al. 1998). Much of the teacher's task requires immediate decisions about immediate situations. Stone (1993) uses the postmodern term 'contingency' to characterize the same phenomenon. Fenwick's (1998) characterization of the teacher's work as the management of energy is one way in which this immediacy is enacted. Drawing on Koerner's (1992) description of the body electric classroom, Fenwick argues that, 'A group of adolescents in a classroom appear at times to be a bubbly cauldron of physical energy' (Fenwick 1998: 624–5).

As Fenwick suggests, part of the teacher's daily task is to direct this energy, in innovative ways, often responding to immediate and unpredictable situations. Thus the need for immediacy is accompanied (at least on the surface) by individual teacher autonomy. The layout of the school, with classrooms often physically isolated from one another, means that professional colleagues and seniors are often out of reach in the everyday life of the teacher 'at the chalkface'. How teachers respond to immediate situations – what goes on behind the classroom door – is for the realm of each individual teacher – albeit within professional and institutional parameters. The world of the classroom can thus be a very private world. This apparent autonomous (and relatively powerful) position of the classroom teacher has come under threat in recent years, as educational policy has increasingly dictated what should be taught and how teachers should go about that task (Acker 1989, 1994, Apple 1986, Ball 1990, Gray et al. 1999). For example, the introduction of a national curriculum in England and Wales, and an accompanyingly more rigorous school (and teaching) inspection system (Apple 1998, Gray et al. 1999) has served to challenge the position of the classroom teacher as autonomous professional.

The challenges to the autonomy of the classroom teacher, and the twin requirements of responding to immediate situations combined with an increasingly centralized controlling of classroom work, is complicated further when viewed from a feminist perspective. The immediacy and privacy of the classroom also means that it is an isolated environment and one in which teachers can be extremely vulnerable (Delamont 1983). This vulnerability can be both intellectual (for example, threats to the control of knowledge make teachers extremely vulnerable) *and* physical. The classroom can be a physically frightening environment for the lone teacher – male or female. The isolation of the classroom also means an immediate lack of collegial support and available consultation. This can compound feelings of loneliness and isolation. Aside from the difficulties teachers have in providing mutual, immediate support for each other; the physical layout of the school, and increasing everyday burdens of the classroom teacher, make school-based classroom initiatives difficult to organize. This includes initiatives on gender, which have been relatively unsuccessful partly because of the pressures of time and the inherent difficulties in organizing classroom teachers (Acker 1994). One way in which teachers manage classroom space is through the establishing of routines and planned arrangements (Fenwick 1998). The management of the unpredictability of student energy relies to a large extent on the predictability of the teacher. Any extra initiatives, however deserving, create extra burdens on individual teachers, which are often too much to bear.

A feminist perspective here should also draw attention to the disjunction between autonomy and power. While teachers may have considerable autonomy in the classroom, women teachers, particularly, do not experience the same power within the school and education system generally. Studies have highlighted the structural powerlessness of women teachers (Acker 1994, Boulton and Coldron 1998, Cunnison 1989, Riddell 1992, Weiner 1994). These rather pessimistic observations should however be balanced by an alternative, feminist position. The relative autonomy of the classroom teacher to organize and control the classroom, and to organize the effective delivery of a curriculum (albeit one that has been imposed rather than planned) can provide opportunities for empowerment, as well as potential isolation. The teacher in the classroom must still undertake a considerable amount of autonomous decision-making. Ironically, while women teachers may remain relatively powerless in the wider school, the classroom can provide female space and place. In most primary school classrooms, and a considerable number of secondary school classrooms, the 'chalkface' remains a female domain. This is compounded by *others* who take part in the everyday life of the classroom. Classroom assistants and parent volunteers are usually women; there is the potential for the classroom to provide opportunities for women to work with other women. So while the external pressures of the work of the teacher, accompanied by the physical layout of the school and compounded by the power structures of the school, may threaten autonomy and promote isolation, a different scenario is also possible. It remains important to note that the everyday ethos of the classroom and the reproduction of knowledge in the classroom is, more often than not, in the hands of women teachers.

Talk and Control of Talk

A key element of the everyday work of the teacher is managing interaction and talk. The classroom is an interactive and verbal environment and the teacher's work in this context involves talk and the control of talk (of pupils and students). Much of what the teacher actually does involves talking to pupils, individually and collectively, and creating a learning environment by balancing quiet and talk (Fenwick 1998). A feminist perspective can examine this aspect of the teacher's work on at least two levels: the type of speech/talk that is advocated by and acceptable to the teacher; and the inter-actions between teachers and pupils. The feminist research on language and talk has centred on both sexist terminology in our everyday language (Ehrlich and King 1992, Spender 1985) and on the nature (and difference) of male and female discourse (Coates and Cameron 1989, Graddol and Swann 1989, Lakoff 1975). The first of these – the adoption of 'masculine' words and terms as universal – such as 'her', 'man', 'master' and so on – has been a focus of the liberal feminist approach to equal opportunities in education. The adoption of gender-neutral, non-sexist linguistic practice is by no means universal and complete, however. The dominance and acceptability of male-defined models of language practice and use still needs to be addressed in the context of talk and language used and 'approved' in the classroom setting (Shuy 1986; see also Chapter 3 for a discussion of discursive prac-tices and the school curriculum).

In terms of male and female discourse use, there is evidence that males and females have different conversational styles (Cameron 1995, Tannen 1991). The ways men and women, and boys and girls, talk are different. This feminist approach to sociolinguistics notes that men and women use language in different ways to different ends. Deborah Tannen (1991) differ-entiates between 'rapport-talk' as a female conversational style, which stresses connectedness and sharing, and 'report-talk' as a male conversa-tional style, which stresses independence and a more instrumental approach. Deborah Cameron (1995) locates these kinds of discursive differences into a broader model of gendered identities and power, stressing that language styles are socially produced as feminine and masculine, and that individuals adopt these in the process of constructing their gendered selves. We can think of this in terms of styles of conversation, but also in terms of male–female interaction (Tannen 1991). There is evidence, for example, of inequalities in male and female discourse, and the control of language in primary schools. Fisher (1994) notes from her observations of primary school classrooms that boys dominate talk, speak mainly to each other, and their verbalized ideas are treated more seriously (by boys and girls) in mixed-gendered, collaborative work situations.

Providing a feminist analysis and critique of research on gender differ-ences in teacher–student/pupil interaction is problematic, not least because the research is inconclusive, and to some extent contradictory. Most of the published studies on teacher–pupil interaction and gender are of two types. There are some well-cited studies by feminists which report very small-scale projects, often without sufficient reflexivity to meet contemporary standards. In contrast there are some large-scale projects carried out using positivist methods that are grounded in malestream epistemologies (see Chapter 9). These two broad types of study are frequently contradictory in their conclusions, and each demonstrates the disadvantages of its paradigm. In the following discussion we have drawn on both, despite inadequacies, because classroom interaction is so central to all inquiries into gender equity, educational processes and the everyday work of the teacher.

Two of the earliest feminist studies of teachers' interaction with male and female students were done in English secondary classrooms by Dale Spender (1982) and Michelle Stanworth (1981). They both claimed that teachers devote a greater proportion of classroom talk and attention to boys. Stanworth's was a single-handed project in one school, and Spender's claims are based on ten lessons she herself taught in a London school. No serious classroom researcher of the positivist tradition would dream of making a sweeping claim about teacher or pupil behaviour based on such an inadequate sample. Flanders (1970) stated that any generalization about a teacher needed to be drawn from at least six hours of observation. The UK-based ORACLE project on elementary school teaching, for example, made 47,000 observations of fifty-eight teachers and 84,000 observations of 489 target pupils (Galton et al. 1980; also see Galton et al. 1999) before they drew any conclusions about teaching styles. However the studies and conclusions of Stanworth and Spender are particularly well cited, and perhaps justifiably so. Even if one discounts their findings because of inadequate methods, sample size, or lack of reflexivity, similar conclusions have been drawn by other researchers whose methods are superior. French and French (1984, 1993) and Swann and Graddol (1994) in England and Wales, Evans (1988) in Australia, and Shuy (1986) in the USA all report imbalances in the amount of attention teachers pay to males and females, and in the nature of those interactions. French and French (1984, 1993), for example, provide a detailed analysis of the transcript of a lesson taught by a male elementary school teacher to a class of sixteen girls and thirteen boys. Boys spoke more than girls, and received more attention from the teacher. French and French argue that this is typical of the general run of findings. Teachers (both male and female) pay more attention, in terms of directing their talk, to male pupils than to female ones. If gross counts are made, teacher–male pupil interactions outnumber teacher–female pupil ones.

When the analysis focuses on the *content* of classroom interactions the difference rests on disciplinary and controlling interactions. Male pupils tend to get more teacher attention than female pupils primarily because males get reprimanded and ordered about more than females. Once that behaviour controlling talk is discounted, the academic interactions are not significantly more likely to be directed to males than females. Teachers 'explain' this by arguing that boys are harder to control than girls; boys complain that teachers pick on them even when the girls have caused the disciplinary problems; girls complain that boys are noisy and stop them working. Joan Swann and David Graddol's (1994) analysis of student–teacher interactions in two different classrooms confirms these general conclusions. They found that the turn-taking of talk by boys and girls in the classroom was controlled by the class teacher – by naming students and also by what they refer to as the gaze: the non-verbal means of inviting a student to talk by looking at them. Teachers gaze at boys more than girls, making it more likely that a boy will be 'invited' to speak. Like French and French (1993), Swann and Graddol (1994) partially explain this behaviour in terms of experienced class teachers scanning the classroom constantly to keep a check on emergent discipline problems – and that the more boisterous behaviour of boys channels the teacher's gaze towards them. These findings are paralleled by Terry Evans's (1988) study in two Australian primary schools, where boys had 53 per cent of the total number of interactions with teachers. If these interactions are differentiated by who initiates them (teacher or pupil) then 57 per cent of teacher-initiated contact goes to boys.

At a general level there is evidence that teachers' interactions with girls are less control-orientated, and therefore more positive and directed at educative, rather than discipline, events. It is certainly the case that the ways in which teachers interact with male and female students demonstrate manifest differences. In 1984 William Bennett Jr, then President Reagan's education supremo in the USA, taught a high-school American history class on national television. Roger Shuy (1986), a linguist, transcribed the classroom talk and analysed it. Bennett treated male and female students differently. Male students who answered Bennett's questions were immediately challenged: forced to defend, expand or withdraw their answers (for example 'Why do you say that?'). Women students who spoke got more positive feedback ('terrific', 'very nice') or neutral responses ('OK', 'all right') but were not engaged in further dialogue. No female was asked to defend or amplify her answer. This is, of course, the analysis of only one lesson, and albeit demonstrates a difference in a lesson taught by one, male teacher. Bennett himself did not realize what he was doing, and indeed rejected the importance Shuy attached to the gendered nature of the interactions. A feminist will be struck by Shuy's analysis of Bennett's teaching, but we do not know whether those high-school students noticed, what they thought about it, and how it might have affected their behaviour (see Bossert 1982, Brophy 1985, and the other chapters in Wilkinson and Marrett 1985).

Moving to larger-scale investigations done in a positivist frame, Kelly conducted a meta-analysis of eighty-one studies of classroom interaction and concluded that 'teachers consistently interact more with boys than with girls' (Kelly 1988: 13). She argues that if a student's school career involves 15,000 hours of classroom interaction, a typical boy gets 1,800 hours more teacher attention than a typical girl. However, classrooms differ widely, for reasons that have not been investigated fully. Kelly also found that most of the studies had been conducted in elementary schools, where girls perform better than boys, rather than in secondary schools, where female performance, especially in maths and science, is more disappointing. Despite a range of provisional findings, the research evidence on teacher–pupil interactions is not as robust as it might be, or as it is often assumed to be. Moreover the implications of such findings are not at all clear. Steven Bossert (1982: 173) summarized the results of a number of American studies and concluded:

> These results leave us in a muddle. Teachers do treat girls and boys differently, but the extensiveness of this differential treatment, whether it is perceived by students, and how it might affect their sex-role behaviour and attitudes is unknown.

Gender differences in classroom interaction patterns have not been of sufficient importance to those who fund research for any large-scale studies to be done. For definitive answers we would need a range of studies done of male and female teachers, teaching mixed and single-sex classes across all subjects, the whole age range and all ability and social class levels. We need detailed and robust analyses of teacher–student interaction which addresses the genders of both teachers and students. These need to be done by researchers who are skilled in devising techniques that meet the standards of reliability, validity and reflexivity used by both feminists such as Spender (1982) and sceptics such as Martyn Hammersley (1993). From the research base that we do have we know that 'girls are marginalised in two forms of classroom talk that are important learning contexts: learning through collaborative discussion in mixed groups and class discussion with the teacher' (Paechter 1998: 25).

As far as pupil talk is concerned, it appears that boys participate more than girls. Myra and David Sadker (1985a, 1985b) studied over 100 classes in the USA and found that boys spoke, on average, three times as much as girls. It appears that more boys want to speak, and are more assertive about getting turns, while more girls wish to be silent, or are unable to get into the discourse. It seems that male students at secondary school expect to have the lion's share of the talk, and are rebellious if female students try to participate. These are major issues needing research both at the level of the language used, and as an issue about morality and justice.

Tannen's (1991) insights into gender and discourse demonstrate that this is an issue far beyond the confines of the classroom. She reflects that everyday conversational style is conceptualized by different male and female voices. Carol Gilligan's framework of gender differences in moral reasoning and debate (Gilligan 1982, Gilligan and Attanucci 1988) is also helpful in developing a more sophisticated and feminist understanding of classroom discourse and the perceptions and realities of gender equalities. Gilligan (1982) challenges the ways in which reasoning and moral debate are conceptualized in male-based and 'malestream' ways. In particular she argues that girls and women demonstrate an alternative or different voice, and a different approach to problem solving. This complements the work of sociolinguists like Tannen, and has implications for thinking about gendered discourses in the classroom, by suggesting that there can be many voices in the classroom (and that some are more vocal or silent than others). This multiplicity of voices, and how they are positioned as deficient or dominant and conceptualized as the norm or *Other* (Paechter 1998), sets new agendas for research and analysis.

Discipline and Control

Teachers control their classrooms (as well as the talk in those classrooms). The classroom is a physical and intellectual space to be managed. Teachers must determine routines, rules and sanctions (Coloroso 1982, Denscombe 1985, Gregg 1995, McLaughlin 1991) and manage their classrooms as part of their everyday work.

> Teachers determine rules and routines which, in the classroom of an experienced teacher, function almost invisibly to display teacher expectations for behaviour, and to control student movement and distribution of materials. Teachers also intentionally create physical structures (i.e. arranging desks, sequencing activity, keeping a blackboard list of 'problem students') that encourage or repress certain behaviours.
>
> (Fenwick 1998: 621)

The teacher is involved in defining what acceptable behaviour is and what appropriate sanctions should be taken. Woods (1990) notes that the role of the teacher is a conflictual one. Colleagues judge teachers for their ability to exercise discipline in their classrooms (Gregg 1995, McPherson 1972). As Fenwick (1998) argues, effective classroom management is also about creating the right balance; between work and play, quiet and talk, student responsibility and external control, as well as ensuring that the classroom space is a 'safe place'.

Carrie Paechter (1998) suggests that teachers tend to concentrate on overt forms of disruption in the classroom. That is, they focus on disruption to the overt instructional context of the learning environment. As a consequence, overt and noisy styles of disaffection and disruption, primarily found among boys, are given more teacher attention. Male disruptive behaviour in the classroom – boisterousness, competitiveness – may even be praised (Connell et al. 1982, Kessler et al. 1985). In comparison, teachers often see girls as passive, controllable and submissive and there follows an expectation of good behaviour (Robinson 1992). Paechter (1998) argues that these differential expectations of male and female behaviour have at least five implications. First, teacher articulations of 'problem' students are different for boys and girls (Crozier and Anstiss 1995). Problem boys are often discussed in terms of behaviour and academic performance, while problem girls are commented upon in terms of appearance and (sexual) morality. The assumption of quiet passivity from girls means that overt devi-ation is often gendered by referencing sexual impropriety and appearance. Second, as the overtly disruptive behaviours of boys are given more class-room and teacher time, so boys are more likely to be referred for special needs, or specialized provision (of course, there is also evidence to suggest that boys are more likely to be excluded from school – see Cohen 1998). As a consequence, specialist provision in schools may actually predominantly cater for and be better able to meet the needs of boys. Third, teachers may seek to tackle the potential disruption of boys by gearing lessons more towards the interests of boys, as Mairtin Mac an Ghaill (1994) found, and by allowing boys more control over the space of the classroom (Riddell 1992). Disruptive behaviour then may be self-fulfilling in providing boys with more, rather than less, time and space in the classroom. Fourth, by emphasizing particular kinds of overt disruption, teachers and schools may fail to notice, or deal effectively with, other kinds of disruptive behaviour – such as bullying, name calling, verbal abuse, and sexual harassment (see Jones 1985, Mahony 1989). Studies have demonstrated that sexual harass-ment is prevalent in schools (see Dei et al. 1998, Herbert 1985, Mahony 1989, Riddell 1992), though often not reprimanded by teachers, either in secondary schools (Draper 1991) or in primary schools (Walkerdine 1989). Rather sexual harassment is often tolerated as a natural part of adolescence, or as part of normal 'behaviour'. As Valerie Walkerdine (1989) notes, this may be the case with female as well as male teachers. (Sexual harassment may be part of the teachers' everyday reality too – see Acker 1994, Cunnison 1989, and Chapters 4, 5 and 6 of this volume.) Finally, Paechter suggests that different expectations of behaviour, and teacher emphasis on certain kinds of disruption, can have contradictory consequences for girls. On the one hand assertive girls in the classroom may actually be seen as problem-atic, and not the norm. On the other hand the expectation of well-behaved, quiet girls may actually enable girls to engage in a form of quiet resistance and rebellion. While they run the risk of being categorized as intellectually deficient, by 'keeping quiet and looking busy', they may actually be able to be effective in resisting work. 'Passivity' may in this case actually be a form of resistance.

Thus far we have said very little about the actual ways in which teachers control their class. A common assumption is that a competent teacher is one who can keep a class quiet, for a quiet class is one that can be managed where learning can be achieved (Robinson 1992). A number of studies have argued that the culture and ethos of school discipline often revolves around certain kinds of masculine behaviour (Beynon 1987, Connell 1987, Davies 1992, Shakeshaft 1989). As Robinson (1992) notes, male teachers are more able to use overt forms of discipline and physical force in controlling a class. Beynon (1989) described the ways in which particularly physical coercive measures were used in a South Wales classroom, and were overtly seen in the school as representing good practice in teaching. Pushing, cuffing and shaking were viewed as acceptable everyday forms of discipline by male teachers and pupils alike. Following this particular version of discipline through – good teachers were real men, and the competent teacher was the one who could issue, threaten and display violence – this locates classroom discipline within particular frameworks of masculinity, and of course has far-reaching implications for women teachers. Mac an Ghaill's (1994) ethnographic study of a school in the English midlands locates the different teaching styles of male teachers (and disciplinary mechanisms) within different frameworks of masculinity. While he identifies different kinds of masculine identity and style among the teachers at Parnell School, discipline is central to the shaping of masculinities within the school, for both teachers and students.

> An inability to be powerful and authoritative is a code for an inability to be a 'proper man'. Signs of 'weakness' in many public arenas is associated with femininity. Masculinities in the work place have competence as an essential feature, while incompetence is deemed as failure, weakness or 'womanly'.
>
> (Haywood and Mac an Ghaill 1996: 54)

Davies (1992: 128) argues that the version of masculinity that has come to dominate school management is 'competitive, point scoring, over confident, sporting, career and status conscious' – with pupils clearly identifying discipline with physical intimidation and aggression (Askew and Ross 1988, Bailey 1996). Sheila Cunnison (1985) describes the difficult and contradicting position of women within this kind of school setting. Despite the immediate authority over her classroom, the woman teacher tends to have a largely powerless position within the school. As Cunnison (1989) suggests, a 'macho' culture of discipline flourished in the school she studied. This macho-culture actually marginalized women teachers, who chose not to, or indeed could not, wield the macho-type discipline that was demanded of (senior) staff. The authority of women teachers is often undermined by staff and pupils alike, through ridicule, sexual comment (harassment), gender joking and so forth. Askew and Ross (1988) and Bailey (1996) have argued that male teachers tend to 'look after women teachers', and even where this is not meant to be intimidating or undermining the result is often much the same. Male teachers threatening students who misbehave in the lessons of women teachers are giving a message that the 'lady teacher' cannot cope alone. Cunnison (1989) and Riddell (1992) have both pointed to the ways in which gender joking in the classroom and the staff room, by male staff, and pupils, serves to undermine the authority of women teachers. Sheila Riddell's (1992) study showed how male teachers used male camaraderie and sexual joking to maintain control in the classroom. Teachers also use gender as part of their control strategy in other ways: ridiculing male pupils who misbehave by suggesting they are acting like girls and vice versa; urging the sexes to compete as one way of motivating both sexes; and enforcing gender stereotypes among the pupils. (See Delamont 1990 for ethnographic examples from the UK, and Thorne 1992 and 1993 for parallel examples from the USA.)

This undermining of authority is tantamount to sexual harassment, and certainly works against social justice and gender equality, by supporting a particular kind of school atmosphere (Dixon 1997). As Paechter (1998: 24) writes, 'Male secondary school teachers often tacitly support a more general school atmosphere in which girls and women are positioned as sexual Others and made the object of derision.' The consequences of this for women's strategies for control and cooperation are stark. As Bailey (1996) argues, women often experience difficulties as a consequence of the authoritarian and masculine ethos of the school. Women who attempt more co-operative and democratic approaches in the face of such an ethos may well be seen as a weak authoritarian and disciplinarian by students and colleagues alike. The women teachers working in a boys school (and interviewed by Bailey) confirmed this tension, as one articulated: 'You're always told it's all easy-going discipline, but the impression that I have is that boys are used to being jumped on for minor offences, and you're seen as a soft touch if you don't (Bailey 1996: 176).

One kind of feminist approach to these issues is to argue for girls-only classes, or even a return to single-sex schooling (Deem 1984, Wrigley 1992; also see Daly 1996 for a discussion of the merits of single-sex versus coeducational schooling). Such a motivation impelled one feminist maths teacher in Australia studied by Connell (1985) to leave a public mixed school to teach in a private all-girls' one, where she no longer had to discipline boys in order to help girls learn maths. Other solutions have been to argue for and work towards girl-friendly schooling (Whyte et al. 1988), or anti-sexist schooling (Askew and Ross 1988, Best 1983, Guttentag and Bray 1976). However, gender initiatives such as these have met with resistance in schools, and measuring their outcomes or successes is to say the least problematic.

Beyond the Classroom

As we alluded to at the start of this chapter, the everyday work of the teacher extends beyond the confines of the classroom walls. Here we briefly indicate some of the ways in which the teacher's work can be located in the wider school and the community, and to raise some feminist issues about them. Many of these aspects are expanded upon in the contexts of other chapters. For analytic convenience here we refer to five aspects of the wider role of the teacher – which may be seen as part of their everyday 'work'.

Inside and Outside the School Day

Teachers are responsible for the supervision of pupils over the course of the school day, and beyond the school day – with extracurricular activities, sports, drama rehearsals and so on. This means co-ordinating, supervising and controlling school 'play' as well as school 'work', and ensuring a balance between the two (Fenwick 1998). The issues of interaction and school discourse, discipline and control, and the need for immediacy, are all still pertinent issues. Indeed they may be exaggerated outside the formal contexts and activity of the classroom space. Studies have certainly found that girls experience substantial amounts of sexual harassment in the playground (Jones 1985, Mahony 1989, Thorne 1993), and this often goes unchecked. Boys tend to dominate playground space. Moreover, out-of-hours activities, with half-empty school buildings and little explicit security are ever more isolating and 'risky' environments for the extracurricular teacher – male and female. An understanding of the everyday work of the teacher should recognize that it is not confined to the physical boundaries of the classroom, and extents beyond lesson time.

Staff Rooms

Cunnison (1989) has highlighted how gender joking is common in staff rooms, as a way of preserving male dominance. Jokes may focus on women's femininity, or women's bodies, domesticity, sex or may just poke fun at women in general. Paechter (1998) also notes that the staff room is a distinctive physical and virtual space, with which professional culture and gendered power relations are played out and reproduced (Kainan 1994). Areas of staff rooms may become colonized by particular sub-groups of teachers. Some may become dominated by snooker tables used mainly by male staff. Dominant discourses of sporting prowess can serve to reinforce particular forms of hegemonic masculinity. Paechter (1998: 112) describes a staff room which had an area 'known as the "knitting circle" and was where the feminist teachers sat. In this case the label was used as a put-down for a group that consisted almost entirely of assertive younger women.'

Staff rooms then have important gender dimensions attached to them –

in terms of both discourse and space, which a feminist analysis of the everyday reality of the teacher should take account of.

Meetings and Management

We have already suggested that the style of discipline and control pervasive in the classroom will often reflect the management (male) ethos of the school (Davies 1992). As Riddell (1992) and others have noted (see Boulton and Coldron 1998), women are often excluded from positions of power with the school, and therefore may have little influence on the administration and ethos of the school. As we discuss in Chapter 5, men manage education and those women who do become managers face dilemmas of working with the system or seeking to challenge or change it.

The day-to-day running of the school, and the sharing of information and ideas, is often enacted through daily or weekly staff meetings. Askew and Ross (1988) argue that the contributions of women are often ignored, undermined or reiterated by a man. Hence, in so far as staff meetings are decision-making forums, women are excluded, or prevented from participating as fully as their male colleagues. Bailey's (1996) account of women teachers working in a boys' school to some extent reinforces this view – not least as one woman teacher had been expected to take the minutes at staff meetings – serving as a secretary. Thus we should be aware of the administrative, as well as teaching, loads and discursive practices within which teachers routinely operate.

The Teacher and the Community

The relationship between the school and the community it serves and in which it is located is complex and multifaceted. In terms of the everyday work of the teacher this may mean regular encounters and interactions with parents (Vincent 1996), governors, local businesses, public services and often the community at large. There has been important work undertaken on the relationships of parents, especially mothers, to the school, and this has emphasized the gendered dimensions of educational decision-making (see David 1993). We should be aware that the relationships of schooling extend beyond classroom and staff-room interactions. The everyday world of the classroom teacher is situated in local organizational, institutional and community frameworks.

Teachers' Work and Identity Work

Work on teachers' lives and careers has sought to locate the everyday realities of teaching alongside the everyday identity work in which teachers are routinely engaged – both collectively and individually. In Fenwick's study of junior high teachers in Edmonton, Canada:

> a common trait shared among the teachers was a vivid sense of identity in their work, reflected in the centre entire construction of the classroom space. Many talked about the self in relation to the ambiguity, contingency, and multiplicity of the environment in which they floated.
>
> (Fenwick 1998: 627)

We explore this dimension in Chapter 5, where we draw on the body of work that has been done on the narrative and (auto)biographical dimensions of the teacher's work, to explore the identity work of women (and feminist) teachers. Through their work practices and experiences, teachers are involved in constructing and reconstructing their identities, and those of their students – as gendered, racialized, sexualized, (dis)abled and situated. In the context of this chapter we should be aware of the individual and collective ways in which the work of the teacher contributes to the (re)construction and (re)production of identities and selves.

Conclusion

In this chapter we have concentrated on the everyday work of the teacher in the classroom. In particular we have chosen to emphasize the classroom management elements of the teacher's job, and to draw out gendered dimensions of those elements. Our primary aim has been to review the available research on classroom talk and 'control' rather than to offer alternative and distinctively feminist visions. However, it is clear that a feminist critique also offers the potential for different readings and alternative classroom practices: for example, seeing the 'privacy' of the classroom as opportunity rather than risk; adopting classroom space strategies to encourage collaboration and create feminized spaces; undertaking management strategies that foster democratic and social justice values. Later chapters return to these issues and explore the potential and problematics of such strategies. In the next chapter we turn to the intellectual work of the teacher – as 'receiver' and transmitter of knowledge. By exploring what gets taught and how it gets taught, the chapter provides a feminist critique of 'school' knowledge and gives some suggestions for alternative readings and pedagogies.

Knowing things differently ...

It is a Tuesday morning at Ledchester University. Arlette Traherne is teaching the first-year course 'Introduction to Women's Studies'. The class has been reading the life of Barbara McClintock, the Nobel Prize-winner. One member of the class, Elvira Luker, asks: 'Why didn't we learn about McClintock at school – I never knew there *were* any women geneticists'.

3 (Re)producing and (Re)defining Knowledge(s)

> Feminism as the source of new knowledge, that which runs counter; as the source of action which is based upon such knowledge; as a means of turning analytic attention upon the objects of knowledge – production; as a source which redefines who and what is subject, who it is that can know, as well as what it is that is known. Feminism as the analysis of old knowledge and the source of new knowledge.
>
> (Stanley 1997: 1)

Introduction

The everyday work of the classroom teacher cannot be separated from the reproduction, transmission and control of knowledge(s). The omnipresence of the teacher (Woods 1990), and the expectation that they 'know' everything, is caught up with the role of the teacher in defining what is valid and relevant information, and in deciding how that information should be packaged to students. Teachers can be perceived as definers of curricula at both explicit and implicit levels; or at least the mechanisms and means through which *the curriculum* is effectively transmitted to students and pupils. Of course, 'official' school knowledge taught via a curriculum is only part of the knowledge base that is reproduced and transmitted in the school and in the classroom. Teachers and the school are also vehicles for the reproduction and transmission of social values, knowledge in the realm of personal and social education, and folk knowledge about social norms such as sex roles and gender relations. Thus the school is the site and teachers the source of multiple knowledge(s).

The new sociology of education (Bernstein 1971, Esland 1971, Young 1971) was crucial in placing knowledge as central to the education experience. Education through the teacher was inextricably linked to social control over knowledge and cultural reproduction. The original theorists who proposed the 'new' sociology of education were not concerned about gender at all, and the work produced on the sociology of the school curriculum did not make the 'malestream' nature of that curriculum problematic. When analysing the everyday work of the teacher as a controller of knowledge from a feminist perspective this demands that we question both the basis and content of school knowledge(s). Stanley and Wise (1993) use the phrase 'situated knowledge' to locate knowledge within a social and cultural context. The feminist critique of knowledge and of what counts as knowledge (Caine et al. 1988) stresses the social location and production of knowledge. Put simply, teachers' control over knowledge should be accompanied by questions about whose knowledge is being given priority and coverage. Some knowledge claims are seen as superordinate in relation to others (Bourdieu 1993). The case can be made that what is seen as the knowledge is that which is defined by men, who are defining male experience as universal on the basis of all-male samples (Stanley and Wise 1993). Paechter (1998: 64) relates this argument to what she describes as the 'hegemony of reason and rational thought'. She argues that the knowledge taught in schools is reason, or decontextualized knowledge. She suggests that it is decontextualized knowledge that is valued in the school and that takes precedent over knowledge situated in everyday practices. In comparison, alternatives to reason and decontextualized knowledge – contextualized knowledge, emotion, non-rationality – are conceptualized in negative frames. Hence power is caught up and controlled by the control and transmission of certain (masculinized, hegemonic) forms of knowledge.

The legitimation and reproduction of school knowledge is inscribed in the voices and actions of teachers (especially white, middle-class males) argues Giroux (1988). However, we would wish to add to that the argument that the teacher's control over 'classroom' knowledge has always been questionable, as teachers are, more often than not, working within state regulatory education systems, and with existing, prescribed texts. Teachers' control over knowledge (and indeed how it is to be delivered) has, for example, come into question as a result of the introduction of a national or core curriculum in England and Wales. Teacher unions in particular have been extremely vocal in protesting against such moves, which they have perceived as reducing the autonomy (and power) of teachers to decide the curriculum and how to ensure its delivery.

From a feminist perspective the arguments remain consistent, even with a national curriculum. Questions about who defines the knowledge that should be included and reproduced in a national curriculum are just as valid as questions about what knowledge an autonomous teacher chooses to reproduce in her classroom. Feminist scholars and educationalists have undertaken a critique of knowledges. This has not simply been about documenting gender bias and establishing some kind of alternative unbiased or 'feminist' knowledge base. Rather it has acknowledged the situatedness and social positioning of all knowledge claims, locating knowledge in a political process of certification, superordination and subordination. Weiner locates this approach firmly within a post-structuralist feminism critique of dominant discourses of knowledge, where 'the knowledge that is produced as fruit is the knowledge that is linked to the system of power which produces and sustains it' (Weiner 1994: 99).

In this chapter we aim to explore the nature and delivery of classroom knowledge from a feminist perspective. In doing so we have two broad aims: to provide a summary of the feminist critique of classroom knowledges and curricula (to *deconstruct*), and to discuss examples of feminist pedagogy and approaches to the curriculum (to *reconstruct*). The chapter is in four main sections. First, there is an overview of the ways in which gender relations are enmeshed in the discourses and practices of the curriculum. Second, we turn our attention more specifically to the curricula of specific school subjects and disciplines. Third, examples of feminist curriculum practice and pedagogy are discussed as a way of engaging with the transformative, as well as the critical, aspects of the feminist rethinking of knowledge. Fourth, we conclude with a brief discussion of the role of the school in the reproduction and transmission of 'non-academic' and folk knowledge.

The Gendered Curriculum

While the school curriculum is often conceptualized around particular subjects, it is worthwhile noting that across subject specialities the curriculum is inscribed in a set of linguistic practices and dominant discourses (Paechter 1998, Weiner 1994). School curricula present a package of knowledge, scripted and transmitted in particular ways. Moreover, the curriculum that is encompassed within the everyday realities of teacher and student is often a gendered one.

> [The curriculum can be characterized] as a set of discursive practices in which girls and boys, teachers and pupils, different racial groups are differently and variably constituted as powerful or powerless, good or bad, feminine or masculine, workers or mothers ...
>
> (Weiner 1994: 98)

The school curriculum can be conceptualized as one in which dominant discourses seek to normalize some knowledges, and regulate or mute other knowledges. And with this conceptualization, gender relations are enmeshed within the content and delivery of the curriculum.

It is relatively unusual for students to be presented with the problematics of knowledge, or asked how ideas come to be seen as dominant or normal. Rather it is still the case that school students are presented with knowledges that are desituated and decontextualized, presented as truths and universals (Paechter 1998, Walkerdine 1988, 1989). The discourses of learning and understanding transmit, rather than seek to challenge, accepted and dominant understandings of the social world and academic disciplines. Particular ideas and sets of knowledges are imparted without critical attention to how they got there or why they are being privileged over other ideas or sets of knowledges. These arguments, then, are not about the content of particular curriculum subjects, but rather the specific discourses and practices that shape the teaching and learning of them. There are at least three aspects of this that are particularly relevant to a feminist critique. First, language is central to the meanings imparted through the school curriculum. Language and associated linguistic practices guide the ways in which curricula are understood and reproduced. This has both pedagogic and content significance. At perhaps the crudest level, yet still a pervasive one, feminist scholars have provided a critique of the generic 'man' used in linguistic practices and conventions. (See Chapter 2 for a more detailed discussion of language and talk.) Dictionaries say that 'man' can be used to mean both the human race (the generic usage) and the male of the species. Feminists have pointed out that this can result in considerable ambiguity in the classroom. When William Bennett Jr taught the high school American history class he chose one of the Federalist Papers as his subject matter (Shuy 1986). Throughout the whole lesson, Bennett totally failed to unpick for the students the use of the term 'man' in the Federalist Papers. Not only that, but the four American male researchers who analysed Bennett's teaching failed to pick up this aspect (Delamont 1986). Yet there is ample research (Thorne et al. 1983) to show that pupils do not understand the generic man but think it means male. Forty-four articles are cited on this point in Thorne et al. (1983), including Harrison (1975), who discovered some American adolescents studying 'the evolution of man' who believed that only males had evolved!

Second, the body of knowledge that is presented and the levels of understanding that are assumed are caught up in gender-power conceptualizations and relations (Foucault 1977). Walkerdine's (1988) work on the implications of gender relations in the knowledge and understanding base of the discourse of mathematical education is an example here. Walkerdine (1988) suggests that the language of mathematics, and the teachers' judgements of performance in mathematics, position boys and girls differently and unequally. The work on images of science and scientists also reveal that students represent these in gendered ways, perhaps as a result of the gendered discourse of school science (see Soloman 1993, Tuckey 1992; also Matthews 1996). Walford (1980) analysed the content of British school textbooks in physics, and found that women were outnumbered four to one in the pictures (compared to men). Where women were pictured it was as stereotyped 'non-scientists' (housewives, nurses, cooks), or they were presented as frightened or amazed.

Science and maths are a particular 'problem'. The more a discipline is believed to be 'objective' in its methods and content, the less likely it is that feminist critiques and alternative contents will be treated seriously. The discourse of English literature, for example, allows for a debate about different, gendered, readings of, say, *Jane Eyre* or *A Passage to India*, and so it is not hard for a teacher to make space for such discussions. Science and maths teachers are overwhelmingly committed to a belief that their subjects are impersonal, objective and gender-neutral. There is no space in the discourse for the social constructivist ideas of scholars such as Collins (1985), Harding (1993) or Keller (1985). For a science teacher to discuss the possibility of science being gendered is, in important ways, a denial of the science itself, and hence an undermining of the teacher's subject identity. Sanders (1995) raises these issues for maths teachers, Bentley and Watts (1994) for science. There have been calls for 'girl-friendly' science (see Whyte 1986) but the idea of *feminist* content for science and maths lessons is a problematic one.

Third, the 'normalizing' and 'regulating' aspects of dominant curriculum discourses (Weiner 1994) is further cause for feminist concern. The advent of a national curriculum in England and Wales, following the 1988 Education Reform Act, provides explicit evidence of the symbolic link between school knowledge and the needs of the state. One possible feminist reading of the national curriculum that ensued actually welcomed the effective curtailment of curriculum choice up to sixteen years, effectively seeking to end gender differences in subject take up and choice. Indeed, research for the Equal Opportunities Commission in England and Wales (Arnot et al. 1996, Salisbury 1996) provided concrete evidence of this. (It is worth noting that choice has subsequently been reintroduced at fourteen plus, and this has led some to speculate that conventional gender patterns will re-establish themselves as a result – see Paechter 1998.) However, if we turn from subject take-up to discourse and pedagogy, then any recourse to equality or gendered understandings is lost anyway. The new curriculum formations have come on the back of New Right attacks of educational philosophy and practice. Significantly, schooling has increasingly, rather than decreasingly, become viewed as an important site for cultural trans-mission. And as a result, new curricula that have been formulated appear retrogressive. There is an implicit assumption that knowledge can be carved up and packaged under discrete headings. There is the linked assumption that the knowledge can be examined and assessed routinely and satisfacto-rily. The knowledge that is (re)presented actually denies rather than recognizes both teachers and students as creators of knowledges, and constructors of experience. The implications for social justice and equity – never mind feminist pedagogy and understandings of knowledge – are to say the least grave.

In the discussion so far we have only touched on the actual content of school subjects and disciplines. In the next section we therefore turn our attention to a more detailed exploration of the school curriculum as a set of discrete, and decontextualized, disciplinary subjects – with associated schemata and texts.

Contents and Readings

The school curriculum has been the subject of feminist and gender-sensitive research since the 1970s. It is fair to say that much of the early research was more concerned with gender representation and sex stereotyping than with providing a more radical feminist critique of the relationships between the curriculum, knowledge and power. Nevertheless, the early findings, substantiated and developed by later work, provide an important element to the overall picture of the everyday work of the teacher – that of explicitly teaching disciplinary and educational knowledge through the use of schemes, texts and other classroom paraphernalia. Even a cursory glance at the literature would lead us to the conclusion that the explosion of feminist work in the academy (Evans 1997) – if we are to believe we are experiencing one – has not been matched by an explosion at the level of the school curriculum. In fact, some would argue that with the advent of various curriculum reforms, for example in England and Wales, gender may actually be being taken out of, rather than integrated into, everyday school subjects and curriculum practices. As Weiner points out in a reading of the English and Welsh national curriculum documentation, the commitment to equal opportunities was rather rhetorical and 'the newly created world of the national curriculum was also to be virtually "woman-free"' (Weiner 1994: 116).

Research has been carried out at both primary and secondary school levels, examining the content of curriculum schemes and textbooks that are used in the classroom as part of the process of knowledge transmission. Much of this research was carried out in the 1970s and early 1980s, although later research tends to substantiate rather than fundamentally challenge their early claims. Analysis of primary school materials and literature concludes that gender stereotyping is prevalent, both numerically in terms of numbers of males and females represented in texts, and in the tasks and roles that are assigned and demonstrated. Primary reading schemes in the UK were studied by Lobban (1974, 1975), and reading books studied by Stacey et al. (1974), and Maccia et al. (1975). Their conclusions were similar, with analyses of books and schemes revealing clear roles for boys and girls. Boys were almost always pictured and described as more adventurous and active, girls as passive and homemakers. Men tended to have jobs in the paid labour market, while women were predominantly given domestic roles in the home. Classic children's authors, such as Enid Blyton, have been heavily criticized as gender-biased, as have fairy stories (Carter 1990 provides authoritative feminist readings of classic tales) and comics (Delamont 1990, Sharpe 1976). We are aware in making reference to this literature that such analyses were a staple of feminist research in the 1970s and 1980s, but have now ceased to be fashionable. We would hope that many of the blanket gender stereotyping in the reading materials for pre-adolescents have now been removed. However, there is no systematic review to substantiate this claim.

Primary school textbooks (as opposed to 'fiction' reading books and schemes) have been less heavily studied, although research that has been done is able to document similar issues of gendered representation and activity. Early studies of US elementary textbooks (see Nilson 1975) concluded that, in both non-fiction and fiction texts, boys and men were the dominant figures. More recent studies of subject-specific texts, for examples in primary mathematics (Northam 1982) and history (Cairns and Inglis 1989) in the UK, draw similar conclusions. In maths texts (Northam 1982), males and females were shown in stereotypical roles – with girls being accurate recorders and having appropriate standards of behaviour and boys being more inventive and more likely to be shown solving problems and taking the initiative. The Cairns and Inglis (1989) analysis of primary history texts is equally discouraging: economic, social, cultural and religious histories were relatively neglected (where we would expect to find more women), with military and political history dominating the narratives and historical accounts. Where women are shown and discussed, they were in relatively passive, domestic and fashion roles.

Secondary school curriculum materials have also been analysed in terms of gender. Buswell's (1981) study of UK lower school humanities is well cited as an example of extreme under-representation and misrepresentation of women. Abraham (1989) examined mathematics, French and English texts used in an English comprehensive school in the mid-1980s and concluded that, among other things, the mathematics and French texts and materials were overly male-dominated. Similar patterns have also been found in examination and assessment materials (see Hendry 1987). Recent critical attention has been paid by researchers and some teachers/authors to the secondary school history curriculum, in particular to the inclusion (exclusion) of female history. At a simple level it may be argued that women are now more included as significant social actors in history materials and classes. However, an increase in women's names mentioned and in pictures of women in texts does not in and of itself fundamentally challenge the taken-for-granted knowledge base.

We pause here to take a more detailed look at history curricula and texts, as an example of a gendered content curriculum. Michelle Commeyras and Donna Alvermann (1996) analysed the content on women in three secondary school history textbooks in the USA, while Gaby Weiner (1993) examined school history in England. Both studies are timely given contemporary developments in the study of women's history, and simultaneous debates over history curricula. The 1990s saw substantial efforts to (re)introduce national history curricula both in the USA and in England and Wales. Importantly, on both sides of the Atlantic, these moves have heralded the explicit support of a history enmeshed in particular understandings of nationhood and identity. The development of the national history curriculum in England and Wales came on the back of New Right back-lashes of so-called radical history, accused of denigrating the history of the nation (Thomas 1979) and criticisms of political correctness. In North America, similar debates ensued – emphasizing national triumph and lamenting the de-emphasis of studying chronology and great men (see Weiner 1994).

> The criticism from both nations echoes the same basic concern that students will learn more about historical wrongs than the triumphs of their respective countries. The conservative backlash on both continents against a more inclusive multicultural and gender-balanced history curriculum has serious implications for the studies made to date to re-envision the contributions women have made to history.
>
> (Commeyras and Alvermann 1996: 33)

Commeyras and Alvermann examined the content and language in world history textbooks used in the classroom, and in particular how these served to position women. Their micro-analyses of content and language revealed that an androcentric view of history continued to be presented. The language of the texts positioned women in stereotypical ways.

> Efforts to integrate women into a history divided into time periods that revolve around exploration, conquest, consolidation of power and the politics of ruling expanding empires are accomplished by adding subsections on famous women, paragraphs about women's status and rights in these time periods, and sentences about their enabling contri-butions as wives and mothers of famous men.
>
> (Commeyras and Alverman 1996: 46–7)

Weiner (1993) provides a similar analysis of English school history in the new national curriculum. She specifically analysed the documentation of the national curriculum available during the early 1990s. Her analysis included a review of equality and social justice issues, including gender – which we concentrate on for our purposes here. The final report of the national curriculum history working group (DES 1989), tasked with developing the 'new' history curriculum, did pay some attention to equality concerns, though this was rather limited. Only four paragraphs were given over to gender – under the guise of equal opportunities (though, as Weiner points out, multiculturalism and race come off worse, with only two paragraphs and an assumption that the more ethnically diverse the population the more case there is for *British* history within the curriculum). On gender, the working party provided advice on 'the evils of stereotyping and the bias of "heroic" history' (Weiner 1993: 91). But the prescribed *content* of the history units to be taught in schools were gender-biased, and did little to present re-visioned historical accounts of women. In the core course (taken by all students), only two out of thirty-one named historical individuals were women, and in optional units only nine out of ninety-three named figures were women. Similar biases were prevalent with regard to race and ethnicity; which led Gill (1990) to conclude that the history of great white men still dominated the new curriculum. Moreover:

> there is no topic devoted entirely to women (even the Suffragettes appear to have lost their usual place), although some of the optional units e.g. HSU13 Domestic Life, Families and Childhood in Roman and Victorian Times seem designed to focus more on women's traditional domestic role historically.
>
> (Weiner 1993: 92)

Weiner locates her analyses alongside other trends evident in the history curriculum – the lack of radical or feminist historical perspectives; an emphasis on content and fact, rather than analytical and historical skills; the favouring of political and military history at the expense of social and cultural history, and the centring of a positive British history. In short the 'new' history curriculum still presents a decontextualized 'malestream' knowledge.

This brief look at the school history curriculum in the US and in England is a salutary reminder that feminist knowledges have not impacted on the taken-for-granted knowledges of schooling as much as one would have liked or hoped for. However, this does not necessarily mean that feminist teachers are without resources, nor that they do not mount challenges to what legitimately counts as knowledge. But it should be acknowledged that feminist curricula and attendant pedagogic practice are still battling at the margins rather than having a major impact on the mainstream (malestream) curricula. In the next section we turn our attention to feminist curriculum practice – both what it is and what it might be.

Feminist Curriculum Practice

There are a number of ways in which feminist educators and teachers can and do work with and beyond existing curricula contents and practice. These include challenging the content of the curriculum, and disrupting the teaching and learning processes that are embodied within curriculum practices. For our discussion here we have chosen to divide these into three levels of approach or action: curriculum content; feminist pedagogy; and feminist communication and collaboration. These are by no means exhaustive categories, but do give some indications of the range of action and possibilities.

Curriculum Content

Given the gendered bias of school curricula, one of the prime aims of feminist curriculum practice has been to challenge and change the content of taken-for-granted school knowledge(s). As we have already suggested, it is not enough simply to argue for more representations of women, or for the simple addition of women in areas of the curriculum. However, it is important that the certainties, 'facts' and universalities of the accepted school curriculum are challenged. There is already some evidence of this occurring – for example, drawing on the work of feminist historians to provide more girl- or women-friendly histories, or including the writing of women in historical and contemporary studies of literature. However, the (small) triumphs of feminist educators to place women and the problematic of gender on the curricula of higher education (see James 1998, Martin 1985, Rosser 1998) have not been paralleled in the school sector, partly because of the regulatory frameworks of national curricula. And it is even rarer to see sexuality, as well as gender, as part of an enlightened curriculum (see Warren 1998 on feminist critiques and transformations of the curriculum). So the examples provided by Boutilier (1994) on teaching lesbian literature at high school in the USA and Blinick (1994) on the inclusion of lesbian and gay issues in school histories of topics such as the US civil rights movement and the Holocaust are exceptions rather than accepted.

The key point to emphasize here is that any challenge to the confines of the curriculum requires feminist (and other) teachers to build up resources in addition to those currently available (Joyce 1987, Paechter 1998). This places additional pressures on the time and energy of teachers and students, who run the risk of ridicule and overt hostility (Acker 1988). Mounting a challenge to the dominant preoccupations of school knowledge and formal understandings of the curriculum can be a risky and tiring business.

Feminist Pedagogy

Feminist curriculum practice must be about offering new readings and challenges to what counts as knowledge, as well as continuing to critique existing curriculum practices. A key to this is the development and maintenance of effective feminist pedagogies: ways of teaching, learning and knowing (Cohee et al. 1998). Commeyras and Alvermann (1996) conclude their analysis of school history texts with suggestions of alternative ways of reading such texts – specifically reading the subtext, and becoming a resistant reader. They argue that textbooks can and should be read subtextually, in their case from a critical perspective, rather than taken at face value: 'Engaging in reading subtexts as human artefact meets the challenge feminist scholars have posed to educators, namely to present gender as a problematic area of study rather than as the natural order of things' (Commeyras and Alverman 1996: 45).

Reading the subtext is part of their broader understanding of becoming a resistant reader (Fetterley 1978, Flynn and Schweickart 1986; also see Bartlett 1998 for a discussion of the re-reading of feminist literature), which Commeyras and Alvermann argue that students need to be encouraged to engage in.

> There is a need for teachers to become proactive in the way they help students deal with age-old myths surrounding the dominance of men in relation to women … it is imperative that we find ways of teaching students to recognise unstated assumptions, subtleties of language and why some individuals are championed while others are omitted [from historical accounts].
>
> (Commeyras and Alvermann 1996: 46–7)

This is part of what may be seen as a feminist (though not necessarily so) pedagogical approach that enables students to develop understanding and meaning, rather than a simple internalization of curriculum 'facts'. This may include providing the means to different and varied interpretations, as well as more collaborative and experientially based work and reading. Crucially, however, any such approach must also acknowledge resistances to feminism – which can be mounted from both teachers and students. The calls for a feminist pedagogy from scholars such as Weiler (1991), Weiner (1993, 1994) and Cohee et al. (1998) must take into account such resistances.

Lewis (1990) considers the transformative potential of feminist pedagogy in the classroom – that is, seeing such an approach as 'celebratory as well as critical' (Weiner 1994: 126). The pedagogical movements Lewis identifies are instances where the gendered context of the classroom can be illuminated and shared. Feminist pedagogy here is about an overall approach to the classroom and to the teaching, rather than specific concerns with curriculum content. Thus the challenge and potential for change is in the approaches to the classroom and the curriculum – and the ways in which these approaches lend themselves to the critical (as well as celebratory) expansion of alternative educational understandings, and discursive practices.

Communication and Collaboration

Implicit in the development of curriculum spaces and feminist (alternative) pedagogies is the desire and need for collaboration and communication between and beyond feminist educators, teachers, practitioners, curriculum developers, policy makers and so forth. This is something with which feminist educators and teachers are familiar (Joyce 1987). In the UK, for example, there are active (local and national) groups of feminist teachers across a range of school subject disciplines. This is one important area of collaboration, although for feminist curriculum practices to have any lasting impact, collaboration and communication is also vital beyond the corpus of self-identified feminist teachers. Debates over and challenges to the curriculum are social justice and equality issues rather than simply feminist issues. The development and ongoing collaboration and communication with colleagues, the academy, policy makers and parents will be vital for any long-term goals to challenge and change the curricula and taken-for-granted knowledge of schooling:

> [F]eminist teachers, whether they like it or not, are in the cultural front-line when it comes to resisting the unacceptable or pushing the necessary changes that will improve girls' and womens' future educational experiences and life chances. Exhaustion notwithstanding, time alone will tell how effective they can be.
>
> (Weiner 1993: 98)

To summarize, feminist challenges to the knowledge base of schooling are not at all mainstream, although there are instances of good practice. It is vital that a feminist perspective of school knowledge does not just concentrate on providing a sustained critique, however valuable, valid and necessary that critique might be. It is equally important to construct new ways of conceptualizing knowledge, and in transmitting that knowledge through the frameworks of the educational institution. In working with these frameworks, feminists should also seek to challenge the boundaries of them.

Other Knowledge(s)

Thus far we have focused upon the academic, 'official' knowledges in education. Before leaving this topic we turn our attention to the everyday, mundane and 'non-academic' knowledges that also permeate schools and form part of the teacher's work. Alongside those knowledges that are enshrined in the official curriculum are other knowledges that teachers (and students/pupils) bring to school, and reproduce within school. These can be differentiated on at least two levels. First there is the distinction between academic and 'other' non-academic school subjects. And second there is the distinction between the formalized and the mundane (or hidden) curricula of schooling.

Commentators have distinguished between academic and non-academic school subjects, or between dominant and marginal subjects (Attar 1990, Paechter 1998, Sparkes et al. 1990). Paechter's (1998) analysis concentrates on the 'otherness' of marginal subjects in the curriculum. She focuses on craft, design and technology (CDT), which incorporates 'craft' skills and home economics, and physical education (PE). She locates the low status of these subjects within their gendered and social class histories (working-class girls learning how to cook, working-class boys learning to do manual labour; the differential emphasis of boys' and girls' physical education over time, and so on). She points to the ways in which subjects like CDT and PE have also been linked to the less able, the disaffected (and in some cases particular ethnic groups – see Carrington and Wood 1983). The low academic status of these subjects has often meant that they have been excluded from studies of gender and schooling (see Riddell (1992), who ignored PE). Moreover, subject specialists in these areas have been shown to have relatively weak voices with the school and the educational arena more generally. Paechter's analysis suggests that in these non-academic areas of the curriculum some groups, especially girls, black boys and less able students, are constructed as *Other*, and the content modified to reflect this. For example, gendered versions of CDT and PE are normalized in the school curriculum.

> The cases of [CDT and PE] make it clear that it is quite possible for alternative male and female forms of a subject to develop and flourish more or less independently for decades, even in mixed schools. The subjects where this has happened however, are those that are themselves Other within the school curriculum; they are of low status, and generally aimed at those, often working class, students who are seen as 'less-able'. Higher status subjects only come in one main form; there are no gendered alternatives.
>
> (Paechter 1998: 90)

Thus so-called non-academic subjects in the school curriculum are themselves enshrined with gendered connotations. Ironically, the development of separate (though not necessarily girl-friendly or feminist) subject curricula for boys and girls has been located in the marginal rather than mainstream (malestream/dominant) subjects. So while we have separate, gender-specific PE, we do not have accepted separate, gender-specific mathematics or science or geography.

Teachers and pupils also bring to the school, and reproduce within the school, mundane or everyday knowledges. Teachers have beliefs about how society functions that permeate schools, as do pupils. Such knowledges appear in many contexts, such as meal times, physical education lessons, and public 'homilies'. Measor (1984), for example, showed how female pupils' 'folk' beliefs about femininity impeded their science teacher's attempt to get them to do experiments, and Delamont (1998) analysed the folk models of gender offered by PE teachers to 12-year-old girls. Riseborough's (1988) account of a cookery teacher in an orthodox Jewish school, where the staff and pupils shared a set of knowledge about the world that was more powerful than the official curriculum, is another classic example.

Feminist teachers are likely to have a very different set of beliefs about the way the society works from non-feminist colleagues, which may be revealed in non-academic contexts. A feminist PE teacher observed by Delamont (1990) deliberately sent six girls to fetch a piece of equipment from another hall to challenge gendered assumptions about 'strength'. The man in the other hall sent the girls back empty-handed, with six boys from his class carrying the 'heavy' items because he believed 'girls shouldn't carry things, Miss'. Ethnographies of everyday life in schools frequently show the power of the 'hidden' curriculum and everyday knowledges. Many commentators, from Becker (1952a) onwards, have emphasized the 'classist' nature of such beliefs and knowledges. Gender issues are equally pertinent, however: the teacher who 'knows' females are 'naturally' better at childcare is deploying knowledge just as much as the geography graduate using an atlas. Feminists, with their basic belief that the personal is political, that the mundane (housework) is as important as the exotic (the sales conference in New York), that the implicit matters alongside the explicit, have conducted research on how the mundane 'knowledge' of teachers is powerfully deployed in the school.

Aspects of this concern with the personal and how that permeates the curriculum content and process are present within analyses that concentrates on the relationship between caring and knowledge (see Noddings 1984, 1992). Webb and Blond (1995), for example, argue that caring is part of teacher knowledge, and that this knowledge impacts upon pedagogy and curriculum. In an innovative study where one (Webb) undertook participant observation in the others (Blond's) classroom, Webb and Blond collaborated on a narrative inquiry of caring knowledge in the classroom. They argue that caring for the person is central to the teacher's training, and that this caring knowledge is part of the practical knowledge of teaching. This clearly has implications for a feminist understanding of the realities of the classroom and the kinds of knowledge that permeates those realities.

> Our claim is not that every teacher cares, nor that every student responds to a teacher's caring. Our concern is to demonstrate the level of subjectivity that exists in the relation between two persons (teacher and student) – a level of subjectivity and knowing which involves both bodies and minds.
>
> (Webb and Blond 1995: 624)

Conclusion

In conclusion, we would want to emphasize that the teacher's everyday work is fundamentally about the reproduction and transmission of knowledge(s). These incorporate both academic and non-academic, formal and mundane. Moreover a feminist perspective of school knowledge reveals critique, broader understandings and new ways of knowing. In the next two chapters we turn our attention to the relationships between gender and the career of teaching. In Chapter 4 we examine the teaching labour force, the process of promotion and women in educational administration, before focusing more on experiences and biographies of women teachers in Chapter 5.

All the headships …

Carlotta Comperton is at her Ed.D. course, at Ledchester University. This module is on the European Union law on discrimination, and the class have been working on judgements on racial discrimination cases. Next comes sex discrimination, and members of Carlotta's group are having coffee. Bruce Fossett and Connor Fulpurse, both heads of PE at local schools, are having a moan about promotion in Ledshire. They are muttering that 'all the headships' are going to women. Carlotta looks at Fern Codrington, a geography teacher at Abbotsleigh, and gestures at the statistics on women and promotion in teaching displayed on a wall poster. They do not bother to say anything.

4 Gender and the Teacher's Career

> Many individual feminists suffered professional burn-out under this pressure
> to love and nurture all their students (no matter how repulsive some of those
> 'little individuals' were).
>
> (Mercer 1997: 41)

Introduction

This chapter concentrates on the position of women within the career of
teaching. In doing so it addresses two particular issues. Firstly, as Hilary
Burgess (1989) has pointed out, while teaching is a good *job* for a woman it
is a *career* with prospects for men. In the course of this chapter we hope to
explore that position – both by addressing the gendered structuration of
teaching and by considering the opportunities and realities of career
advancement for women in teaching. Second, teaching is often conceptualized as an occupation that has been feminized – that is, it is one of the
liberal professions that has undergone feminization. The feminization thesis
– that the gender balance of a profession is skewing towards women – has at
least two meanings: that of numbers and that of ethos. While we are able to
say with some confidence that the first kind of feminization is visible (the
majority of the international teaching force is female), the second kind of
feminization – suggesting new structures, organizations and ways of
seeing/working – is harder to delineate. In the course of this chapter we draw
some conclusions about the extent of feminization within the teaching
profession.

   The chapter is organized into three general sections: (1) an overview of
women in the teaching profession; (2) career trajectories and promotion; (3)
leadership, administration and management. These sections all contribute to
a general aim of attempting to map relationships between gender and the
division of labour in teaching. By concentrating on teaching as a job and as
a career we are attempting to locate the experiences of (women) teachers
within the educational labour market and world of work. In doing so we do
not elaborate on the everyday experiences of teachers as they go about their

work and the construction of their identities and biographies through their work (although we do include some data on the experiences of promotion and of educational management). We concentrate much more on individual experiences and biographies in Chapter 5.

Women and Teaching

The position of men and women in the teaching profession as a whole mirrors their position within international labour markets. A gendered division of labour exists with the teaching profession (Acker 1994). There are more women in teaching than men, and women are an increasing majority within the teaching profession. In principle, 'teaching is a career in which women and men enjoy equal opportunities' (Measor and Sikes 1992: 111). However the numbers of women securing senior teaching posts remain disproportionately and disappointingly low (Acker 1989 and 1994, Bell and Chase 1993, Boulton and Coldron 1998, De Lyon and Migniuolo 1989). In England and Wales, for example, women make up over 65 per cent of all teachers, and yet account for less than 45 per cent of head teachers (DfEE 1998).

On the whole (and of course there are exceptions – some women do reach the high echelons of the teaching profession), women teachers remain clustered in lower, unpromoted ranks of the teaching profession, and often in particular (traditional/feminine) subject areas and school arenas. Women are under-represented in headships, senior teacher roles, educational leadership and administration. In the USA, for example, men make up over 90 per cent of school superintendents (head teachers) (Chase 1995), and women are not proportionately represented in educational administration.

> Male dominance of the occupation is striking because superintendents rise from the ranks of teachers, seventy percent of whom are women. While the presence of women in the prestigious professions of medicine and law has increased slowly over the last twenty years, the superintendency has remained resistant to women's integration, despite the fact that half the graduate students in programs of educational administration are now women.
>
> (Chase 1995: 30)

This is a familiar story, echoed and sustained elsewhere. In Canada, while three-quarters of elementary school teachers are women, three-quarters of the principals are men. While almost half of secondary school teachers are women, over 85 per cent of secondary school principals are men (Taylor 1995). This general position is also evident among the policy ranks of teaching. Turner et al. (1995) highlighted the gendered divisions within Her Majesties Inspectorate (HMI) of schools in Scotland. The HMI is responsible for the auditing and government inspection of schools. In 1994 there were thirteen senior management/chief inspectors in Scotland, of which only one was a woman. And in the Scottish inspectorate more generally, women made up only 20 per cent of the total. This picture was also reflected by Adler et al. (1993), who noted that out of 108 chief education officers in England and Wales only sixteen were women. There are exceptions to this familiar tale, for example, and ironically, in the Irish education system (Lynch 1991). Ireland has both a religious (mainly Catholic) school system and a lay (or secular) school system. Teachers drawn from religious orders (nuns, priests and brothers) do not compete for senior posts in the open educational labour market. Religious schools draw senior posts from within their own members. Hence within the Irish Catholic school system in particular you do find many (religious) women who hold senior educational posts. However, in the lay system the picture is less promising (and more predictable). In Ireland, like elsewhere, women are under-represented at most senior management levels in schools (Lynch 1991). Golding and Chen (1993) present a complex picture of school principalship in Israel, which has undergone considerable feminization in terms of numbers. Between 1972 and 1989 the numbers of women securing principalships in Israel rose dramatically; women now make up 67 per cent of elementary level principals and 37 per cent of secondary school principals. Golding and Chen (1993) note that this trend has been paralleled by two further trends: that of the dramatic erosion of the occupational prestige of the teaching profession as a whole in Israel *and* the steady increase in the education attainment levels of school principals. Hence the scenario is that highly educated women are moving into school principalships at the same time as the social status of the teaching profession in Israel is decreasing.

The issue of seniority or promotion within teaching is even more complex if one considers subject specialism and school type. Women make up the overwhelming majority of teachers of nursery and primary (elementary) age children (over 80 per cent in England and Wales, 75 per cent in Ireland). However, the numbers of female principals in these sectors do not mirror this. For example, in Ireland in 1988–89 only 8 per cent of women in primary teaching were principals, compared with almost 40 per cent of men (Lynch 1991). In secondary education the pattern is less marked, though still significant. In England and Wales women account for over half of all secondary classroom teachers, and they only secure 22 per cent of headships in that sector (DfEE 1998). Lynch (1991) has argued that one of the major problems is that few women actually apply for principalships (less than 32 per cent of all applicants). She has pointed out that those who do apply fare reasonably well. The problem seems to be the level of application rather than the quality of the applicants (we return to this as a factor of promotion later in this chapter). Other commentators have noted this scenario (see Acker 1994, Boulton and Coldron 1998, Hilsum and Start 1974). We explore the relationships between gender and promotion in the teaching profession in more detail later in this chapter.

Many of the senior posts that are held by women correspond to what may be considered to be traditional sex-typed or feminine areas of the educational spectrum. When women do reach senior posts in teaching these tend to correspond to 'traditional feminine' educational areas. Men tend to be heads of faculty, heads of sixth form, deputy heads and head teachers. Promoted women tend to be heads of year, heads of lower and upper schools, and heads of special education. That is, women are concentrated in promoted posts that are mainly pastoral in nature (Torrington and Weightman 1989). Where women teachers are promoted to deputy principalships they are more likely to be promoted to posts with a special remit for pastoral care. As with the high numbers of primary school teachers who are women, this seems to confirm the notion that women tend to be found in posts that combine teaching with caring roles (Mercer 1997). Where women do become subject heads, heads of sections or departments, it is still more likely for them to do so with what might be perceived as traditional subject boundaries. In mathematics and science subject areas, for example, women are still under-represented both in terms of actual numbers and in terms of senior posts, despite such educational projects as, for example, Girls into Science and Technology (GIST) and Women in Science and Engineering (WISE) in the UK (Henwood 1996, Whyte 1986). These projects were aimed at encouraging girls into science and technological subjects at school and as an educational career. Indeed, the overall success of such initiatives has been called into question. A report commissioned by the UK government (HMSO 1994) noted the only partial success of WISE. Felicity Henwood's (1996) discussion of the WISE initiative indicates that the limited success rests, in part at least, in the ways in which the 'WISE discourse' defined the 'problem' of women as one of ignoring opportunities and lacking information, rather than concentrating on structural inequalities, and gendered discourses with science and engineering occupations and sub-specialities. Henwood concludes thus:

> We need to understand more about the relationship between gender, sexuality and work and the ways in which both gender and (hetero)sexuality are produced through the construction of difference at work. Only by exploring these relationships more systematically can we begin to understand how and why any radical or transformatory potential of equal opportunities initiatives such as WISE is constantly undermined.
>
> (Henwood 1996: 212–3)

To summarize, in terms of the numbers of qualified and practising teachers, and student teachers (see Chapter 6), women are in a majority. Children in formal education are being educated in the school classroom by women.

However the evidence suggests that women do not appear to have access to the power and policy-making within the education system (nor are they able to influence, in any uniform or sustained way, the knowledge base that forms the bedrock of teacher education – see Chapter 6). In that sense teaching, while becoming increasingly *feminized* (in terms of numbers), is not becoming distinctly *feminist* (in terms of career trajectories, discourse and ethos).

A case could be made that, as it has been demoted in terms of prestige, the teaching profession has been ever more willing to encourage women to apply. The parallel trends that teaching has become more feminized (at the junior and younger ranks especially) while being conceptualized as a semi-profession (Acker 1983, 1994 and Chapter 8 of this volume) has meant that the aspirations of feminism in terms of labour-market opportunities have perhaps not been met here (yet). While the majority of new recruits to teaching are women, that does not necessarily translate into a majority of women holding permanent posts. In Ireland in 1987, for example, females constituted the great majority of education graduates. However, when it came to obtaining permanent teaching appointments on qualifying, the male graduates fared better. Twenty per cent of male graduates in both primary and secondary education got permanent jobs, compared with only 9 per cent of female graduates. Conversely, over 80 per cent of female graduates of education secured part-time or temporary work, compared with 65 per cent of the male graduating student teachers (Lynch 1991). There are, of course, equal opportunities policies and codes of practice within schools (for a summary of these in the UK see Turner et al. 1995, Arnot et al. 1996, Salisbury 1996). Local education authorities in the UK, responsible for state schooling, routinely collect equal opportunities data on race, gender, family circumstances and so on as part of the application and recruitment process. This acts as a monitoring mechanism. However the actual impact it may have on the actual recruitment and interview process is difficult to assess. In Greece, primary and secondary school teachers are hired according to official procedures that stipulate that lists of applicants should be ranked according to date of university graduation. Again this accords with an equal opportunities ideal and may benefit women (who form the majority of recent education graduates) (Kontogiannopoulou-Polydorides 1991).

Teacher unions have also taken up the mantle of equal opportunities within the profession. In Britain, the National Union of Teachers (NUT) resolved to campaign for equal pay as early as 1904 (Oram 1987, Partington 1976). More generally, women teachers have been active in teacher unions as a way of seeking to challenge male hierarchies and place feminist issues on union agendas (Rowbotham 1989, Weiner 1994). However, battles over equal pay and equal status have been drawn out and, at times, bitter (Delamont 1990). During the 1950s and 1960s the National Association of

School Masters (a men-only union) argued to reverse the decision of the principle of equal pay and set a tone for a gendered division within the ranks of the teaching profession.

The teacher unions have not provided an alternative source of career advancement and job satisfaction for women, as might have been the case. In the UK, women teachers had separate unions (as did men) prior to the 1975 Sex Discrimination Act, and, through unions such as the National Union of Women Teachers, they sought to establish equal worth, and career recognition. Indeed some of the early women teacher unions could be said to have been distinctly feminist in their outlook and action. However, with the 1975 Act, single-sex unions disappeared and merged, a consequence of which could actually be seen to be the demotion rather than increasing prominence of gender and equal opportunities issues. Top jobs within teacher unions tend to be held by men. Women's sections within the established teacher unions have not been mainstreamed. Women teachers in the NUT, for example, began a sub-group in the late 1970s to seek to establish a place for women's rights issues and to analyse the domination of men within the union. And while they were successful in getting the NUT, together with the Equal Opportunities Commission, to undertake a survey of promotion and the women teacher (NUT 1981), it is fair to say that the equality agenda has not been pursued very strongly by the teacher unions. There has certainly not been any sustained or lasting impact of union activity that has permeated to the teaching profession as a whole.

Before considering the explanations for and experiences of the gendered career trajectories within the teaching profession, it is worth noting that this picture is a familiar one throughout the broader education system. As we explore in Chapter 6, men effectively manage teacher education. Although the number of women academics working with university education departments is greater than in some other higher education fields, women are seldom in a position to dictate policy, as they are mainly concentrated with the lower ranks of the profession. This is a picture mirrored in further education (Leonard 1998) and higher education (Acker 1994, Brown 1999, Lie and Malik 1994, Masson and Simonton 1996). Brown's (1999) analysis of men and women at the decision-making levels in British higher education (1996–97), for example, is a salutary tale: 42 per cent of higher education colleges and universities in Britain had no women in any of the five senior academic positions (vice-chancellor/principal; pro-vice-chancellor/deputy principal; registrar or equivalent; bursar (or equivalent) and university librarian). Only twenty out of 146 institutions analysed (that is, only 14 per cent) had more than one senior female academic officer. There were no senior women in six of the eight colleges in the University of Wales. Similar patterns are evident among the academic ranks. For every ninety-six male professors in Britain, there are only four women, and in some disciplines it is hard to find a woman professor at all.

Careers and Promotion

It remains the case that women are disproportionately under-represented in the 'career' of teaching, while remaining a majority of the teaching labour force. There have been a number of explanations put forward to explain or account for the under-representation of women in school management and senior educational posts. As Boulton and Coldron (1998) have pointed out, these explanations have been built around assumptions about gender and career. Literature on women's career patterns and under-performance in teaching has been located in assumptions of a deficit model of women and the labour market, and in a pervasive ideology of individual choice. Hence the arguments have been made that women have not succeeded in achieving promotion because (a) they lack the necessary aspirations, qualities and skills and (b) they choose not to put themselves forward for promotion. Feminist scholars have challenged these assumptions – proving them to be inadequate and masking a far more complex positioning of women within the career of teaching. Indeed it has also been suggested that assumptions that women lack ambition and promotional qualities are more a part of the folklore of the staff room (Delamont 1990, Measor and Sikes 1992) than the experienced reality of women teachers (Boulton and Coldron 1998).

Bloot and Browne (1996) identified nine clusters of factors in the literature as possible explanations for the under-representation of women in promoted positions in education:

- policies and regulations
- patriarchy within the education system
- gender role stereotyping
- male models of leadership
- family commitments
- low promotional connotations for women
- women's own perceptions
- lack of skills and experience
- lack of encouragement and support.

These clusters lend themselves to three overarching sets of arguments: (1) women's commitment to promotion and career advancement have been systematically called into question; (2) the process of promotion has been pointed to as malestream and inequitable, and dependent upon (male) sponsorships and networking; (3) school management has been perceived as based on male models of leadership and discipline – thereby negating the skills, experiences and leadership qualities of women teachers. We now turn to a brief discussion of each of these as the basis for exploring the relationships between gender and career (non-)advancement in teaching.

merit and selling oneself may also be disadvantageous to females. As an experienced female PE teacher in Australia told Bloot and Browne:

> It is obviously the gift of the gab ... it's just how referees filled out and how you fill out forms, you know, 'blab' about yourself. You can go and do courses on how to write your resumé and all that sort of thing ... on how to butter yourself up ... it's wrong.
>
> (Bloot and Browne 1996: 88)

Bloot and Browne (1996) suggest that women are traditionally portrayed as less adept at promoting themselves, and hence systems of promotion that rely on this, like the Australian system, may be 'mixed in its potential to change the present standing of women'.

There are also much more informal aspects to the process of promotion: the role of networks, sponsors, role models, and general encouragement. A number of commentators have noted the importance of networks and sponsorships in the pursuance of career advancement in teaching (Evetts 1990) and of the reality that women may be less well plugged into networks that count (that is, 'male' networks) (Boulton and Coldron 1998, Delamont 1990, De Lyon and Migniuolo 1989, Measor and Sikes 1992). The lack of mentors and role models is given by Bloot and Browne (1996) as a significant factor in the under-representation of females at head-of-department level in Australian schools. Those that had succeeded in obtaining promotion had been actively encouraged to do so by significant others (peers, but more significantly those in positions of power – administrators, other heads, superintendents and so forth).

Models and Conceptualizations of School and Educational Management

A management ethos that values discipline, control and competition is often perceived as the model of management, predominant in education and schools. As such it is often conceptualized as a male model of leadership, with authority derived from an authoritarian approach. This tendency to present educational leadership as one encapsulating competition, regulation and control has been criticized as dismissing what have been perceived to be feminine management styles – based on collaboration, participation, and negotiation (Adler et al. 1993, Davies 1990). This interpretation is open to debate; there is some dispute as to whether women and men do display distinctly different management styles. Equally it has been argued that alternative visions of educational management – based on collaboration and negotiation – are possible, and desirable (Blackmore 1999, De Lyon and Migniuolo 1989, Shakeshaft 1989). Although, as Bloot and Browne (1996: 90) point out, 'because there are so few females in leadership roles there is

Commitment and Ambition

It is the case that fewer women than men apply for promotion in educe
(Acker 1994, Boulton and Coldron 1998, Lynch 1991). This has, in the j
been linked to low promotional connotations for women and a lac
ambition and commitment. Yet on closer analysis women's commitmer
teaching is on a par with that of men's. As Measor and Sikes (1992)
noted, assumptions about women taking excessive career breaks are m
ical rather than real. Women teachers take nowhere near as much time
as is often suggested (Evetts 1990). In addition, they do take part in a
school activities, and in-service courses (often thought to be impo
elements of a promotion application). While they may apply for promc
less than their male colleagues, this does not and should not equate w
lack of ambition. Davidson (1985) found little difference between the a
tion of male and female teachers, although women often felt their cha
of success were poorer. This may go some way to account for the l
numbers of applications. While early explanations proposed that this
of interest' was linked to gender stereotyping, later commentators
suggested that this is an oversimplification. Davies (1990) and Bloot
Browne (1996) suggest that gender roles and family responsibilities
actually be used as convenient and stereotypically acceptable excuse
conceal more powerful deterrents to apply for promotion. Sandra A
(1983, 1994), for example, argues that a lack of awareness of the prom
system and a lack of confidence that they will succeed are more l
reasons for low application rates.

The Promotion Process

The process of promotion can be conceptualized in at least two way:
formal and the informal. It is difficult to provide concrete evidence
formal promotion procedures are biased, or that they intentionally disc
nate against women. In many countries, such as the UK and Aust
schools and educational authorities are governed by statutory legislati(
gender equality in employment (such as the UK Sex Discrimination
1975). As we have noted earlier in this chapter, equal opportunities r
toring is now a routine in many educational work contexts – and certa
normal routine element of recruitment processing. However, there are
ably aspects of the procedure that may continue to serve to disadva
female applicants. It is still the case that most interview panels will h
majority male membership. Male dominance of the senior echelo
teaching and school management mean that the educational and c
decision-makers are mostly men (although school governors, espe
parent governors, do have a significant female membership – see David
Vincent 1996). Furthermore, promotion systems that are based on

limited opportunity to demonstrate the benefits of female management, and the well-entrenched traditional model remains as the "norm" '.

Recent changes to the education system in England and Wales, which have been mirrored elsewhere (Mahony 1997), have brought the issue of educational management to the fore – with consequences for women educationalists. Pauline Leonard's (1998) analysis of the further education sector in the UK (post-16 education/tertiary education) points to the re(positioning) of male management values and culture as a result of recent shifts.

> The cultural shift in educational philosophy from professional concerns to the economic principles of marketisation, unit autonomy and performance targets has been seen by many men involved in the running of FE as an opportunity to reclaim these organisations as both male-dominated and masculine.
>
> (Leonard 1998: 82)

Leonard argues that the shifts in education and schooling towards a market-orientated economic model actually serve to exacerbate precisely those elements of educational management perceived as masculine. If this is so, then the opportunities for new stages of management with which women may feel more comfortable may become less rather than more likely.

Choice or Constraint?

The account presented by Boulton and Coldron (1998) of one well-qualified teacher choosing not to apply for internal promotion to a management position contextualizes the gendered politics of promotion. In particular, their account addresses the explanation of individual choice with regard to the decision to apply for promotion (or not to apply). Boulton and Coldron (1998) provide a narrative of one woman, Lesley, and her 'decision' not to apply for a position of deputy head teacher of a school in England. A series of events and key decisions by the school and head teacher led to Lesley's 'choice' to decline to apply for this internal promotion, despite assumptions from many colleagues and the head teacher that she would and should apply. The appointment of a temporary deputy head (a male who was also head of sixth form) pending the permanent appointment and the decision not to advertise the post externally were key factors influencing Lesley's decision. She was loyal to the temporary deputy head (who would also apply for the position and with whom she would have to work afterwards); the temporary appointment itself and consequent decision to advertise the post internally as deputy head and head of sixth form (the post held by the temporary appointee) indicated to Lesley a lack of institutional support for her to apply. Lesley also identified a lack of support among some colleagues, and did not feel willing to cope with this. Furthermore, Lesley felt unhappy about a purely internal recruitment process – and would have felt more at ease competing with external candidates rather than internal colleagues. In the end, individual agency actually played little part in Lesley's choice not to apply – structural and financial decisions and the perceived (lack of) support within the school channelled her decision. This is particularly pertinent as an example of internal promotion politics. It should be noted that the school had a genuine commitment to equal opportunities and yet it was still possible for an able and confident woman to feel isolated and disadvantaged. The internal promotion dynamic presented by Boulton and Coldron is particularly striking when:

> women more often than men will be restricted to internal or local promotion ... issues of staff support assume far greater importance, and in schools where the management style is at least partly collegiate, this is accentuated. Explicit support and encouragement for candidates needs in this context to go beyond assurance of having the right experience and skills to do the job. Lesley herself identified the gender dimension of this when she spoke of being more concerned about lack of support than a man would be. Sponsorship, shown to be important for women particularly when exercised by those of 'gatekeeper' status, can also be even more influential in an internal context. The difficulties that arise when all those of gatekeeper status are male is demonstrated in this study.
>
> (Boulton and Coldron 1998: 159–60)

The far-reaching point of Boulton and Coldron's study is that 'choosing' to apply or not to apply for promotion is not simply about individual choice. Rather the politics of promotion and situated contexts in which career advancement is made may actually constrain rather than promote real choice. It is certainly the case that gendered assumptions about women teachers' lack of ambition and commitment remain wholly inadequate explanations for the lack of women within the higher echelons of the teaching profession.

Thus far we have concentrated on teaching, gender and career advancement in rather negative terms. That is why we have emphasized the gendered division of labour with the profession and the explanations for the lack of proportional and representational career advancement. To redress the balance we now turn our attention to women managers within teaching.

Experiences and Narratives of Educational Leadership

In a review of the literature on teacher leadership, Smylie (1997) does not mention gender at all – either in general or in relation to educational leaders, administrators and managers who are women. This ignores and dismisses the experiences and narratives of women who do succeed in obtaining management positions in the educational (and school) arena. In a still relatively small literature on women and educational leadership a number of themes are recurrent. Here we deal with three sets of issues:

- the contradictory position of women within educational management and how it is accounted for;
- educational leadership and emotional labour;
- leadership and educational change.

Ambiguous Empowerment

Ambiguous empowerment is a phrase coined by Susan Chase (1995) to capture the contradicting experiences of power and subjection of women school superintendents (head teachers) in the United States. Through collecting and presenting the work narratives of these women head teachers, Chase argues that women educational leaders develop a range of narrative strategies for coping with and articulating their ambiguous empowerment – that is, their professional achievements and power in a context of a white- and male-dominated profession. This concept of ambiguous empowerment resonates with the so-called impossible fiction of the woman teacher, as described by Walkerdine (1990) and Munro (1998): to be a teacher is to possess power, authority and knowledge while to be a woman is to lack power, authority and knowledge.

Chase (1995) concentrates on a small number of the twenty-seven work history narratives she collected from women school superintendents. She uses these narratives to illustrate various overlapping narrative strategies articulated by women superintendents to account for their position. The importance of professional identity and professional discourse is particularly evident. Success is articulated as the ability to do the work well, and in fitting in with established patterns of the world of teaching. Some, like Ana, highlighted their competence and skills through professional discourse, and played down or excluded experiences of subjection and inequality. Others utilize their gendered and racialized experiences and identities to both expose vulnerability and draw strength. In doing so, 'they partially dismantle and partially preserve the individualistic, gender-and-race-neutral character of the discursive realm of professional work' (Chase 1995: 180). Thus, like student teachers and teacher educators (see Chapter 6 of this volume), these school superintendents draw on professional ideologies of neutrality as a means of both accounting for subjection and establishing a means of empowerment.

A central theme of Chase's work is the ways in which women superintendents are totally committed to their work and to 'what needs doing'. This does not mean that they did not recognize discrimination (of gender and race) and the collective nature of their subjection. Rather it illustrates the high level of primary commitment to their work task. Equality issues are part of but not central to that task: 'The individual struggle for equality is essential, but also secondary, to the primary commitment to professional work. While professional commitment is an end in itself, the struggle for equality is a means to that end' (Chase 1995: 183).

The importance of support comes across in the narratives that Chase presents. Support is presented in contradictory rather than straightforward ways. Further, it reinforces the idea that success is tied to an involvement in certain kinds of (male) networks. Margaret, for example, contextualized her success through the mentorship of powerful men and derived her own personal strength in the context of vulnerability to men's greater power. Karen noted her desire for integration with her male colleagues as part of her work. Twenty-five of the women Chase interviewed spoke of the importance of support from women peers and colleagues. But while there was enthusiasm about support in general – the limits of informal female networks and participation was well recognized. This kind of support often lacked a power base, and while such networks were a base from which to request equal access, and share experiences, they were not seen as effective mechanisms for demanding radical changes. Relations with fellow women held little power and many of the superintendents sought individual solutions when they themselves were personally confronted by discrimination. That is, they did not rely on collective action to issues of equality.

The Emotional Work of Educational Leadership

A number of commentators have highlighted the 'emotional labour of leadership' (Sachs and Blackmore 1998: 270), and the ways in which this is articulated and managed by women educational managers. Caring, more generally in education, 'tends to be dismissed as a "warm fuzzy". Too difficult to analyse or categorize, impossible to put a number on' (Webb and Blond 1995: 611–2). Yet as Noddings (1984, 1992), Gerver and Hart (1991), and Webb and Blond (1995) emphasize, caring is important to the everyday work and 'knowledge' of education and teaching. This is equally so within educational leadership, and explicitly acknowledged by women managers and feminist commentators. In a study of women in leadership roles in primary and secondary schools in Australia, Judyth Sachs and Jill Blackmore (1998) argue that effective leadership entails the management of emotions. In part this means implicit management, whereby emotions are rendered invisible and held below the surface. Managing emotions effectively means that you never show you cannot cope, and you always appear in control and 'professional'. Sachs and Blackmore contrast the expected emotions of care, patience, calm, control with the experienced emotions of grief, frustration, satisfaction, guilt. As Blackmore (1999: 164) notes, 'women principals are expected to manage their own and others' negative emotions, often denying their negative emotions of passion and anger for their own survival, for fear of being seen to be "weak", non-rational and psychologically inadequate'.

The complexity of emotional labour can also be compounded by physical costs, as Sachs and Blackmore (1998) discovered. Many of the women principals they interviewed had had extended sick leave while others complained of feeling constantly tired or exhausted. The most extreme example they found was that of Alice, who recounted: 'I vomited every morning coming to work, I'd get up and be sick. I didn't want to come to work, lived in dread and fear of staff meetings' (Sachs and Blackmore 1998: 277). They note the loneliness and isolation of educational management, as do a number of the women interviewed by Chase (1995). This is illustrated in the ways in which women educational managers seek individual solutions to collective problems of inequality.

In emphasizing the caring work and emotional labour of women managers in teaching we are not arguing that only women experience these aspects of educational leadership. An anti-feminist stance might well make of this that women should not manage precisely *because* they get emotional about the work they do. We would provide the counter-argument that the emotional work of teaching should be openly acknowledged and seen as a strength rather than a weakness of women managers in teaching. It certainly negates arguments about a lack of commitment and motivation for the role.

Resistance and Change

Women educational managers orchestrate resistance to inequality and social injustice and are engaged in educational change. Blackmore presents a range of strategies that were employed by the women principals she studied in Australia when they were 'confronted with political, ethical and moral dilemmas in their work, to counter feelings of anger, frustration and isolation as their early enthusiasm and energy waned' (Blackmore 1999: 165). These strategies included working harder (and longer), becoming highly task-orientated, focusing on procedures and process, or opting out and leaving altogether. One of the women superintendents highlighted by Chase (1995) was in the process of leaving the superintendency. Denise described the superintendency as a greedy institution, and defined her move as reclaiming a life of her own. The lack of institutional support and detrimental aspects of commitment to the job had led her to the decision to leave. This decision was accompanied by worries about her responsibility to other ambitious women, and the perceived need to debunk any idea of professional failure. Denise wished to achieve a better balance of work and family commitments, and in a way her decision to leave was itself a form of resistance. Her ambition had been satisfied and the process of deciding to leave was itself empowering.

Cleo, one of the women teachers interviewed by Petra Munro (1998), had moved into administration, and in a way this move was also a form of rebellion and resistance. As Munro (1998: 77–8) notes, 'moving into administration was an example of how women disrupt the stereotypes of women teachers as lacking motivation and career aspirations'. Yet Cleo did not attempt to challenge or change the system; rather she engaged with and worked with the system, exacting change through conventional channels rather than attempting to overthrow the system. Administration as a form of resistance was in and of itself. So leaving educational management *and* being an educational manager can be articulations of resistance.

Other narratives and accounts present women educational leaders not only as resisting but also as agents for change. Taylor's (1995) account of school boards in Canada illustrates the ways in which women in educational administration strive to make equality a reality – by articulating agendas for change and resisting oppressive practices. Karen, a US superintendent, saw part of her role as educating sexist men and in resisting blatant discrimination. Institutionalized male dominance was part of her active agenda for change, albeit within a context of integration. Blackmore describes the work of feminist administrators committed to educational change in Australia. Referring particularly to women working within the ministry of education, Blackmore (1999: 205) highlights how 'femocrats' are working to 'disrupt the discourse of bureaucratic rationality' and attempting to utilize feminist practice to enact educational social change. Blackmore concludes that feminists in educational management face contradictory goals between being a 'good woman' and being a 'good teacher', and between being a bad or good feminist.

> Women leaders sought to create safe havens for their colleagues in quite non-supportive work environments, often at risk to themselves professionally and personally, by acting as a buffer against reforms that many felt were antithetic to good education and social justice. They worked as 'outsiders inside' cultural discourse that were often alienating and antagonistic.
>
> (Blackmore 1999: 205–6)

Blackmore argues that there is no essential style of female leadership, but does suggest that feminist discourses about women and educational management 'have the potential for cooption by as well as subversion of, hegemonic discourses in educational administration' (1999: 221). Furthermore, Blackmore is sceptical of the potential for reconceptualizations and social change within education, while a particular understanding of the qualities and practices of leadership is strived for.

Feminists in educational administration ... need to focus beyond the issue of women and leadership, to contextualize it and to politicize it by linking leadership more transparently to wider educational debates about social inequality, educational reform and issues of social justice .... It also means problematizing leadership as a key concept in educational administration and policy – redefining it and even rejecting it – for perhaps the focus upon leadership is itself the biggest barrier to gender equality.

(Blackmore 1999: 222)

Conclusion

In this chapter we have concentrated on gender and the career of teaching. We have done so as a way of highlighting the gendered division of labour within the teaching profession. We have sought to explore the discourses that surround the issue of women and career advancement within teaching, by suggesting that the picture is more complex than some accounts would have us believe. We have ended the chapter by giving some indications of what it is like to be a female educational manager. The ambiguity and emotional labour of the role is counterbalanced by the potential for active resistance and educational change. While it is difficult to ascertain particular feminine styles of management it is clear that women educational managers are committed to their task, their career and their colleagues, as well as to wider issues of equality and social change. However, the immediacy and authoritative nature of the management task may serve to weaken their potential to be active agents for change in what is still a male-dominated, hegemonic discourse of educational leadership. In the next chapter we stay with the contradictory experiences of women teachers by exploring the biographical and identity work of teaching.

Teaching is my life ...

It is lunchtime at Deeping primary school. Two dinner ladies – Glenys and Hester – are clearing up after the school dinner. They comment on how tired all the teachers are looking, although it is five weeks till half term. Glenys says: 'I asked Jaquetta if she'd been out clubbing, but she said it took her till midnight to do all the paperwork, and Kathleen's twins have got measles so she was up all night.' Hester nods and points out that the headmistress's mother is dying, so she is off to Newcastle every weekend to be with her. They agree that between the children, the parents, the paperwork, and everything they would not want to teach.

5 Experiences and Biographies

I like Virginia Woolf's notion of women inhabiting a separate women's country, but perhaps that concept is too false and cosy, draping and disguising our important differences ... all we share are multiple borderlands where snow and big city meet tropical rain and rapid garden with ambiguous results.

(Mercer 1997: 32)

Introduction

In this chapter we explore some of the biographical, experiential aspects of teaching, and relate these to wider issues of understanding and documenting the lives of teachers, their everyday realities and the context of the teaching profession. The concept of 'career' can be located in both individual and structural experiences. As we document in Chapter 4, career can be conceptualized in terms of organizational processes and sequences: as structural progression; as a series of stages through which to progress; perhaps ultimately towards leadership and success. These structural dimensions are also experienced on individual and personal levels (Nias 1989). Careers may be structurally contextualized but they also encapsulate personal lives and individual stories. Individual biographies and personal trajectories are key to the collective biography and experiences of any occupation or profession – such as teaching.

The social sciences have increasingly explored the links between 'science' and biography. Personal narratives and stories have developed as a main strand of qualitative work, with an assumption that they offer data grounded in biographical experiences and social contexts (Atkinson and Silverman 1997). Stanley and Morgan (1993) highlights the role of biography and autobiography in sociological inquiry, and suggests that a critical exploration can be fruitful. By conceptualizing biography and autobiography as topics of investigation rather than unproblematic resources, we can reject:

conventional sharp distinctions between structure and action, and, relatedly, individual and collective, as presenting an over-dichotomised view of social life. It means rejecting any notion that 'a life' can be understood as a representation of a single life in isolation from networks of interwoven biographies. In spite of the widespread assumption that autobiography is concerned with a single life, in practice it is a very rare autobiography that is not replete with the potted biographies of significant others in the subject's life.

(Stanley and Morgan 1993: 2)

The 'biographizing' of social structure and 'structuralizing' of biography (Stanley 1992 and 1993) has been taken up and used by feminists. A feminist construction of the world has centralized women's voices and women's lives (Personal Narratives Group 1989, Heilbrun 1988). Feminists have taken up the mantle of documenting the past and present lives of women, as one mechanism for making visible previously invisible and silent history and lives, as well as a strategy for exploring relationships between structure and agency. As Blackmore reminds us, feminist research places emphasis on lived experience: 'the representation of self emerges as an issue in the messy nexus of research, theory and feminist practice' (Blackmore 1999: 62). Evans (1993) has pointed out that feminist reasons for this interest in the personal and the intimate are several-fold. Discussions of the limits of the so-called 'grand narrative' of theory (Evans 1993), coupled with the postmodern emphasis on the particular rather than the general, has led to increased emphasis on the local, the small scale, the personal.

The feminist concern with documenting the lives and voices of women can then be seen as part of a broader trend towards contextualizing social life through an appreciation of individual experiences and biographies. 'By focusing upon the similarity amongst women through biography and autobiography, feminists have produced new collective truths which, in turn, frame other women's stories' (Blackmore 1999: 66). For the documentation of the teaching profession this has meant, in practice, an increasing concern with the need to listen to and learn from the experiences of women teachers of the past and present – within a context of the wider appreciation of the relationships between teachers' careers, identities, histories and biographies (Connelly and Clandinin 1995, Kehily 1995, Maclure 1993). This has helped to reinforce the premise of feminist theory and praxis that the personal, the political and the professional are interwoven. As Blackmore (1999) points out, however, it is important that the gathering and reading of women's narratives (including teacher narratives) does not overly valorize biographical work and treat the personal, political and professional as one.

There is no utopian terrain upon which women's biographies exist. The danger is that the life narrative genre, with its recursive production of 'woman', can produce a normative definition of subjectivity ... if the discussion is left at the level of women's experience disconnected from a broader sense of gender politics and context.

(Blackmore 1999: 64)

We use this as a starting point for our brief exploration of teachers' lives and identities, treating the experiences of teachers as personal and structural. We discuss the ways in which a life-history or narrative approach has been used to articulate teachers and their teaching experiences. In particular, we draw out the specific analytic features of such an approach. The chapter then goes on to consider some of the themes that have emerged from studying the contemporary lives of teachers, specifically women (feminist) teachers.

Histories, Herstories, Narratives and the Lives of Teachers

Life histories and narratives have been collected and analysed as a mechanism for understanding the lived realities of schools and of teaching (Connelly and Clandinin 1995, Rust 1999). Some choose to distinguish between, on the one hand, the stories, biographies and life histories of individual teachers and, on the other hand, perspectives that aim 'to create accounts not of individual careers or professional lives, but of patterns in the career paths taken by the teachers studied and of the dynamics that explain these patterns' (Huberman et al. 1997: 14). Such a distinction is useful in articulating the situated and structural contexts of individual experiences. The collection of personal biographies and narratives gives voice to teachers and their teaching; the collectivity of narratives and biographies can lead into the broader picture(s) of teaching careers and the teaching profession (Goodson 1981, 1997).

> Studies of the teacher's life and work develop structural insights which locate the teacher's life within the deeply structured and embedded environments of schooling …. [I]t is true that personal data can be irrelevant, eccentric and essentially redundant. But the point that needs to be grasped is that these features are not the inevitable collection of that which is personal. Moreover that which is personal at the point of collection may not remain personal. After all a good deal of social science is concerned with the collection of a range of other personal insights and events and the elucidation of more collective and generalisable proffering and processes.

(Goodson 1997: 145)

The collection and analysis of personal narratives has become an increasingly common strategy for making sense of the social world. Social scientists, including those working in the fields of education, have often utilized the biographical approach (Atkinson and Silverman 1997, Franzosa 1992, Kehily 1995). There is a widespread assumption that narratives offer uniquely privileged data, grounded in biographical experiences and social contexts. It is often assumed that these data embodied reciprocity and the potential for empowerment, themselves seen as key aspects of a feminist approach to social research (see Atkinson and Silverman 1997, Coffey 1999, Maynard 1996, McLaughlin and Tierney 1993). As Munro (1998) and others have pointed out (see Atkinson and Silverman 1997), however, the narrative method is not without its critiques and potential problems. Narrative research can serve to romanticize the individual and their stories, or indeed can privilege the narrator (and their analyses) to the detriment of the individual and personal biographies. There is nothing inherently liberating or empowering about the narrative method *per se*. Like all research, life-history research is implicated in power relations, although, as Munro (1998), Goodson (1992) and others have pointed out, narrative inquiry and a life-history approach also have the potential to highlight and illuminate gendered constructions of power. In cautioning us about narrative research, Munro (1998: 12) concludes that 'these cautionary tales are intended to keep us suspicious of all claims of privilege. What they suggest is complex ways in which narrative both contests and reproduces positivistic notions of power, knowledge and subjectivity despite claims to the contrary'.

Nevertheless, there has been a sustained project to collect, document and analyse the life stories and everyday experiences of teachers. Certainly since the 1980s there has been a trend towards life-history and narrative research in education, mirroring the more general trends in the social sciences (Connell 1985, Connelly and Clandinin 1988, Cortazzi 1991, Goodson 1988, Sikes et al. 1985). The collecting of biographical narratives has given meaning and temporal quality to the work and career of the teacher. The teacher's work has come to be seen as biographically, as well as organizationally and socially, structured. Moreover, such data have revealed the identity work that teachers routinely engage in through their work and teaching experiences (Fenwick 1998, Kehily 1995).

Ivor Goodson (1997) summarizes the themes and features of the studying of teachers' lives by adopting a life-history, narrative, experiential approach. He highlights a number of overarching principles of such work. These are as follows:

- *Respect for the (auto)biographical and the teachers' voice.* This treats personal experiences and individual voices as valuable and insightful ways of understanding the everyday realities of teaching.
- *Understanding the relationships between teaching experience and the accounts of teachers.* Recognizing that teaching is replete with stories and narratives, and these can reveal complex and diverse experiences of teaching.

- *Recognizing the importance of life experiences and backgrounds to the everyday practice of teaching.* The lives and biographies of teachers cannot be separated from the work they do. A life-history, narrative approach ensures that teachers' backgrounds and experiences are treated seriously.

- *Understanding the relationships between the teachers' lifestyles, latent identities and cultures.* This recognizes that identities are complex, fragmented and shaped by understandings of lifestyle and culture. Gathering teacher narratives can help to make sense of the complexity of teacher-identity construction and teacher culture.

- *Recognizing the importance of life cycle for the perceptions and practice of teaching.* A biographical, life-history approach is sensitive to the relationships between the everyday realities of teaching and parameters such as age and generation, social status and parenthood.

- *Documenting the importance of decisions and critical incidents.* Narratives and stories provide conventions and frameworks for articulating and making sense of the teaching career and experiences. They enable the identification of key figures, incidents and turning points, and thus enable the charting of decisions and progressions.

The biographical and narrative approach to teaching necessarily embodies a concern with the construction and articulation of teacher selves (Nias 1989), and engages with a postmodern premise that selves are created and multiple. Goodson (1997: 150) describes this as the self-creation of selves that are 'free floating and multiple, subject to constant flux and changes', and argues that in adopting such an approach we should be cautious. Goodson has been a key figure in proposing and utilizing a life-history and biographical approach to understanding teachers' lives. He clearly sees a place for the articulation of the identity work and negotiation with which teachers are routinely engaged in a grounded analysis of the work realities of teachers. But Goodson also reminds us of the structural value of studying individual lives and experiences – that is, ensuring that personal narratives, individual lives and experiences are located within the situated, political and local contexts of education and schools. Simply to follow a postmodernist perspective of multiple, negotiated, free-floating selves ignores what Goodson (1997: 150) describes as 'the circumscribed spaces and socialised trajectories' of teacher's lives. Strategies for self-formation therefore take place in juxtaposition to the institutionalized and socialized practices of schooling, and a concern with the processes and spaces of teacher identity-work must engage with both the individual and the structural.

Having sketched out some of the general justifications and themes of interest in the study of the lives and narratives of teachers, the remainder of this chapter draws on work that specifically highlights the life and work experiences of women teachers. We do not attempt here to provide an exhaustive or systematic review, nor have we only referred to data that explicitly draws on a narrative or life-history approach. Rather our intention is to draw on a growing body of work in order to illuminate general themes and shared experiences. We are most concerned with exploring how women teachers experience their work, and how they articulate those experiences.

Women (Feminist) Teachers

Feminism has been a strong influence and exponent of an educational interest in documenting and exploring the lives of teachers – not least because studying the lives of women teachers is a mechanism through which the gendered epistemologies, experiences, and agencies of teaching can be explored. The resultant literature is a growing one, but at the moment it is still relatively small. For a profession predominantly made up of women we know surprisingly little about the experiences of women teachers – their daily lives and the meanings they attach to their teaching work (Apple 1983, Joyce 1987, Tyack 1974).

There is a literature on women writing for themselves, especially collaborations between feminist educationalists and women teachers sharing experiences and strategies for change. The clearest examples of this are to be found in the action research field (Burchall and Millman 1989, De Lyon and Migniuolo 1989, Jones and Mahony 1989, Weiner 1989). There are some well-cited works on the careers and lives of teachers, which deal with both men and women teachers, and treat gender as analytically valuable (see, for example, Connell 1985, Sikes et al. 1985). Some researchers, like Jennifer Nias (1989), have deliberately not placed particular emphasis upon gender. In her study of primary teachers (men and women) talking about their work, Nias only mentioned gender issues if the teachers themselves raised them. While she did not find support for gender stereotyping in such aspects as women's emotional commitment or men's liking for organization, gender was relevant to articulations of career, power and promotion, although, as she comments, the lack of a feminist perspective is problematic: 'Of course, to avoid directly addressing the gender implications of what these teachers said is to ignore the possibility that they and I are the victims of false consciousness' (Nias 1989: 4).

The relative absence of research on the lives of women teachers, given their majority within the profession, has been the subject of some discussion. Petra Munro (1998), for example, offers a number of possible contributory factors to explain the neglect of women's voices in research on teaching:

> First, the gendered construction of teaching as ideologically congruent with women's supposed innate nurturing capacities has obscured the agency of women's lives. Second, the sexual stereotyping and gendered

occupational structures resulting from the rhetoric of 'women's true profession' has resulted in representations of women teachers as objects of knowledge, and rarely as subjects.

(Munro 1998: 3)

Munro's (1998) own work on women teachers and life-history narratives is the latest in a series of monographs that attempt to rectify this deficit, by giving voice to women teachers, using teachers' own narratives to (re)present their lives, and the meanings they attach to them. Like Hoffman (1981), Casey (1993) and Chase (1995), Munro's work is based on the narratives of teachers based in the United States. In presenting and analysing the life-history narratives of three women – Agnes, Cleo and Bonnie – Munro takes seriously their lives and experiences, and provides an understanding of the politics of identity and the corollary concepts of resistance and subjectivity (McLaughlin and Tierney 1993, Munro 1998, Smith 1993). The generational differences, teaching experiences and career progressions of Agnes, Cleo and Bonnie help Munro to document educational pasts, presents and futures. Their stories provide insights into the meanings these women give to their work. In Munro's analyses of these stories, concepts of agency and structure, power and resistance are explored. A pertinent factor that she stresses is the way in which these women challenge the dominant discourse of teaching as 'women's true profession' (compare Hoffman 1981). Agnes, Cleo and Bonnie all tell stories of resistance in their accounts of becoming teachers; their stories of administration (often working with, rather than against, the system) encapsulate the enactments of change and resistance. Their narratives articulate some of the key premises of Goodson's (1992) life-history approach to understanding teachers' lives. Agnes, Cleo and Bonnie do not present their teaching careers as planned and necessarily strategic, so much as ones of luck, significant others, and critical incidents. Their personal experiences of teaching, and of educational management, situate their accounts of the teaching profession. Their biographies and backgrounds shaped their identities as teachers, and their reflections of those identities. Age and generation (Peterson 1964), as well as gender and race were key to the negotiated meanings of their teaching and teacher identity (re)construction.

Schulz (1998) uses the metaphors of path and journey to make sense of being and becoming a woman teacher. She collected and shared the stories of Nepalese women teachers – and these stories revealed 'the path taken, the helping hand, the walking without stumbling, the taken-for-granted not seeing of the women, and the new vistas at every step' (Schulz 1998: 181). Schulz's study is particularly powerful in placing the stories and lives of women teachers in situated contexts – of culture, society, time and space. Women teachers' reflecting upon their routes to teaching was something with which Schulz (1998: 164) could empathize and share – as a teacher who too had 'experienced the path taken'. This encapsulates a key function and place for the narratives of women teachers – that is, the sharing and collectivity of them. In that sense they form part of a shared feminist research project. Within that project there have been some studies that have specifically addressed the life and work experiences of teachers who self-identify as feminist.

Feminist Teachers

Life-history and biographical research with feminist teachers has taken place (see, for example, Coulter 1995, Joyce 1987, Middleton 1987, 1989 and 1993, Sparkes 1994, Weiler 1988). Furthermore, feminist teachers (in collaboration with academics and other educational practitioners) have periodically engaged in action research, with a strong emphasis on the biographical – documenting how they are striving to work towards change within education (see, for example, Adler et al. 1993, Browne and France 1986, De Lyon and Migniuolo 1989). However, there has been little systematic empirical research on the working lives of feminist teachers in school classrooms. What available material has demonstrated is that it is important to pay attention to feminist accounts of teaching. Such accounts convey the lived realities of feminist struggle within patriarchal educational institutions, as well as the ways in which feminist teachers negotiate their identities and daily work. Joyce (1987) interviewed a small number of white, feminist teachers, mainly located in inner London. Joyce explored with the teachers the impact that their feminism had on how they taught and on the relationships they had at work. All of the teachers 'had problems in their working lives, from being treated as a joke because of their views, to being openly criticised or deviously undermined' (Joyce 1987: 76). These teachers who self-identified as feminist encountered negative responses each working day, and often experienced feelings of isolation. Rebecca Coulter's (1995) study of the experiences of feminist first-year teachers in Canada demonstrates these same dimensions.

> The individual threads of each woman's experiences are important in and of themselves for what they reveal about the work world of teaching and the culture of schools. But the knots of sexism, misogyny and anti-feminism which tie these threads together and structure the pattern become increasingly visible also.
>
> (Coulter 1995: 47)

The young feminist teachers whom Coulter studied had to contend with sexual harassment, everyday school events that in themselves revealed deep-rooted hostilities toward women, sustained male comments about their appearance and objectification and sexualization from male colleagues.

Inside the classroom they were forced to struggle with patriarchal gender relations. As feminists who chose to be teachers they were also committed to change – which was not an easy path to follow. Yet Coulter takes heart from their experiences:

> The uncertainties they feel, the odds they face, the victories they achieve, the setbacks they suffer are part of the pattern of experiences that must inform the efforts of women's movement activists, teacher educators, teacher unionists and others committed to anti-sexist education.
>
> (Coulter 1995: 47)

In terms of the work that feminist teachers do, it is important to stress that subscription to a feminist agenda does not necessarily alter the process of classroom teaching. Children still have to be taught and children enthused (and disciplined), examinations and curricula worked towards (for discussions of feminism and the school curriculum see Chapter 3). What a feminist agenda may do is change the goals of classroom teaching rather than the process of that teaching. That said, feminist teachers do find themselves having to make difficult choices over what and how they teach, often coping without adequate 'gender-sensitive' classroom resources, as Joyce (1987) noted. For example, Nina Baym (1990) suggests that as a feminist teacher of literature one has to expose students to new texts and new readings of old texts. Baym argues that feminist practice in the classroom is at best difficult and problematic. This is partly because feminist teachers are teachers usually teaching institutionally defined subjects in institutionally defined ways, using 'second nature' conventions. With the best will in the world even dedicated feminist teachers operate within conventionally understood perceptions about their subject areas. Baym's point is more strongly made in her articulation of what feminism is. Feminism cannot be simply equated with gender and translated into gender-sensitive classroom praxis: 'Feminism *per se* does not require that gender be the most important factor; feminism is ultimately a practical decision about where to direct one's limited energies and powers in the effort to make a more liveable world' (Baym 1990: 62).

The US Journal *Feminist Teacher*, started in Indiana University in the 1980s and arising out of a feminist teacher collective, bears testimony to these difficulties, and to the ways in which feminist teachers have been innovative in addressing what it means to be feminist in the school, college and university classroom. *The Feminist Teacher Anthology* (Cohee et al. 1998) brings together a number of papers from *Feminist Teacher* that particularly address feminist pedagogies and classroom strategies. We addressed the relationships between feminist teaching and the production and transmission of knowledge in Chapter 3. More generally in the context here, the articles brought together in *The Feminist Teacher Anthology* raise issues about the lived realities of feminist teaching and praxis in the classroom in order to:

> ... move beyond analysis of the abstracts and the frustrations of femi-
> nist teaching and feminist administering to proposing detailed strategies
> and resources for raising students' (and teachers') consciousness about
> gender, race, class and sexuality; ... for transforming larger institutional
> environments to make them more equitable, democratic places for the
> collective construction of knowledge.
>
> (Cohee et al. 1998: 7)

While the overall picture is far from rosy for feminist teachers, there are positive examples of actively seeking change. *The Feminist Teacher Anthology* makes particular strengths of the enhancing feminist pedagogy, the development of feminist teaching strategies and the everyday realities of the feminist classroom. In the UK, also, there are examples of women teachers striving for change. Well-documented initiatives such as GIST – Girls Into Science and Technology (Whyte 1986) – and GAOC – Girls And Occupation Choice (Holland 1988) – were early action-research projects influenced by a liberal feminist agenda of equal opportunities, subject choice and career destinations (we discuss action research in more detail in Chapter 9). More individualized initiatives are also in evidence. For example, Adler et al. (1993) demonstrate how women who have been promoted within the school context have applied feminist theories to their daily professional practice. These women, who self-identify as feminists, view styles of teaching, learning and managing through 'a different lens'. However, Adler et al. (1993) accept that educational establishments within which these women work are constrained by the structures of male hierarchy. Therefore, working with a theoretical framework of liberal feminism and equal oppor-tunities is more acceptable and likely to be more successful than more radical approaches. Similarly Browne and France (1986) present a series of papers on how women (some of whom self-identify as feminists) are working to change practice in nursery education; again the emphasis is liberal and equal-opportunity based. There is also commentary of how feminist teachers (and researchers) are addressing, challenging and changing the schooling experience of boys (see Askew and Ross 1988, Bailey 1996, Epstein et al. 1998; Raphael Reed 1999, Skelton 1996 and 1998). Sue Askew and Carol Ross (1988) argued that anti-sexist education cannot and should not just be about improving the experience of girls' education, and that feminists in the classroom cannot and should not ignore boys. Bailey's (1996) account of women teachers working in a boys school highlights the ways in which their presence both challenged and reinforced the male ethos of the school. As numbers of women teachers increased in the school, the more dynamic this process became:

> [T]his ... is not the story of a school radically feminised, but of the women who negotiated a place for themselves within its male structure. It is difficult to see in this account the herald of a new and equal society, and this would not have been the intention of many of the women involved. Rather the slide toward feminisation was the consequence of interaction and negotiation.
>
> (Bailey 1996: 184)

Overall feminist teachers remain a marginal voice within education – although some have been successful in disseminating their ideas and influencing/challenging/changing classroom strategies and institutional practice. As Joyce (1987) concluded, feminist teachers have a:

> quite phenomenal level of commitment, energy and persistence. Much of their work is ignored or even derided, and although all of them recounted instances of positive feedback from other staff or pupils, sometimes years later, plainly the personal cost of such dedication is high.
>
> (Joyce 1987: 86)

We suspect that there are many more feminist teachers than the rather sparse literature would suggest, working within and beyond the classroom for change, often in the face of hostility or disinterest, and personal cost. Joyce (1987) suggested that if being a feminist teacher is hard, then being a feminist lesbian teacher is even harder.

Lesbian Teachers

The absence of research material on feminist teachers in general is matched by a dearth of literature on lesbian (and indeed gay) teachers (Squirrell 1989). Like the material on feminist teachers, much of the literature on lesbian teachers is practitioner-orientated and initiated. Lesbian feminist teachers have described how their positions as feminists and teachers are compounded by their sexual identity (Clarke 1996, Epstein 1994, Griffin 1991, Khayatt 1992, Scott 1989). The literature that is available on lesbian teachers deals with at least three sets of issues: (1) the management of identity and self-disclosure; (2) 'teaching' sexuality and providing role models in the classroom; (3) 'queering' the curriculum: that is, how lesbian teachers manage their identity in the face of homophobia, heterosexism and hostility; how sexuality is tackled in the classroom, and the central importance of providing positive role models; and critiques and reconfigurations of the curriculum, to take into account lesbian epistemologies, perspectives, literatures and stories.

There are rich descriptions of the everyday experiences of lesbian teachers – how they manage their identities, often in the face of homophobia and heterosexism in the school and education system. Ferfolja's (1998) study of the sexual harassment experiences of Australian lesbian teachers vividly illustrates this. These teachers experienced overt harassment, as well as underhand comments, and 'some took stress leave as a result' (Ferfolja 1998: 405).

The relationships between the public (teaching) life and personal (lesbian) life are complex. In autobiographical accounts, 'coming out' in the context of the school and conversely how 'passing strategies' are acquired in order to keep lesbian identities from colleagues and pupils are revealed (Clarke 1996, Epstein 1994, Khayatt 1997, Sparkes 1994, Squirrell 1989). In (re)presenting his life-history interviews with Jessica, a lesbian physical education teacher in the UK, Andrew Sparkes (1994) notes the ways in which Jessica felt the need to separate her personal and professional life. Resigned to the patriarchal cultural rules and resources that shape interactions in the staffroom, Jessica's

> … identity management strategy, is framed within the 'professional' expectation held by many of her colleagues, that one's private home life should be kept separate from one's public work life. In particular, issues of sexual identity are commonly assumed to be 'private' affairs that should not be brought into the public and professional world of work.
>
> (Sparkes 1994: 111)

Jessica's enforced silence about her sexuality made her question her ability to teach, and left her unable to challenge sexism in the staffroom and classroom. Gill Clarke's (1996) in-depth interviews with lesbian physical education student/teachers and qualified teachers in England reveal similar tensions. Clarke notes that the subject matter of physical education – and the centrality of the body to that – exacerbates the identity management issues for lesbian PE teachers. Clarke (1996) documents how lesbian teacher identities are often construed and shaped by heterosexual *others* (see Paechter 1998). Lesbian teachers often straddle the dual identities of lesbian and pseudo-heterosexual. In concealing their lesbian identities from colleagues and pupils, the teachers Clarke interviewed employed mechanisms and strategies to 'cover tracks' and deflect attention from their sexual identity. Staff-room conversations were managed to minimize discussions of homelife and partners, intimate friendships with school colleagues were avoided, as were general conversations about homosexuality. Homophobic and heterosexist comments were not challenged, but rather endured for fear of 'drawing attention'. Some also adopted strategies to put colleagues 'off the scent' – being overly flirtatious with male colleagues, for example. These staff-room strategies carried over into the everyday realities and interactions of the classroom. The lesbian teachers were ambiguous in discussions about 'significant' others, and where possible (within the particular confines of the physical nature of their subject) avoided physical contact and situations that might be perceived as having sexual connotations. Clarke counters the negativity of her accounts of these lesbian teachers' experiences with the observation that successful 'passing' as a pseudo-heterosexual may also be perceived as a form of active resistance by suggesting that 'getting away with it becomes a means of resisting and challenging, albeit in perhaps a rather hidden way, this too is another paradox of their identities' (Clarke 1996: 205). (It is worth noting here that pupil folklore and stories are replete with tales of the lesbian or gay PE teacher and the attendant concerns of the body – see, for example, Pugsley et al. 1996b, Paechter 1998).

Unlike the lesbians of Clarke's study, many lesbians 'choose' to reveal their lesbian identity, and 'come out' to colleagues and students (see Beck 1994, Klages 1994, Wright 1998). Adams and Emery (1994) share anecdotes and strategies of classroom coming-out stories and provide advice on ways and means. They locate coming out in a broader context of creating an open and safe classroom space – in which coming out is part of the process – a moment rather than an end. Barbara Blinick (1994) provides an account of her coming out – and how she prepared for the day, including choosing what to wear (a frilly dress and pearls) and how to wear her hair (loose and on her shoulders). She highlights a position – one that will have resonance among many other women (black/(dis)abled) teachers – of how she found herself being extra-good and extra-dedicated – a kind of super-teacher – in order to prove how wonderful lesbian teachers are. Blinick (1994) also relates coming out to the more general issue of providing role models and teaching sexuality in the classroom. She felt she had a responsibility to come out: 'I felt it was crucial for young people – especially those questioning their sexual orientation or who already knew they were lesbian, gay, or bisexual – to see another healthy, happy and productive lesbian' (Blinick 1994: 143).

This is an issue that Clarke also addresses. Not only were the lesbian teachers she talked to 'forced to suffer in silence but pupils are also denied the opportunity for lesbian role models' (Clarke 1996: 204). Janet Wright (1998) presents her coming-out story in such a context – as one strategy for fighting homophobia and heterosexism – by providing a dialogue that can be simultaneously empowering and difficult, even frightening. In commenting on her article which first appeared in 1993, Wright underlines this mix of the personal and the professional:

> I am more aware now than I was when I originally write this article of the emotional toll that coming out in the classroom takes on me. In this article I emphasise the positive effects of coming out both on myself and on my students – who so clearly benefited from authenticity. I remain convinced that the benefits outweighed the costs for me, as well. However, I am struck and challenged by the fact that it hasn't gotten

any easier for me over the years and that the initial experience of coming out still leaves me feeling raw and vulnerable.

(Wright 1998: 191)

Lesbian (and gay) teachers have also documented and reflected upon the ways in which they have challenged and changed the curriculum of schooling (see, for example, Blinick 1994, Nieb 1994, Kitch 1994). In common with feminist teachers more generally, working within a 'malestream' and 'heterosexual' knowledge base is the starting point for lesbian teachers in the classroom. Challenging heterosexism, argues Scott (1989), is a challenge that must be addressed by all who are involved in teaching.

All education workers, parents and governors have a part to play in challenging the myths. While inevitably teachers are in the front line in presenting alternatives, schoolkeepers, technicians, cooks, media resource officers, clerical and canteen workers can all ensure that hetero-sexism never goes unchallenged.

(Scott 1989: 266)

The dual identities as instructors and queers (Barale 1994) has proved both opportunities and dilemmas for the transmission and (re)production of curriculum knowledge, as we document and explore in Chapter 3. The strategies for feminist curriculum practice such as resistance reading, providing alternative texts and interpretations, integrating rather than simply 'adding on' women's experiences, stories and his(her)stories, also have extra connotations for the lesbian educator in the classroom and beyond the classroom.

Conclusion

The most vivid picture that emerges from the literature on feminist teachers is the difficulties they face in combining their politics and beliefs with the classroom and staff-room realities. Many self-identified feminist teachers resist being openly identified as feminist (Coulter 1995), in the same way that lesbian teachers often resist or actively mute a lesbian label, fearing it 'dangerous' or a catalyst for further ridicule. There are many stories of ridicule, hostility from male (and some female) colleagues, misogyny, sexism and anti-feminism discourse (Coulter 1995, Cunnison 1985 and 1989, Middleton 1987). Further, action aimed at change is also described with some disillusionment. The first-year Canadian feminist teachers in Coulter's study described how they did not find it easy to stand up to long-standing teachers, nor openly to fight sexism in schools. They found it difficult to initiate anything at a school level, and also had to deal with the rigours of a first year of teaching. They found they had to ration energies and enthusiasms in a bid to survive in the classroom, and had to work away at sexism at an individual and *ad hoc* level. Similar stories have been told elsewhere (see Acker 1983 and 1989, Coffey and Acker 1991, Joyce 1987).

As we have highlighted in this book, feminism and teaching have a long joint history. Yet the lived reality of feminist teachers is a very mixed one (Thompson 1989). Our intention in this chapter has been to explore the lives and experiences of women/feminist/lesbian teachers, particularly focusing on the identity-work that they engage in. Often, the concerns about gender and teaching are located at structural and curriculum levels – concerned with equal opportunities, a gender-free or gender-aware curriculum, and non-sexist practice, rather than promoting anti-sexist practice, tackling school hierarchies and the shaping of educational policy. These locations are central to our understanding of gender and teaching, and to any aims at positive change, as we indicate in the book as a whole. However these concerns and perspectives can mask the individual lives and work of teachers. A focus on biographies and lives of women/feminist/lesbian teachers reveals important connections between personal and public lives, actions and experiences. Our concentration on particular aspects of the teacher's identity and identity-work – as woman, feminist, lesbian – inevitably silences other aspects that are equally valid to the experiences and negotiations of teachers in their everyday work. For example, age and life cycle (George and Maguire 1998, Peterson 1964), parent(mother)hood and family (see Cunnison 1994, George and Maguire 1998, Sikes 1997, Vincent 1996), 'race' and ethnicity (Brah and Minhas 1985, Fordham 1996, Haw 1998, McKellar 1989) have all been revealed to be useful and valuable in articulating the lived realities of teachers and teaching. By listening to and making sense of teachers' experiences and accounts we are better placed to understand those everyday teaching realities. The 'work' of teaching is not only about managing the classroom and delivering the curriculum, it is also about managing and negotiating biographies, identities and selves. And a feminist perspective is a useful way of going about understanding that work.

In the next chapter we turn our attention towards the recruitment and initial training of teachers. We are concerned here with exploring why teaching and teachers are the way they are. That is, how does the training and education teachers receive contribute to their understandings and perceptions of the teaching profession and teaching work? In exploring these issues we also reveal the difficulties of incorporating feminist practice into the teacher-education curriculum.

Longing to teach ...

Arlette is talking to two final-year students in the queue in the coffee shop. They are both specializing in French, but she knows them from staffing the university's rape crisis phone line. She asks what they plan to do after graduation. Lois Elvery says she's applied for teacher training, Meade Colesfort for an MA in medieval French. Arlette and Meade say they would not want to teach. Lois replies that she's always wanted to be a teacher, and enjoyed teaching in France during her year abroad. She adds: 'Anyway I'm not ambitious, or career-minded: a job at Prior's End Girls' School will do me'.

6   Recruitment, Initial Training and Socialization

> To be alone in a corridor of empty rooms on a Saturday evening became my greatest fear. It seemed to presage a life-long loneliness. So I leapt gratefully into the arms of the first attractive man who offered release from this prospect. I decided to teach because it seemed convenient for a married woman and it meant I could stay in Oxford to do a 'Dip.Ed.'. I then taught in schools, but I did not look ahead to a career as a teacher.
>
> (Alberti 1997: 145)

Introduction

The careers and experiences of teachers, and the profession of teaching in general, cannot be separated from the processes of recruitment and training. In order to make sense of the dynamics of teachers and their work, there needs to be some understanding and analysis of who joins the profession *and* how they learn the techniques, strategies and everyday realities of teaching. The beginning of a teaching career has been documented and described as a classic socialization story (see Bullough 1997, Huberman 1993, Lacey 1977). Various chronologies or phases have been identified as elements of the route to professional teacher status. The early work of Colin Lacey (1977), for example, described a narrative or chronology for becoming a teacher through initial training. Lacey identified four distinct phases in the process of becoming a teacher:

- the honeymoon period – a phase of new experiences and optimism;
- the search – the shift towards the need to search for materials and ways of teaching and managing the classroom;
- the crisis – a loss of confidence and optimism, a sense of failure and lack of control;
- 'learning to get by' – displacing the blame of failure and developing the strategies for coping in the classroom.

Variations on this chronological approach to teacher training are evident in more contemporary literature. Huberman (1993), for example, describes a three-part pattern, from certainty through experimentation to stabilization. And Bullough (1997), in a recent review of initial teacher education, suggests that beginning teachers move from a trial-and-error approach to teaching towards a more systematic development of teaching strategies – 'a clashing of conceptions of self with institutional role expectations and of an eventual but not always happy resolution' (Bullough 1997: 80).

The experiences of teacher training, or occupational socialization into the teaching profession, are not, of course, as uniform as such schemata inevitably suggest. Typologies and generalizations always mask a much richer and more varied reality. Establishing the transition to becoming a teacher as a *process*, with a narrative or storied quality (Wood and Geddis 1999), enables an understanding of teacher training as experiential, biographical and contextual. Thus teacher training is cast as both individual and collective – individual in the sense that beginning teachers are complex selves, bringing to and taking from teaching their beliefs, understandings, emotions and experiences (Nias 1989); collective in that teacher training is a shared experience of cohorts, learners and teachers, novices and mentors. (See Hatch 1999 for a useful discussion of the potential role of studies of teachers' work in socialization of new recruits to teaching.) Overshadowing these is a broader policy and educational context of teacher recruitment and training, set within the parameters of schooling and of higher education.

In this chapter we consider these personal, collective and contextual aspects of teacher recruitment, education and training. In particular, we explore the ways in which a gendered analysis and a feminist lens can aid our understandings of the beginnings of the teaching career. The chapter covers both who is recruited into the teaching profession and the processes of initial teacher education and socialization. Attention is also paid to the institutional and policy context of teacher education, and to those who are responsible for providing that education 'on the ground'. We have organized our material into five sections: initial recruitment, the policy context, discourse of teacher education, teacher educators, and feminist practice.

Initial Recruitment into Teaching

The lower echelons of the teaching profession are predominantly female. This should not come as a startling revelation, nor is it a new trend. As Apple (1985) points out, the feminization of teaching is seen in data from England and the United States going back to the beginning of the twentieth century. It is without doubt the case that the majority of new entrants to teaching are women. This phenomenon is both international and sustained. Initial teacher recruitment (and training) in the UK has two main routes (although other routes to qualified teacher status are now possible and are discussed later in this chapter). The postgraduate certificate of education (PGCE) is a one-year, post-first-degree qualification. The bachelor of education (B.Ed.) is a four-year undergraduate programme, primarily catering for primary (elementary) teacher training. While there are almost equal numbers of men and women undertaking the PGCE, the B.Ed. programmes are almost exclusively taken up by women. The primary age focus of the majority of B.Eds may account for this, as there have been few attempts to attract men into the primary education field (De Lyon and Migniuolo 1989). At the time of writing, the most recent available figures for the UK (DfEE 1998) were for the year 1994–5. Out of a total primary education teacher recruitment of 217,000, only 36,000 were men. In initial teacher recruitment in the UK overall, women account for over 88 per cent of new entrants. This general gender trend is repeated elsewhere. In Denmark, for example, 75 per cent of students at teacher-training college are female (Jørgensen 1995); in the United States women make up over 65 per cent of all student teachers, in Greece 70 per cent (Kontogiannopoulou-Polydorides 1991).

It is difficult to assess whether these trends have anything to do with feminism *per se*. The high status of the profession as a whole, which was accorded before the late nineteenth century, no longer seems to apply. It could be argued that this is because it is now a female profession. The conundrum of the relationship between the changing gender distribution within, and the shifting status of the profession, is complex and cannot be judged in simple causal terms. However the seemingly parallel trends of increasing female numbers and fall of professional status is a tendency not confined to Europe or the United States. For example, Golding and Chen (1993) document that, in Israel, a dramatic erosion of the occupational prestige of all of the educational professions has been coupled with a 'rapid feminization' of those professions (see Chapter 4). It does appear that, as women have consistently applied to become qualified teachers, the prestige of the profession has reduced. Indeed it could be argued that, as teaching has become 'feminized' (especially among its younger ranks), the aspirations of feminism for increased and enhanced labour market opportunities have shifted rather than met head on. Despite being the majority of new recruits to teaching, women also secure less permanent or promoted posts than their male counterparts. In general terms, female access to high positions within the teaching profession has proved far more difficult than access at recruitment level. More specifically in the context of this chapter, first destination posts for few qualified teachers also show marked gendered distributions (see Chapter 4).

To summarize, the majority of recruits into initial teacher education are female. This trend has international dimensions and shows little sign of reversing. Indeed the high female recruitment into teacher education is more robust than ever. In this sense the feminization of teaching (and teacher training) is secure. Despite this, there is some evidence to suggest that male teacher education graduates do better in securing immediate and permanent employment following the initial period of training. Indeed this might be precisely because they are perceived to be a strategic resource, for which schools are keen to secure whatever (and whoever) they can. Recent debates over the relationships between masculinity and schooling (Connell 1995, Haywood and Mac an Ghaill 1996, Kenway 1996, Mac an Ghaill 1994, 1996, Thorne 1993) and the perceived underachievement of boys in the school system (Delamont 1999, Epstein et al. 1998, Raphael Reed 1999) have placed increasing emphasis on positive male role models. With the trend firmly set towards a largely female teaching profession, male teacher education graduates ironically look set to be in an ever stronger position to compete for teaching posts. This is equally applicable whether masculinities are seen as fragmented, reconstituted or in need of restoration (Epstein et al. 1998, Martino 1995, Parker 1996, Raphael Reed 1999).

The Policy of Teacher Education

As with education systems generally, teacher education has undergone dramatic changes in the past few decades (Edwards 1990, Furlong et al. 1988, Gosden 1990, Maguire 1995, Mahony 1997). These changes have fundamentally set about reforming teacher education. Moreover, as Pat Mahony (1997) argues, these reforms have international comparability and reflect not only local (national) educational climates, but more general international changes in the public sector. In practical terms, institutions have been closed, merged and reconstituted; alternative routes into teaching (for example, licensed and articled teachers, see Furlong et al. 1996) have been approved; tighter teaching standards have been developed and introduced; and a tightening of control over what is taught has been put in place. Changes have affected the structure, organization, curriculum and ethos of teacher recruitment and training. Teacher education has been vulnerable to demographic and economic contexts, and to political fluctuations in educational policy.

Teacher education has also been recast within a discourse of educational effectiveness (Mahony and Hexhall 1997). In England and Wales (and mirrored elsewhere) emphasis has increasingly been placed on the practical, competence-based skills of teaching, and the consequent restructuring of teacher education to provide them. As Maguire notes:

> In the UK the teacher is being reconstructed as the practical person, the doer not the thinker, the manager not the scholar. This new teacher will be cheaper to produce because what is required is more practical experience and less theoretical interrogation of schooling and pedagogy.
>
> (Maguire 1995: 119)

The sustained attack on teacher education, primarily by the New Right, and an increasing emphasis on what Mahony (1997) calls 'The New Public Management' (NPM) approach in teacher education has promoted an understanding that the initial education of teachers should be more concerned with attributes and skills for practice, rather than be theoretically informed. This assures that skills and attributes can be standardized and controlled, monitored and checked. In England and Wales, the establishment of the Council for the Accreditation of Teacher Education (CATE) in 1984 began this trend toward standardization and overt assessment. CATE assessed initial teacher education programmes, using criteria that pertained to a number of parameters such as selection procedures, teacher educators and content of the curriculum. Superseded by the Teacher Training Agency (TTA) in 1994, there has been an increasing emphasis on control over what is taught as well as how it is taught. The shift in content has been dramatic, with an increasing concentration on the teacher's operational and utilitarian role within the classroom, and a downplaying of theoretical perspectives and social contexts. The virtual removal of theory (Acker 1994, for example, notes the virtual disappearance of sociology from the curriculum of teacher education) has been combined with an increasingly centralized curriculum. New models of teacher education are befitting of a workplace training model with the emphasis upon training on the job and studying in school (Furlong et al. 1996, Hodkinson and Hodkinson 1999). In this sense teaching can be seen as being reconceptualized as a job requiring common sense, practical experience and training, rather than necessarily a graduate-style higher education. Within this has been an increasing emphasis on partnership between higher education institutions and schools (Edwards 1995, Goodlad 1991). Bullough (1997), and Nance and Fawns (1993) note similar trends in USA and Australia respectively.

Any systematic feminist analysis of these changes to teacher education has been slow to develop. Mahony (1997: 88) suggests that one reason for this has been that 'feminist teacher educators are too busy trying to survive the changes to write about them'. Nevertheless there are important things to be said about the changes, with regard to gender and feminism. It would not have been unthinkable that gender equality should form a key criteria in any reviews of teacher education organization and curriculum. Indeed, an increased emphasis on the standards of teaching might well have had central to it issues of equal opportunity, gender equality and other fundamental issues of social justice. Yet the reforms have impeded rather than aided attempts at integrating theory and practice, and have perhaps generated more apathy than action. CATE, in the UK, never prioritized gender, choosing to refer to it only under more general guises of equal opportunities, personal and social education and so forth – to be permeated rather than prioritized in the teaching curriculum. While CATE increased its reference to gender over the years, taking advice from the Equal Opportunities Commission (see, for example, EOC 1989), its overall commitment remained rather low. Gender still holds a tenuous and marginal position in a full and time-constrained teacher training curriculum (Acker 1994, Coffey 1992, EOC 1989, Skelton and Hanson 1989).

To some extent the issue has been tackled more directly in Europe. The European Commission's Council of Ministers for Education agreed a resolution in 1990 on the enhanced treatment of equality of educational opportunity for girls and boys in initial and in-service education of teachers (EC 1990). This put forward the view that equal opportunities and a consideration of gender issues in education should be perceived as good practice in teaching. This can be seen as part of a wider cycle of activity initiated by the European Commission aimed at reforming teacher education, including the formation of the Teacher Education Network (TENET) project in eleven EC countries between 1988 and 1991. The main aim of the TENET research project was to integrate equal opportunities into the teacher education curriculum. A similar project was undertaken in the Nordic countries, again aimed at stimulating the development of an equal opportunities perspective in the content and methods of teacher training and education (Boulton and Coldron 1993). Both these projects were informed by a commitment to equal opportunities and gender equality, and therefore may be seen as a consequence of a rise in consciousness coming from a feminist discourse. It is significant that the UK played a marginal role in the EC project. Indeed feminist practitioners in, and commentators of, teacher education in Britain have been particularly critical of the lack of support from central government given to gender equality in teacher education.

In 1994, the UK government established the TTA for England to move the reforms of teacher education forward. Two appointed members of the TTA board were drawn from right-wing educational pressure groups, responsible for the earlier sustained attacks on the theoretical (anti-racist, anti-sexist, feminist) elements of teacher education (see Ball 1990). The TTA remit and consequent restructuring of teacher education made no mention of the needs of teachers in the education of matters relating to social justice, such as gender (Mahony and Hexhall 1997). Raising the standards of teacher education and training did not, it would appear, include an appreciation of the political, social and cultural contexts of schooling, education and teaching.

> Teaching involves relationships between people whose personal, social, economic, cultural and political identities and positionings are complex. Negotiating and succeeding within this arena calls for sophisticated everyday repertoires of skills which teachers constantly need to develop. Reference to such creative professionalism is, however, absent from the TTA's documentation, which instead concentrates almost entirely on

concerns about teacher's subject knowledge and pupil performance, both of which are treated as desituated.

(Mahony and Hexhall 1997: 143)

As Mahony and Hexhall (1997) note, the only area in which the TTA specifically acknowledge issues of gender is, in fact, recruitment. Here the priority is given to the problematic of recruiting more men into teaching (TTA 1996b). One implication of this is that the feminization of teaching is seen as part of the 'problem' of the profession, and is not unrelated to the moral panic over the teaching and education of boys (see Delamont 1999, Epstein et al. 1998, Raphael Reed 1999, Skelton 1998).

Ironically, many of the changes we have witnessed in teacher education actually have within them the potential to advance feminist understandings and praxis of pedagogy. They *could* have been harnessed to preserve and promote feminist insights into teaching and teacher education. Mahony's analysis of the so-called new public management ethos demonstrates this potential, while at the same time addressing key hindrances. While some schools of education within UK universities boost feminist managers (Heads of Department), the volume of work actually cuts them off from teaching more about the ways feminists can and do act in non-oppressive ways from relative power strongholds. Management training, Mahony (1997) notes, is not geared to their needs as feminists, and it is inevitable that a distinction is drawn between their feminist presence (which is, of course, worth while in itself) and the power to act in feminist ways (not easy, or possible, in the majority of cases). Other aspects of the NPM, like the move towards a heavy emphasis on standards and outputs, also have feminist potential, though not in their present incarnation. Feminist perspectives are marginalized and there have been few attempts at a participatory consultation process. Issues of gender and social justice, the emotional dimensions of teaching and learning, and the social and political contexts of teaching are missing rather then integrated at the heart of such measures. Rendered invisible are precisely the kinds of issues that feminists would argue should be present in national standards and profiles of educational outcomes.

Finally, it is worth noting that these trends in teacher education must be seen with a framework of higher education more generally. For example, teacher education institutions, and education departments in the University sector in the UK have been pushed to adapt and survive. Alongside the development of initial (and in-service) teacher education provision, they have been subjected to the more general changes of higher education. This has required (among other things) a requirement that they seek additional sources of funding (for example, by recruiting overseas students onto advanced courses), and maintaining (and developing in many instances) a robust publishing and research grant base. This has further increased the workload and pressures on staff, who have also been hit by the same destabilizing forces affecting all of higher education, making long-term planning of staffing and courses problematic (Gosden 1990). At the same time, educational research has shown signs of altering in the direction of, on the one hand, small-scale, practical, school-based projects and, on the other hand, government-commissioned policy-orientated evaluations and test development. It is increasingly difficult to find funding for basic research with a traditional base in the academic disciplines. Money available is increasingly tied to policy purposes. Some of these trends could be used to raise the profile of gender issues – for example, small-scale teacher research – or policy questions could easily focus on gender. However, unless gender is prioritized in guidance from government and NPM (and highlighted in teacher training curricula) such work is always likely to stay on the margins of research endeavour. Indeed, overemphasis on school practice may actually hamper the dissemination of the larger body of theoretical and empirically grounded scholarship on gender.

The Discourses of Teacher Education

The policy climate and consequent reforms of teacher education have done little to either maintain (place?) gender on the agenda, or promote feminist insights and pedagogy. That gender occupies only a marginal place in the initial training of teachers should come as no surprise, however, for reasons other than (as well as) the institutional context and official guidelines. There is no reason to assume, for example, that (beginning) teachers will be immune to the values and currents of the wider society, which in themselves have gendered consequences. What is clear is that teacher education apparently fails to provide effective and sustained challenges to the dominant discourses. The discourses of teacher education are pervasive in formulating traditional ('ungendered') teacher ideologies. Sustained commitments to, for example, child-centred learning, political neutrality and professionalism, often unmarked by concomitant commitments to opposing systematic injustice and inequality, may impede attempts at reform. Furthermore, the framing of teaching as women's work may actually run in contradiction to a feminist agenda. The analysis that follows draws on the work of Coffey and Acker (1991) and particularly relates to the UK experience, although the points are sustainable in an international context, where similar discourses can be identified.

Childcentredness and Individualism

Childcentredness encourages individualism and actively resists *any* categorization of pupils (including by gender). Such an ideology is prevalent in many teacher education courses, where student teachers are encouraged to emphasize children's individual needs and differences, and to avoid stereo-typing (Skelton 1989, Thompson 1989). Riddell (1989, 1992) found secondary school teachers also uncomfortable with a categorization by gender. (Carrington and Short 1987 make a similar argument to explain teacher's resistance to anti-racist strategies.) Commitments to individualism, while worthy, may actually hamper efforts at reform. Focusing on individual children and individual teachers stresses a role for teacher education which de-emphasizes the social and political context in which teaching operates. In doing so it can mask social justice issues and the structural dimensions of gender in and out of the classroom.

Political (Social) Neutrality

The teaching profession has always engaged in an often difficult dialogue over the issue of neutrality. A number of studies (see, for example, Pratt 1985, Riddell 1989 and 1992, Whyte 1986) have documented that teachers prefer to remain neutral rather than venture into what they consider to be potentially controversial political territory. Moles (1995), for example, argues that in the Republic of Ireland the teaching of 'value added' material (aside from moral teaching of the church) is not seen as part of the job of teaching. Hence there is resistance to moving beyond the teaching of 'factual' material. In practice, this means that it is easier for teachers to support a 'gender-free' or gender-neutral approach than one that seeks to actively support change (Acker 1988). Neutrality in this form has been criti-cized as promoting a gender blindness, rather than an engagement with issues of social justice. The irony of this gender-blind or gender-free approach is that it can qualify as a form of equal opportunity, and is often used implicitly as an equal opportunities strategy of default (choice?) in schools. Not to pay special attention to gender differences can be a strategy for improving things for girls and women in some cases, although it is a risky strategy. Of course, one of the timeless dilemmas of feminism is whether to stress equality (sameness) or difference (specialness) when compared to men (Snitow 1990). Many people, including some feminists, believe that to make special provision for women and girls (positive-action measures) is a form of reverse discrimination, and indeed may even be insulting in segregating out femaleness as a state requiring compensation. Nevertheless the practical outcomes of such views can be systematically disadvantageous, perhaps for both sexes or all genders.

A neutral stance, however well intentioned, that ignores considerations of gender can have discriminatory consequences. However, finding alternative stances is far from easy. As Sandra Acker (1988) has argued, it is worth remembering that teachers' belief in neutrality is not without virtue. The consequences of such views and a reflexive approach to them, however, should form part of an agenda of teacher education, as well as teacher consciousness. To remain uncritical is to provide positive reinforcement for existing practices (both good as well as bad).

Professionalism

Ideologies such as neutrality and childcentredness cannot, of course, be separated from the discourse of professionalism with and of teaching, and teachers. Teachers regard themselves as professionals (see Chapter 8 on the profession of teaching). In the public arena teachers have been keen to portray a professional persona. This has implications for innovation and reform in both teaching and teacher education (Shen and Hsieh 1999). It is not our intention here to elaborate on the sociology of the professions (see Chapter 8); suffice it to say that there is a debate over the definition and value of the professional (see, for example, discussions in Hoyle and Megarry 1980, Ginsburg 1987). On a simple level, being 'professional' can be taken to mean doing one's job competently. However, it also has connotations of detachment and neutrality, being uncontroversial, apolitical and protective of occupational autonomy. Some have argued that also carries connotations of being masculine (see, for example, Delamont and Atkinson 1990, Ozga and Lawn 1988, Witz 1992). Professional ideology is and can be used by teachers in defence of their work practices, and against reforms that serve to weaken or threaten their autonomy. Equally professional ideology can be used against teachers, as when the public rejects their attempts at industrial action as unprofessional (Burgess 1986). It may also encourage caution *vis-à-vis* radical innovations that may be perceived as threatening the standing of the profession. The identification of gender equality in some countries, such as the UK, with fringe social and political movements (like feminism!) may also mean that occupations that consider themselves 'professions' will be reluctant to actively embrace and action such a goal.

This ideology is not without its contradictions (Ginsburg 1987). Entrusting teachers with the responsibility for the future of the nation while treating them as incompetent and in need of close direction is a case in point. Whitty et al. (1987) suggested that student teachers themselves will see the contradictions between professionalism on the one hand and less than satisfactory material conditions and fluctuating teacher morale on the other. The increasing emphasis on the school-based experience brings this contradiction to the fore, and indeed may create the opportunity for radical teacher educators to encourage students towards greater critical reflection of issues, such as social justice and gender.

Teaching as Women's Work

As we indicated in Chapter 4, the gender divisions in teaching are marked. Indeed the division of labour between men and women in the profession should now be a familiar tale. What are the consequences of these realities for teacher recruitment and education? One outcome of the identification of teaching as a predominantly female field is that, ironically, gender bias is *less* likely to be seen as an educational problem (Spencer 1997). Teaching is manifestly not seen as a male craft, and has not excluded women or hindered their progression in the way that some professions have. Research has demonstrated that women teachers often adopt a fatalistic, rather than feminist, stance in response to inequalities they encounter in their everyday work (Acker 1990). They often account for inequalities, for example with regard to promotion in terms of the balance of the staff room, or the need to provide male role models.

A further consequence of teaching as a female-majority profession is that it might actually discourage the recruitment of precisely those women who may be in a position to, or especially feel able to, challenge gender stereo-types and conventional sex roles. This may be especially so as the opportunities for women within the professions generally have increased. While initial teacher education relegates gender to the periphery of the curriculum, research has shown that many recruits to teaching (male as well as female) have relatively conventional (perhaps acceptable) ideas about sex roles (Delamont 1990). That is not to deny that some enter teaching with feminist, anti-sexist and more radical ideas about sex roles, although they may find it hard to maintain those positions in schools. Perceptions of teacher imagery and the pressures to conform are inherent in learning to teach (Hawkey 1996). It has been observed that 'If pupils and older colleagues try to train new teachers into established ways over such things as christmas decorations in each classroom, deviations from conventional behaviour about sex roles are likely to be much more heavily punished' (Delamont, 1990: 75).

More specifically, conventional views of sex roles and the lack of a critical mass of gender in teacher training may account for teaching not being concep-tualized as a rebellion and not necessarily perceived as a challenge to male-dominated settings (or hierarchies). Ironically, teaching is perceived already as feminized space. Given all the constraints and barriers in other occu-pations, teaching is still seen as a relatively 'good job for women', rather than one riddled with bias and discrimination against them. A consequence of this may be that teaching may not be attracting those individuals who wish to chal-lenge and change gendered divisions of labour, and systems of social justice.

The dominance of men in management roles in schools (especially beyond primary levels) and in higher education (see Chapter 4) further diminishes the chances of gender and anti-sexism being placed high on the agenda of initial training and subsequent teacher employment. Studies suggest that women teachers as a group, especially in secondary school, lack power and influence (Cunnison 1985, Riddell 1989). A similar story is told in institutions of higher education. Coffey and Acker (1991) reported on the difficulties and antagonisms encountered by women teacher educators, arising from both male colleagues and student teachers (both male and female). Profiling the issue of gender in class was often problematic and met by hostility or the 'negative' label of positive discrimination. Similarly, colleagues were often defensive if gender was raised informally or formally in meetings, resulting in individual women being typecast rather than an effective challenge to a prevailing orthodoxy.

The discourses of childcentredness, neutrality, professionalism and 'teaching as women's work' all have within them the potential for challenge and change – with regard to both putting gender on the agenda and making positive contributions to furthering issues of social justice more generally. However they can also all serve to work against such ambitions – both within teacher education and beyond into the work of teaching. In the context of this chapter we would suggest that initial teacher education has the task of transmitting and reproducing the ideologies of teaching, providing a discourse of professionalism, alongside providing the increasingly prioritized practical skills of teaching.

Hidden Teachers – Reluctant Reformers?

Referred to by Maguire (1995) as the hidden teachers, teacher educators are central to (and vulnerable in) the reconstitution and reorganization of initial teacher training. As reforms increasingly centre this training in schools, teacher educators within higher education become increasingly vulnerable as staffing strategies shift. Although men still outnumber women in HE schools of education (the conventional home of initial teacher education and training in the UK) there are more women here than in many other academic fields. Higher education generally does not have a strong track record of promoting women. Women are seldom in a position to dictate policy. Goodlad (1991) argues that increasingly education faculty are distancing themselves from teacher education and the careers of teachers. This is perhaps not surprising given that the policies that govern teacher education are now set outside of higher education (although it remains a moot point whether it was ever thus). Teacher educators have very little autonomy over curricular and academic development. In the UK, and elsewhere, this has meant a diminishing of the role of higher education in the training of the classroom teacher. Whitehead et al. (1996) note that as student teachers spend less time in higher education institutions, teacher educators face reductions in their staffing base. They report the non-replacement of staff, the use of temporary appointments, earlier retirement packages and the employment of 'visiting' lecturers paid on an hourly basis, as evidence of a move to an increasing casualized and transient teacher education work-force. While policy rhetoric may rephrase this in terms of flexibility, the outcome is much the same. One of the conventional auspices for women working within higher education may be in the process of contracting and reconstituting. Ironically the resultant higher education labour market opportunities – 'flexible' (temporary) contracts, or 'visiting' rather than permanent status – may increase the feminization process of the teacher education work-force. It is well documented that women are more likely to be found in such 'transient' and usually insecure employment.

This restructuring of the teacher education work-force is compounded by a refocusing of higher education more generally. Inside the university sector, certainly in the UK, few rewards are offered to those involved in the training and education of occupational groups such as teachers. An increasingly dominant emphasis on research funding and output makes it increasingly unattractive (and non-viable) to be a department or individual mainly concerned with teaching and learning at all. This is compounded by the ever more stringent quality requirements within higher education – teaching quality assessments, lengthy documentation, recognizable and measurable aims and objectives and so forth. As Acker (1994: 18) notes, 'Schools of education have had to face *both* the incursions into academic freedom and security suffered by higher education *and* the fallout from the government's educational reforms in the schools and alterations of teacher education.' These may actually work against, rather than for, innovation, theoretical input and approaching difficult or sensitive issues.

Maguire (1995) argues that there is still a commitment to a theoretical base in teacher education among teacher educators. But in their everyday reality, teacher educators are faced with a new dominant discourse of the 'practical', which both idealizes and misrepresents practice and limits learning to the reproduction of the immediate and routine (Maguire 1995: 127). Maguire points to factors such as the perceived need for immediacy, the time constraints of initial teacher training programmes, and the 'survival' skills approach to early teaching experiences, as compounding the difficulties that teacher educators have in reconciling theory and practice. In attempting to meet the longer-term professional needs of student teachers, while helping them 'survive' the first year(s) of school, it is more often than not the matters of reflection, interpersonal relationships, values and theoret-ically informed 'professional' knowledge that will fall by the wayside. This, of course, means a privileging of the technical on-the-job skills of the class-room and subject-specialist knowledge, and in consequence enormous difficulty of putting and keeping broader individual issues such as gender on the agenda.

Like teachers themselves, teacher educators' conditions of work are also a factor in the resistance to gender-equality initiatives. As we have docu-mented in Chapter 2, teachers' conditions include lack of time, and the new and ever demanding pressures of reforms to education and the teacher's work serve to exacerbate this (Coffey 1992). In schools it is easy to see how survival becomes a prominent goal, displacing ideas about innovation in 'optional' areas like anti-racism, anti-sexism and social justice. The conditions of work in institutions charged with preparing teachers for the world of work are faced with similar challenges – again requiring an emphasis on survival and the immediate. Initial teacher education courses have often been criticized for being too short to include all that is desirable as well as all that is required. Survival thus is not only prioritized on teacher education courses but is also a lived reality for teacher educators. Given current pressures on teachers and teacher educators it is unsurprising that there is a preference for simple, non-controversial teaching strategies (Shah 1989). Survival becomes the goal, rather than the development of a critical, social-justice perspective on classroom practice.

Feminist Challenge(r)s

Thus far we have highlighted the contexts and climates in which teacher education is placed. The gender regimes of teacher education have received relatively little attention (compared, for example, to those in schools). The pressures on both the teachers and the learners – the teacher educators and the novice teachers – remain severe. There is still little critical engagement nor possible curricular time given over to innovations and reflection, particularly with regard to gender and other areas of social justice. A combination of teacher ideologies, material conditions of work, and policy direction incline towards a prioritizing of survival rather than innovation, of practice rather than theoretical or disciplinary engagement. Institutions responsible for educating teachers share many features with schools, and can be experienced as discouraging environments by feminists with them. Nevertheless there is some evidence of efforts by teacher educators to meet these challenges. It is worth noting that strategies do not need to be especially challenging to provoke controversy. Pat Sikes (1991) reports on her own experience of preparing the gender *lecture* (note the singular) as part of the educational issues course of an initial teacher education programme in a English university. She collected life history and biographical material from student teachers prior to giving the lecture. She was keen to draw on the students' own experiences as a resource in planning the content of the lecture. As might have been expected, but it is salutary nevertheless, the data she collected revealed the students' own school experiences differentiated by gender, models of masculinity and femininity, and the gendered division of labour. Sikes used these experiences and starting points to plan and give an introductory lecture on gender. She describes the lecture as relatively straightforward and uncontroversial (she covered gender socialization, basic gender differences in schooling and so forth). Yet there were at least two outcomes or lessons that arose from her experience. First, Sikes questions the one-off big lecture as the most appropriate mechanism for dealing with issues such as gender. However, given time, resource and curricular constraints this is a familiar pattern. Second, in student evaluations many of the male students had found the lecture 'biased' and presenting what Sikes calls a raging feminist view (which Sikes considered it certainly was *not*). In contrast, many of the female students found that the lecture did not go far enough in dealing with issues of gender and feminism. We suspect that these are familiar stories to those teacher educators tasked with 'teaching' issues such as gender (race, disability, sexuality) within the constraints of the formal teacher education and training curriculum.

Mahony (1995) reports on her experiences of developing gender teaching in initial teacher education in London during the 1980s. While she began, like Sikes, with the timetabled format of big lecture followed by small group seminar, she soon realized that this did not provide an optimum or long-lasting impact: 'There would be a couple of weeks intense debate and in some groups uproar would reign, then a majority of students would become preoccupied with other concerns leaving a minority of (mostly) women students committed to change but beleaguered' (Mahony 1995: 41).

Mahony increasingly used and worked with the students' own experiences as part of the teaching and learning. Students were tasked with drawing up a code of conduct of how they wanted people to behave towards each other in seminars to promote learning for everyone. They shared their memories and experiences of humiliation. Feelings were put on the agenda. Mahony argues that working with experiences was an effective way of integrating theory and practice, and made work on sexism and other areas of social justice more meaningful. Equal opportunities stopped being a series of topics to be covered and became more relevant to effective classroom practice, and social life more generally. However, as Mahony notes, this approach did not work with everyone, and for some (staff and students) it was a painful learning experience that could not always be turned into a productive occasion. One huge dilemma, which resonates with feminist praxis in schools, was how to support white, heterosexual, able-bodied, middle-class males as they are asked to treat these categories of their identities as problematic (see Haywood and Mac an Ghaill 1996, Mac an Ghaill 1994; also Berg et al. 1998).

Coffey and Acker (1991) highlighted ways in which those committed to anti-sexism and feminist insight have attempted to integrate these more firmly into teacher education in England and Wales. They reported on a number of strategies, including dedicated gender 'days' or short (usually optional) programmes. The aims of such events are to increase general awareness of gender issues and to facilitate discussion and debate. The lack of official standing of events such as these, and the optional status of them, means that in reality impact may be limited, and may indeed be a case of 'preaching to the converted'. In addition there remains the tension of the relationship between gender and feminism. Research has revealed that 'optional' gender days are attended primarily by women. This may, of course, be desirable, in order to provide a forum for awareness, consciousness-raising, support and so on. It is less desirable, however, if the aim is to provide feminist discourse and anti-sexist practice within the teaching profession as a whole. Other initiatives, such as working with women's studies and feminist teachers, are concerned with encouraging collaborative working across higher education and schools. While important and worthwhile they may still leave gender and feminism at the margins of teacher education and training. Halsaa et al. (1995) report on the development of courses of teacher education programmes in a Norwegian college, as a result of involvement with women's studies. On closer inspection, however, they found that many aspects of the programmes remained gender-neutral or still served to make gender invisible. The student handbook for the programme did not demonstrate a high awareness of gender and only four out of fourteen syllabuses contained gender or related terms. However, there was some evidence of an alternative pedagogy that contained a feminist perspective (project work, problem-based learning, participatory research methods) and all syllabuses contained areas where gender could easily be made to be both relevant and stimulating: 'Our syllabi say very little about gender, but they do have some textual potential for subsuming some vital regendered influences, given there will be situations created in which the subject contenders will be exposed to these problems' (Halsaa et al. 1995: 23).

Women's studies historically has enjoyed a tenuous relationship with the academy. Feminist teachers within schools also experience considerable difficulties. Decreasing isolation and marginalization of women (and feminist educators) and providing a forum for support are vital and worthwhile elements of such collaborations. However, problematizing one's own position ('coming out' as a feminist) and attempting to challenge the orthodox and dominant discourses both come with a price. 'Feminist' is still a controversial label. Other ways of 'getting at gender' in teacher education include using role play and life history strategies and producing statistical material to show how gender pervades school life. All of these strategies have tended to be initiated by individual teacher educators rather than as part of a whole institution response. Many feminist teacher educators remain frustrated with the labels that get attached to their efforts; they are often stereotyped as especially radical, and the result is that their initiatives are often not treated with the seriousness they deserve.

Conclusion

Sharing of feminist scholarship and practice is essential if teaching is to break down its gendered barriers. However, teacher education has tended to avoid rather than seek controversy, and now its timidity has been exacerbated by its vulnerability. New models of teacher education means gender may – ironically – become a non-issue in teacher education. The trends towards school-based teacher education look set to continue; discussing gender and feminism in the context of higher education teacher education programmes may become something of a red herring. The increasing emphasis in schools on education for citizenship (Beck 1996, Gordon 1992, Hall et al. 1998 and 1999, QCA 1998, Williamson 1997) may, however, mean that gender gets a new airing in the training of teachers by the back door. Citizenship cannot be separated from the construction of identity and issues of social justice (Connell 1992), which in turn cannot be separated from gender (Gordon 1992, Arnot and Weiler 1993). And teachers are going to be charged with the task of providing this education, and for that they will need to be educated and trained.

Pioneers and dragons ...

Ledchester University was founded in 1883, and admitted women to study arts subjects from 1884. Arlette's Ph.D. is on the pioneers who campaigned to open the medical, dental and veterinary schools to women, which took till 1898, 1902 and 1922 respectively. In the gym with Carlotta one evening she remarks that the woman who founded the Ladies Training College in Ledchester in 1870 – which eventually vanished into the Education Department in 1961 – would make a good thesis topic for Carlotta's Ed.D. Carlotta is not keen: 'I don't want to study one of those old spinster dragons, full of Christian zeal and piety: I want to do something relevant'.

7 The Foremothers of Today's Teachers

> We may hope that a sufficient number of able and vigorous women will always be found ready to take up the work. They must be properly paid, well treated, and have reasonable security of tenure; otherwise they cannot continue to do efficient work.
>
> (Burstall 1907: 58)

Introduction

Sara Burstall was a pioneering headmistress, who ran a large girls' school in Manchester for many years. In these few lines she sets out the basic tenets of the nineteenth-century feminist position on women and teaching: that it was a worthy and important job that deserved to be seen as a career and to be rewarded accordingly. In this chapter we outline the history of women's entry to teaching in formal, well-organized schools, and provide a feminist analysis of the historical scholarship on women teachers. Our overall aim here is to consider the feminist legacy to teaching, by considering feminist pioneers and early feminist campaigns.

School teaching, whether in the new elite girls' schools opened by feminists or in the government schools for the working class, has never been an easy job: women teaching 150 years ago, like women teaching a century ago or fifty years ago, found it hard work. Eleanor Butler, for example, a feminist who tried school teaching briefly before retreating to Cambridge to do a Ph.D. in German literature, recalled:

> I came down from Cambridge in 1911 determined to have nothing to do with research. But a year's teaching at St Felix School weakened this resolve. However tiresome and tedious research might be, it could not possibly be as exhausting as the lower school, where my feverish attempts to keep order too often ended in a free for all.
>
> (Butler 1959: 42)

St Felix School, Southwold, was a fee-paying girls' boarding school serving the upper middle classes, so if Eleanor Butler could not manage to discipline the thirteen-year-olds in their German lessons at St Felix she was right to return to university research. Women who stayed in teaching are the subject of this chapter. We outline and reassess the lives and achievements of the pioneer women of the teaching profession in the period from 1848 to 1948. Material on teaching from 1948 to 1968, and from 1968 to the present, is to be found in Chapter 8, where we discuss the contemporary teaching profession.

The feminists of the nineteenth century in Britain, the USA, Australia, New Zealand and Canada were active in education in at least three related ways. First, as part of their wider campaigns to get an academically and vocationally worthwhile education for girls and women, feminists started schools, teacher training colleges and universities. Second, these, in turn, provided careers for women as teachers in the schools, teacher training colleges and universities. Third, the feminist educators were responsible for many educational innovations, such as bringing Montessori methods to the English-speaking world, medical inspection in schools, and physical education, which spread beyond the schooling of middle- and upper-class girls to become widespread in the education of males and females of all classes and races. Our chapter addresses these three legacies: women's struggle to get access to an academic education, and their successful strategies for overcoming the barriers placed in their way; the career paths that education provided for women; and the educational innovations introduced by women theorized from a feminist perspective. We address these three legacies in two broad historical periods: the pioneering days of 1848 to 1918; the 'survival' phase of 1918 to 1948. We recall the era of the feminine mystique, 1948 to 1968, in Chapter 8.

The feminist influence on teaching was to be found in two distinct spheres of education: the elementary schools for the working classes for which teachers were trained either through pupil–teacher schemes or in teacher training colleges (Hoffman 1981, Kaufman 1984), and the academic, fee-paying secondary schools for girls from the middle and upper classes for whom teachers were trained via a university education. There were active feminists in both spheres before the 1914–18 War, although they frequently kept their involvement in causes other than education separate from their professional lives (see Copelman 1996, Delamont 1989, 1993a and 1993b, Kean 1990). After 1918, the first wave of feminism lost its major impetus. Once the vote was won, social feminism became the main form. Feminists in teaching concentrated on widening educational opportunities for the working classes, keeping their own jobs and ensuring the survival of their institutions through the years of the depression.

The Pioneering Days (1848–1918)

This section deals with our three legacies in the period from the early stir-rings of nineteenth-century feminism to the end of the 1914–18 War, when women got the vote in most of the Anglophone world. The material is mainly from Great Britain and the USA, but the underlying pattern is similar in Canada, New Zealand and Australia.

Getting In: The Ladies

The middle-class movement established academic secondary schools for girls (teaching the same subjects as equivalent boys' schools), opened higher education and professional training to women, and created careers in both school teaching and higher education (see Dyhouse 1995) that were socially respectable and paid a sufficient salary for a woman to live independently without the economic support of her father, or a husband. To reach those goals, a vicious circle had to be broken. Before 1918 most middle-class and upper-class families wanted to educate daughters for marriage, not economic independence, and they did not want to invest very much money in that education. Therefore the pay women could earn teaching girls was low, and so parents knew that teaching was not an economically secure occupation for women. Because parents wanted their daughters educated so they would 'catch' husbands, and were not prepared to pay much for their daughter's teachers, teachers' salaries remained low. O'Shaughnessy (1979: 7) quotes a government enquiry of 1893 into schooling in Warwickshire, England: 'occupations for women being so few, and salaries paid to women so low, parents are unwilling to pay high fees for the education of their daughters'. One of the first tasks, and the most important successes, of the nineteenth-century feminists was to break this vicious circle. This was an unparalleled achievement, and paved the way for all the other advances, such as the vote.

While feminists in the middle and upper middle classes were breaking the vicious circle, in Britain and the USA, compulsory elementary schooling was being introduced for, and imposed upon, the working class. Because women's wages were lower than men's, these schools employed large numbers of women teachers, many recruited from upper working-class and lower middle-class homes (see Widdowson 1983 on the UK, Hoffman 1981 on the USA, and Prentice and Theobald 1991 for Canada and Australia). Women's wages were half those of male teachers, but teaching was a more attractive job than domestic service or factory work. Many of these women had little or no training in the nineteenth century, although by 1918 a teacher training college diploma was becoming a requirement. These two sorts of teachers – ladies with a higher education grounded in Latin and Greek in the elite, fee-paying schools, and largely untrained women with the '3Rs' in the state schools – had little in common before 1918, and only began to converge in the years after 1918. The middle-class pioneers are dealt with first, then those who taught the working classes.

The feminist pioneers who opened academic secondary schools and colleges for young ladies in the second half of the nineteenth century did so against a body of medical opinion, religious orthodoxy, and widespread belief among their potential clientele (that is, middle- and upper middle-class parents) that such institutions were dangerous. A pupil or a member of staff at an academic secondary school or in a college was held to be in phys-ical danger (her health would suffer, she might become subfertile or die of brain fever), in moral danger (away from the control of her mother she might meet anybody) and liable to forfeit her marriage prospects, for men would not want a wife who knew algebra. To deal with these dangers, schools and colleges took action to safeguard pupils and staff. The dangers to physical health were countered by medical inspection and physical educa-tion. The moral risks were dealt with by imposing strict rules about social interactions and behaviour in the schools and colleges. The fears about marriage were challenged by statements that education would actually improve women's performance of family duties and reminders that unedu-cated spinsters could easily sink into destitution. Enough parents were convinced by the educational pioneers to make the early schools financially viable and then pay for a university education for young women, but each strategy to safeguard the pupil's reputations as ladies brought its own controversies. For example, the new activities of gym, field hockey and cricket introduced to improve young women's health and fitness were, in turn, attacked by opponents of schooling (see Delamont 1989, 1993a).

Feminists in education who forget their history are in danger of losing the gains of the previous generations. We have sketched in the main strategy used by the first-wave feminists to disarm critics of female education – the 'double conformity strategy' – because it is partly by revealing successful feminist strategies of the past that future feminist strategies can be envisaged (Delamont 1989). Double conformity meant that women did all the academic work expected of equivalent men and adhered strictly to the conservative rules of ladylike behaviour. So the pupils, students and teachers worked like men but dressed and lived like ladies. This dimension of the pioneer feminist teachers' work is, today, frequently misunderstood. Scholars of women's educational history have revealed, often in vivid detail, exactly how clever the pioneers of female schooling were in using the double conformity strategy to gain their objectives.

To rediscover the realities of the teachers' work in the second half of the nineteenth century, in order to recognize its feminist dimensions or offer a feminist analysis of it, we need contemporary sources, such as autobiogra-phies by pioneering teachers and pupils who lived through the early days – Sara Burstall (1911, 1933), for example, who became headmistress of the Manchester High School for Girls – or study the virulent attacks on the girls' schools by critics such as Meyrick Booth (1927, 1932) and Arabella Kenealy (1899, 1920) in the UK or G. Stanley Hall (1904) in the USA. There are fewer sources of this kind from which to reconstruct the social worlds of the women who taught the working classes. They wrote fewer books, left fewer archives, and figure in fewer memoirs. What is known follows in the next section.

Getting In: The Working-class Teachers

Whether our images of working-class women in nineteenth-century England come from Mrs Gaskell, Catherine Cookson, or films about Jack the Ripper, education is unlikely to figure prominently. We can conjure up servants and seamstresses, factory workers and farm labourers, exhausted wives and mothers, or the alcoholic prostitutes of London's East End. The elementary school teacher and the student of a Mechanics' Institute literacy class are not familiar figures in our minds. June Purvis's (1989) book *Hard Lessons*, with its vivid evocation of such working-class women, is unusual precisely because it focuses on an otherwise neglected subject. Dina Copelman (1996) uses fictional sources, as well as archival and autobiographical materials, in her exemplary study of London teachers from 1870 to 1930. Purvis's main achievement was detailed documentation of the presence of working-class women in various types of schooling, and adult institutions. She has shown how they gained admission, what they paid, what facilities they received (no votes in the Institutes, and no access to newspapers, for example), and what curricula they studied. The archives of both mixed and single-sex institutions have been explored to provide rich data on a hitherto neglected aspect of English educational history. Research such as that of Purvis (1989), Kean (1990) and Widdowson (1983) suggests that the women who entered elementary school teaching were not faced with the same barriers as middle-class women. For the working-class recruits, teaching was more respectable and less damaging to health and marriage prospects than factory work, shop work or domestic service. However, the rules of respectability – appropriate dress, chaperonage, and segregation by religious denomination and class – were also to be found in the teacher training colleges for such women. In employment, the managers of schools expected a high degree of respectability and exercised detailed surveillance over women teachers. Copelman (1996) makes these constraints clear, as do Oram (1987) and Hunt (1987) for Britain. Kaufman (1984), and Hoffman (1981) make the same points for the USA.

The conditions under which the women trained to teach the working classes were generally harsher. If they were residential, the women lived in spartan accommodation, and were often expected to do domestic work in their college as well. Those who used the pupil–teacher route, or lived at home when attending college, faced domestic work and family duties, as well as modest home circumstances. The records of the training institutions include cases of women who had to leave training due to family poverty, or to nurse sick relatives, and those who were expelled for breaking the many rules governing their behaviour. Respectability was enforced on these women, just as it was on the 'ladies'.

Careers

The middle-class ladies who obtained an academic secondary education, went on to university and then entered teaching in the fee-paying sector had three career routes available in education. First, they could choose to stay in schools, aiming to be head of a subject (the senior classics mistress, the senior scientist) or a headmistress. Alternatively they could move into teacher training, becoming perhaps the principal of a Ladies Training College such as St Mary's at Cheltenham. Third, they could move into university teaching, either in their own subject or into the education department (see Dyhouse 1995). These three sectors were more open to ladies moving between them in the 1848–1918 period than we can envisage today. Each of these careers offered a decent salary, the possibility of saving for a pension, and respectability in the surrounding community. Ladies who were such educationalists could become magistrates, served on committees, and were pillars of their church or chapel, and of ladies' circles. Teaching in elite schools was hard work, but the salary and status made it a reasonable choice. The pupils and students taught, and their parents, came from a similar class, and there were common values.

The lives of those who taught the working classes were harder. Salaries were lower, saving less possible, the status lower, and the conditions of work much worse. Classes of forty, in dreadful buildings, with children who would smell, refuse discipline, and exhaust their teachers meant that staying in the job was a brave decision. These teachers did not have the same choices of moving into training colleges, and no access to university work. Copelman (1996: 157) describes the working lives of London teachers between 1870 and 1930, and their hardships parallel those of the pioneer women who went to the American west to operate schools on the prairie (Kaufman 1984). One alternative to a career was to marry. Here we have treated 'marriage' as an alternative career choice.

Widows and Spinsters

Both the ladies in the fee-paying institutions and the women in the state institutions shared one life choice: life without men. They were either spinsters or widows and, in either case, respectable. Married women were rarely found in teaching in Britain or the USA in the nineteenth century. The early women teachers, and the pioneers who set up the universities and teacher training colleges to educate them and the schools in which they could then work, were, in the 1848–1918 period, overwhelmingly heterosexually celibate: either spinsters or widows. At a time when the moral majority demanded that women should marry, the educational pioneers concentrated on creating an alternative role, that of the public, professional, celibate woman, but they did not challenge the domestic dream. In short, celibacy, actual or potential, was the price paid for entry to the male fields of secondary and higher education.

Heterosexual celibacy was a common form of revolt against the traditional female sphere; as John and Robin Haller (1974: xii) argued, the Victorian lady 'sought to achieve a sort of sexual freedom by denying her sexuality, by resorting to marital continence or abstinence in an effort to keep from being considered or treated as a sex object'. Celibacy was, therefore, a form of liberation: 'the woman today flaunts her sexuality to achieve the same end that many Victorian women could only achieve by denying theirs' (Haller and Haller 1974: xii). Herman (1976), in a study based on an analysis of marriage manuals in the USA between 1871 and 1911, points out that for many of their authors women choosing celibacy were employing a form of subversion. 'Celibacy not only meant incompletion; it threatened a sinful life, especially for men' (Herman 1976: 234).

Celibacy played an important and positive part in the educational campaign, especially in the careers of the pioneers who exemplified the new lifestyle they were creating. At the same time, the spectre of enforced celibacy, the fear that the products of the new schools and colleges would scare away potential suitors, haunted the whole enterprise. Thus the pioneers had to establish an alternative sphere for women and change the image of the marriageable woman. The two things were related, for, as Woody (1929) put it: 'a woman is not free to choose her mate so long as she must choose someone'. The pioneers' own lives were conducted along lines of the strictest decorum. In addition, many of them were celibate, either from choice or necessity. Some saw the educational campaign as a higher calling, while others were hostile to sexuality, even in marriage. Thus, for example, 'M. Carey Thomas assumed a conflict between womanliness and intellect' and thought that 'sexual instincts, marriage, and children … interfered with woman's higher achievements' (Cross 1965: 32–3). Indeed, Thomas's biographer Edith Finch (1947: 57) says that she took to calling herself Carey Thomas rather than using her first name (Martha) because 'the added dignity and especially the sexlessness of the name were symbolical'. In Britain, Frances Buss, Dorothea Beale, Emily Davies, C.L. Maynard, Louisa Lumsden, and the Lawrence and MacMillan sisters all stayed single, and they and hundreds like them were taunted in the well-known rhyme:

> Miss Buss and Miss Beale
> Cupid's darts do not feel.

> They are not like us
> Miss Beale and Miss Buss.

In fact it is clear from their biographies that both Dorothea Beale and Frances Buss received proposals, but chose to stay single and work. Rhoda Nunn, in George Gissing's (1893) *The Odd Women*, is a fictional example of such a woman, turning down an eligible husband to work for women's liberation. Roberta Frankfort (1977) draws an interesting distinction between celibacy and domesticity as ideologies among collegiate women in the USA at the turn of the century. She contrasts the lives and beliefs of Alice Freeman Palmer and Carey Thomas, the former epitomizing the 'new' career where the educated woman married an intellectual and shared his interests; the latter embodying the celibate who spent her life in a female community. Frankfort (1977: 33) summarizes Carey Thomas's position: 'she was an isolationist with respect to men, living most of her adult life with close women friends surrounded by a college filled with women students'.

The pioneers, then, chose heterosexual celibacy. Some lived in close relationships with other women, which may or may not have been sexual. In the era under discussion, before Freudian ideas gained credibility in the Anglophone world, their lives were seen as morally superior, celibate, respectable existences. From that base, the pioneers set up morally impregnable schools and higher education institutions in which to educate girls and build their own careers, governed by the double conformity strategy. Finally, for our first period, 1848 to 1918, we turn to those innovations we owe to the feminists of that era.

Feminist Innovation

Many of the features of schooling that are taken for granted in the 1990s owe their existence in Anglophone countries to feminists and/or were pioneered by women in girls' schools. These are of two kinds: innovations in the middle-class schools intended to safeguard the health of the young ladies and those intended to improve the welfare of the working classes brought into their schooling by feminists. Among the middle classes, the three most lasting innovations were (1) systematic medical inspections, (2) callisthenic/gymnastic exercises, and (3) the introduction of loose clothing and the abolition of the whalebone corset. These three developments were all intended to prevent educated ladies from becoming ill by ensuring they were monitored by doctors, took healthy exercise and wore clothes that did not prevent them from breathing properly (see Atkinson 1978, 1984).

Innovations intended to improve the welfare of the working classes included campaigns for school meals, medical and dental inspection, 'fresh air', and the widening of the curriculum to include aesthetic subjects, such as art and music. The pioneering developments associated with Rachel and

Margaret Macmillan are typical here (Steedman 1990). Across all social classes, feminists were instrumental in bringing European ideas of child-centred, progressive, creative pedagogies for young children to the Anglophone world. In Britain and the USA the introduction of ideas from Montessori, Froebel and Pestalozzi came into schooling pioneered by feminists.

We now move on to the years of the Great Depression and the Second World War, when women's careers in teaching were attacked. Once again we focus on women's strategies to keep careers in teaching, their careers and lives, and then their innovations. We keep the separation between the ladies of the elite sector and the women of the mass sector.

The Crisis: The Years 1918–1948

This section labels the 1918–1948 period a crisis for two main reasons, one economic, one ideological. The years between 1918 and 1948 saw an economic depression, which closed some educational institutions for women, and caused widespread unemployment with a backlash against nineteenth-century feminism. Most feminist activity was directed towards welfare reform: social feminism, as J. Stanley Lemons (1973) calls it. The backlash was fuelled intellectually by Freudianism.

Martha Vicinus (1985), in her sensitive discussion of the use of celibacy and all-women communities in the nineteenth-century feminist campaigns, has pointed out that by 1920 celibacy had become distinctly unfashionable. The ideals and practices of the generations of women who had chosen celibacy and all-female communities were challenged by imperialism, eugenics, the depression, and the Freudian revolution. Vicinus states that:

> American historians have noted how singularly ill-prepared Jane Addams and her generation were for the Freudian revolution; they simply could not understand, nor were they sympathetic to, the psychological interpretation of social behaviour. A similar level of misunderstanding seems to have characterized women leaders in England.
>
> (Vicinus 1985: 289)

Vicinus argues that not only did the celibate women find themselves ill prepared for the Freudian onslaught, they had no defence against it. She goes on to say that 'single women had no weapons with which to fight the labelling of their friendships as deviant because they had understood sexual activity as heterosexual' (Vicinus 1985: 291). The growing acceptance of Freudian ideas also raised another 'danger' lurking in schools and colleges to imperil girls – the lesbian. This peril was viciously outlined in a novel by Clemence Dane, *Regiment of Women* (1917).

The 'new' psychological theories were used by Meyrick Booth in the 1920s and 1930s to criticize the education of girls, which he saw as out of date. He characterized the ideology of the girls' schools as 'the sterile rational doctrinairism of the J.S. Mill – Olive Schreiner – Buss and Beale school' (Booth 1932: 143). This sterile doctrine was pernicious, as Booth saw it, because it was not informed by psychology.

> The great boys' schools, despite their defects, embody a long tradition, an immense experience of boyish ways and needs. The girls' schools of today on the other hand, are a new-fangled creation evolved for the most part under the unpsychological ideals of pre-war days.
>
> (Booth 1932: 162)

Booth accused the women running schools of being ignorant of psychology, especially the work of Havelock Ellis and G. Stanley Hall, an American pioneer of adolescent psychology. Their ignorance, he claimed, meant that:

> all over the country countless thousands of young girls are being forced through examinations and encouraged in the playing of all sorts of strenuous games and sports at an age when in the opinion of competent medical men and psychologists, it is essential that they should refrain from all severe mental and physical strain.
>
> (Booth 1932: 169)

Among the 'authorities' Booth cites is Dr Arabella Kenealy, who wrote on similar lines (Kenealy 1920). Booth did not include among the psychologists Helen Bradford Thompson Woolley or Leta Stetter Hollingworth. The former had carried out research that found no consistent sex differences in mental abilities or performance, and Hollingworth showed that menstruation had no effect on women's performance at mental and motor tasks (Rosenberg 1982). Indeed, Booth quite failed to take account of any psychology that differed from G. Stanley Hall's. Booth repeats himself a good deal, claiming that the big girls' high schools were 'dominated by an absolute doctrinairism alien to reality' (Booth 1932:177). He claimed to have correspondence with the head of a teacher training college who did not believe that there were any fundamental sex differences. He accused her and similar women of having 'a large part of her innermost personality violently repressed' (1932: 177). He feared that the girls' schools were not designed to produce wives and mothers and argued that 'it is by preparing girls for celibacy that we make them celibate' (1932: 179). There were then two aspects of Booth's critique: he claimed that the new science of psychology showed the nineteenth-century pioneers to have been wrong; and that spinsters were suppressing, or repressing, their 'true' nature. This latter point was particularly harmful to the cause of women's equality because it is impossible to refute. Similar critiques were launched in the USA, and the heterosexual celibacy which had been respectable became regarded as sinister.

Alongside this ideological assault was the economic recession, which meant that many middle- and upper middle-class families had less money to spend on educating daughters at school or sending them to higher education, and there was also a move to economize on all public services, such as education, designed for the working class. Wages in the public sector fell, and rising male unemployment led to calls to push women out of the labour force. Hence our label of 'crisis' years. We now turn our attention to the lives of women teachers in the period in question.

The Ladies Surviving

The schools and higher education institutions founded in the nineteenth century to educate and provide careers for ladies faced a number of challenges. Apart from the economic recession and the ideological attacks from outsiders, their own pupils, students and younger staff found the institutions 'stuffy' and unduly restrictive (Fass 1977). University students expected to be able to smoke, to meet men, and to wear fashionable clothes. Schoolgirls and younger teachers could not see why the schools had to stay as they were. Older staff who had lived under the double conformity system with enthusiastic compliance to get equality were fierce in their defence of it, fearing that change would lead to old anti-women arguments being reopened. They felt the gains of the nineteenth century were precarious and easily overthrown. Cambridge University, for example, refused to give women degrees in 1897 and 1921 – even though women had been studying there since 1869 – and men rioted in the streets against the idea.

Apart from the generation gap, the schools and universities also faced a problem consequence of their earlier success. Initially only the cleverest and most academically motivated girls had attended schools and higher education. They wanted to learn algebra and Latin, and were both able and interested in academic curricula. Once schools became respectable, and even higher education ceased to be scandalous, families began to send young women who were not so clever and who lacked the passion for the high-status 'male' curriculum. The pioneers had to decide whether or not to open up courses in less academic areas, which meant, in practice, more traditionally female subjects, like home economics, secretarial skills and 'citizenship'. Sara Burstall (1933), for example, opened up such courses at Manchester High School for Girls, while other feminists violently opposed them. Young ladies were even sent to college without the motivation to be there. In *Gaudy Night*, for example, Dorothy L. Sayers (1935) portrays Miss Cattermole, a student at Shrewsbury College for Women in Oxford. She is a young woman whose parents have sent her to Oxford where she is miserable because she would rather have learnt cooking. Such a fictional character would have been inconceivable in 1896.

Surviving the years from 1918 to 1939 was itself a triumph, which is less recognized than the triumph of the pioneers. The ladies who taught in the schools and in higher education in those years had even less opportunity to marry because of the generation of men lost in the 1914–1918 War. However they did still have the career paths of the single-sex education sector, with its school headships, and leadership in teacher training and higher education. The novel *South Riding* by Winifred Holtby (1936) focuses on the life of a headmistress of a girls' secondary school, who is a passionate feminist, a spinster, and has to fight for the survival of her school in the depression.

Teaching the Working Class 1918–1948

The women teachers of the working classes in the crisis years faced pupils whose families were suffering hardship because of the depression, in schools where managers had little money to spend, in a climate hostile to women who had 'taken men's jobs'. However, they did have work, even if equal pay was a distant goal, and the unions to which male teachers belonged were, in the main, fiercely opposed to equal pay. We do, however, have much better data on the teachers of the working classes in this period, particularly because of the rise of women's history. Because women teachers from this era are still alive, feminists have been able to conduct oral history interviews with them.

There are some excellent studies of women in teaching during these years, gathered by life history interview. Rousmaniere (1997) for example, interviewed twenty-one teachers (mainly women) who worked in New York in the 1920s; Peterson's (1964) oldest informants, the women in their sixties, had taught in the twenties, thirties and forties; and Quantz (1985, 1992) has studied women who taught in the 1930s. Kean (1990) has written on the lives of four women (Emily Phipps, Agnes Dawson, Ethel Froud and Theodora Bonwick) who were suffragists, activists in the feminist National Union of Women Teachers and had careers centred on state schooling. Born late in the nineteenth century, they taught through the 1914–18 War and the anti-feminist 1920s. Phipps was the head of a secondary school for working-class girls in Swansea, Bonwick and Dawson taught in London, Froud was a full-time official of the union. The issues that preoccupied them are very similar to those discussed in Rousmaniere's (1997) volume: progressive teaching methods, sex education, local politics, and the roles of inspectors and supervisors.

The everyday working life of an elementary school teacher in an industrial town in Britain is described in a novel by Ruth Adams (1983), originally published in 1938. Adams's novel focuses on her heroine's sexuality and spinsterhood, the daily grind of teaching, and the terrible poverty of the pupils. Like the histories, Adams's novel portrays hard work in badly maintained buildings in a climate hostile to spinsters and to working women. When war broke out in 1939, these problems were overshadowed.

Innovations 1918–1948

The era 1918–1948 was not an innovatory one in the elite sector, but those women working in schools for the masses did campaign for change. The most central campaign for feminists was to extend the opportunity of an academic secondary education to working-class women. In the USA that battle was won early in the period, but in Britain it was not successful until 1944, and then only for those female pupils (about 25 per cent) who went to the grammar rather than the secondary modern school at 11. In Britain in 1918 the idea that a poor girl should attend a school where the taxpayer bore the cost of her Latin lessons was a revolutionary one; after 1944 it had been accepted. This campaign forms one of the subplots of Winifred Holtby's *South Riding* (1936). Other feminist campaigns of the time were for equal pay and an end to the marriage bar for women teachers (Partington 1976). Hence innovations in this context denotes wholesale campaigns in establishing education for all, and equal status for women teachers, rather than particular or specific innovatory methods. Ironically this means that the feminist legacy of the period is even more significant.

Conclusion

This book is primarily about feminism and the contemporary teacher's work and life. But we felt it was important, nevertheless, to provide this historical dimension. We have included this chapter because we feel that women who do not know about their foremothers are likely to make the same mistakes and/or reinvent the same wheels. The women who taught in the 'Wild West', in the virgin territory of Australia, and in the pioneering girls' schools like Wycombe Abbey were heroines, and deserve to be remembered, not least because of the struggles they overcame and the legacies they left. In the next chapter, we finish the historical narrative by focusing on the teaching profession through to the present day. We include an account of women within the profession from 1948, and set our discussions within the sociology of the professions.

Battling on ...

Bruce Fossett and Connor Fulpurse, heads of PE at Westhaven Comprehensive and Holmbury High, are in the pub after an Ed.D. class also discussing their theses. Bruce has decided to study the introduction of mixed soccer into Ledshire primary schools, because his daughter is a keen player and he has had several battles with her primary head and the governors about it. Mixed soccer will be, he argues, an interesting innovation to trace. Connor is thinking of interviewing union activists to see why they devote energy and time to teacher unions. He wonders why teaching in Britain has so many different unions, all fighting each other.

8 Understanding the Profession

> The immediate post-war period saw the consolidation of the traditional model of professionalism, which was oriented towards public service and aspired towards autonomy and self-regulation for the professional groups concerned.
>
> (Nixon et al. 1997: 6)

Introduction

In this chapter we provide an account of the teaching profession, from 1948 to the present day. We have structured the chapter around two sets of issues. First, we summarize the experiences of women in teaching from 1948 to 1968, the era of what we term the feminine mystique. This provides us with the opportunity to foreshadow the contemporary profession. Second, we augment this account with a critique of the sociological writing that has described teaching in general, and women's place within it, during and since those years. This academic writing, which aspired to be scientific and dispassionate, was actually deeply sexist and treated the ideological tenets of the feminine mystique as if they were permanent truths.

Losing Their Way, or Losing Their Friends?

The period straight after the Second World War seemed set to be one of triumph for women and their education. Eighty years after Girton College opened, Cambridge University finally gave in and during 1947–8 the first women became full graduates. This was the victory for which the feminist pioneers had been working for a century, in the face of scepticism and even hostility (McWilliams Tulberg 1998).

Schooling for girls had also made inroads. Martha Vicinus (1985: 210) has argued that in their first fifty years the boarding schools for girls 'were probably the most successful of all women's total communities'. However she counters this argument with the observation that they were not sufficiently 'flexible' in the years after 1948: 'frozen in time, girls' schools became subject to satire and amusement – and worst of all – irrelevance'. Vicinus noticed that 'what had been liberating for one generation', such as the gym slip and lacrosse, 'became stultifying for the next'. Her only source for this condemnation is Judith Okely's (1978) much-cited paper on her life as a pupil at a girls' boarding school in the 1950s. Vicinus (1985: 210) summarizes Okely as follows: 'girls' boarding schools were so narrow and out of date as to destroy all that had once been intellectually exciting and socially freeing'.

The position that Vicinus adopts actually suggests a loss of insight, about which there are several points one can make. Perhaps oddest is her failure to use Mallory Wober's (1971) large body of data on girls' boarding schools. His sexist condemnation of them for concentrating on classics rather than cookery and science rather than sewing would probably have sensitized her to the continuing importance of such schools. They, and only they, kept feminism alive and maintained the supply of women science and maths students during the long period from 1950 to 1980 when co-educational state schools were failing to enthuse girls about science or teach it to them effectively (or both). Vicinus also neglects other published work on the elite girls' schools, but the omission of Wober is the most striking.

The popularity of Okely's paper itself, which has been reprinted several times, is odd, particularly when few commentators have noticed that her school (if she represents it correctly) was rather bad. The way in which many women have sided with Wober to attack the only feminist sector that survived in the UK is startling. Some of the elite girls' schools had allowed the double conformity trap to enslave them, rather than using it as a self-conscious strategy for the advancement of women, but they still taught difficult, academic subjects to high standards. Hours spent on a cold hockey pitch are still a small price to pay for proper maths teaching. Okely's paper is interesting for its total disregard of the fact that the single-girls' school with academic standards actually carried the feminist torch onwards between 1945 and 1980. They may have maintained feminist goals against the will of many pupils, and perhaps unconsciously, but it was extinguished everywhere else. The same phenomenon – the small elite sector being attacked as irrelevant but actually being the only place where good science and maths were well taught to women – can also be seen in Australia (Connell et al. 1982) and in the USA. Proweller (1998) shows this clearly in her ethnography of such a school in an American city, as does Amanda Cross's (1972) fictional portrait of 'The Theban' in New York, and the research by Lawrence-Lightfoot (1983), Susan Lloyd (1979) and the Gilligan team (1990). Of course such schools were of no relevance to the majority of women, but it was from them that most women scientists and many women leaders in other fields came.

In the period from 1948 to 1968 it had become normal for most women teachers to marry, and turnover in the occupation was high because few mothers of young children were in paid employment (see Evetts 1990). The spinster teacher was an object of derision, and in most spheres of education feminist goals were submerged, abandoned or forgotten. By the end of the 1939–45 war, women in both Britain and the USA had lost sight of the original reasons for the regimes of women's colleges and schools, and they were increasingly seen as bizarre, old-fashioned and deeply repressive (as Okely 1978 describes). American examples of this loss of history include the puzzlement felt by freshwomen at the elite 'Seven Sisters' women's colleges in the 1960s faced with the alumnae from cohorts fifty years older (see, for example, Baker 1976 on Radcliffe).

The egalitarian mood of the post-1945 era made fee-paying schools, and especially boarding schools, seem elitist and old-fashioned. For every feminist wanting to preserve high-quality physics teaching in a fee-paying girls' school, there was an equivalent wanting co-education and comprehensiveness. Our perspectives here are similar to that adopted by Elizabeth Wilson (1980) in her history of British women from 1945 to 1968. Wilson is extremely skilful at showing how there were genuine differences of opinion about the merits of every aspect of law and policy relating to gender between women who can all be seen as feminists – but of different types. Wilson does not spend much time on education, but points out that John Newsom's infamous statement about domesticity for the majority of girls was only an elaborated version of 'what feminists such as Eva Hubback were saying after the war' (Wilson 1980: 33). The material on the girls' public and direct-grant schools, on co-education, and on the loss of a career path for women in teaching all has to be understood in this way. What was hailed as liberating by one group of women has also to be seen as destructive of female opportunities by another group.

The achievements of the feminist educational pioneers in establishing the right of young 'ladies' to study nearly every conceivable subject and play a range of sports, plus the organization of a secure and respected career structure for women teachers in the academic girls' schools, were both allowed to run down in a few short years. The cause of the equality of women in education lost out to a 'reform' that was never thoroughly debated: co-education, in secondary and higher education. Not only did some women turn on the elite girls' (boarding) schools and berate them for faults. There was also a widespread revulsion against single-sex education. Sutherland (1985: 155) has pointed out that, although co-education has been 'one of the major changes since the 1944 Act in England', it came about without serious discussion at either local or national levels as an almost 'absent-minded side effect' of comprehensive schooling. Scotland, Wales and Northern Ireland differ from England here, because the former two have traditionally had mixed schools in the maintained sector, while Northern Ireland has kept single-sex schools to the present.

In England the 1944 Education Act produced new secondary modern schools, which were often single-sex. In 1947 there were 1,312 mixed secondary moderns and 1707 single-sex ones. Gradually this pattern changed so that by 1960 most secondary moderns were mixed, and this pattern was followed as comprehensive schools grew. In 1982 there were 2,885 mixed comprehensives and 473 single-sex ones. Single-sex schooling in the maintained sector has been common only in inner London, and in those towns that kept grammar schools. Roman Catholics have been most likely to retain single-sex schooling in denominational schools, because there have been encyclicals (1929 and 1957) condemning co-education. Sutherland (1985) discusses the side effects of this shift towards co-education, and produces a list similar to those of other commentators, such as Shaw (1976 and 1980), Delamont (1980), Walford (1983) and Deem (1984).

Reginald Dale (1969) found that it was women teachers worried about their promotion prospects – or lack of them – in mixed schools who were the most hostile to co-education. Dale's research is a main source of evidence on all aspects of co-education, and what we can say about the issue has to be based partly on his work. Dale concluded that mixed grammar schools were superior to single-sex ones on social and academic grounds. Yet as Shaw (1976: 47) pointed out, 'although Dale ... has dedicated his professional career to championing the cause of co-education and especially to showing that mixed schools are superior to single sex ones on social grounds, the evidence is far from consistent'.

Indeed, as Eggleston (1974) argued, while the evidence that boys do better in mixed schools is overwhelming, it is certainly less convincing for girls. It seems possible to argue that boys benefit socially and academically from going to co-educational schools but girls are better off in single-sex ones. In addition, Walford's (1983) data revealed that the senior staff of those boys' public schools that had admitted girls to the sixth form were motivated not by a desire to improve girls' chances at 'A' level and university entrance – which, given the better science facilities (and classics teaching) available there, would be plausible – but by a desire to counter falling rolls in a manner least disruptive to the school.

When we examine the impact of co-education in schools and colleges on the careers of teachers, it is clear that the fears expressed by Dale's (1969) women respondents were far from groundless. The teachers surveyed about co-education by Dale included women teachers opposed to co-education because of poorer career opportunities for women: 'No men made comments in this section. Typical of the first objection is: One aspect of co-education that seems to me unfair is that in such a school there is less prospect of promotion for women teachers' (Dale 1969: 48). Dale went on to point out that:

> an important section of women teachers in girls' schools oppose co-education for reasons which are not educational ... but are concerned

with careers and promotion, some women feeling strongly that there would be little hope of women gaining headships if ... schools became co-educational.

(Dale 1969: 228)

Dale countered this by proposing that there should be a senior mistress post with deputy head status in co-educational schools, because 'Opinion in the country is not ready for more than the exceptionally good headmistress to be placed permanently in charge of a mixed grammar school, nor do there appear to be many women who would desire it' (Dale 1969: 228–9).

No evidence whatever was offered for either statement, but thirty years later the fears of those women have been confirmed. Women entering schoolteaching, and teacher training institutions, had in 1945 the possibilities of two types of top job. They could aspire to become a headmistress, or the principal of a women's training college. Both were well-paid occupations with considerable social cachet, and led to other work – the magistrate's bench, committees, local councils, and so forth. Even if one did not reach the top of these parallel trees, one could become a head of department in either a school or college. Admittedly, in 1945 in the UK there was no equal pay for women teachers, but there was a career structure. By 1975 equal pay had become legal in theory – although rarely achieved in practice – and the career structure had gone with the coming of co-education.

Sutherland (1985) has pointed out that co-education was adopted as an undiscussed adjunct to going comprehensive. No sustained public debate took place about the consequences of co-education for the careers of women in teaching. Yet what women teachers gained with the award of equal pay they lost with the coming of co-education, because no provisions were made to safeguard their career ladder in the co-educational school. It is easy to forget that teachers only got equal pay in 1961, and that in Scotland, and in England and Wales, there existed men's unions opposed to equal pay up until the 1975 Sex Discrimination Act made single-sex unions illegal. The struggle for equal pay, described by Partington (1976), was long and bitter, and it should not surprise us if entrenched positions adopted during that struggle have not disappeared.

The principle of equal pay in teaching in the UK was first established in 1955, with a settlement then planned to phase it in over six years. The National Association of Schoolmasters (NAS) campaigned to have the decision reversed, while the National Union of Women Teachers (NUWT) campaigned to have equal pay adopted at once. During this period an NAS man wrote in the *Times Educational Supplement* (12 April 1957) that women only came into teaching 'to get a husband to get them out of it. The women's staff room has become a waiting room for the bridal chamber and an ante-room for the maternity home!' The NAS line was that men had dependants to support, and they gradually swung their efforts towards a campaign for a dependants' allowance after 1961. Terry Casey, who later became the NAS general secretary, called for an extra £200 per year for men in 1958. The NUWT disbanded in 1961 and gave its remaining funds to New Hall, a new women's college in Cambridge. Partington argues that the award of equal pay and the failure of the campaign for a dependants' allowance were due to the shortage of teachers, and the high birth rate, in the post-war years, especially the shortage of women teachers (see Evetts 1990). Certainly those who had claimed that giving women teachers equal pay would discourage men from entering the occupation were proved wrong. The number of men becoming teachers, and their proportional share of teaching jobs, both grew between 1955 and 1972, the period when equal pay was newsworthy enough to create interest.

The battle for equal pay was long – it began with a resolution put to the National Union of Teachers conference of 1904 – and extremely bitter, as Partington's history shows. However it would be hard to argue that the sexual inequalities in pay and promotion that are found in schoolteaching and in teacher training institutions today are a legacy of that struggle. Rather the rapid spread of co-education has, as Zimmern (1898) and Clarke (1937) feared, closed the main career and promotion path for the women teacher in the girls' school without providing equality in the co-educational one. The career structure of the girls' grammar and direct grant schools has largely gone, and the suggested safeguards of the senior mistress post at deputy head level are a poor substitute. The career in the women's teacher training college has also been changed out of all recognition by the coming of co-education, and then the closure and merger of colleges. Fletcher (1984) chronicled the changes in the Bedford women's PE training college from a cloistered total institution (see Walker 1983) of the type described in Josephine Tey's *Miss Pym Disposes* (1947), to a mixed, multi-site institute of higher education. Apart from this one account, we are short of information about these college principals and their careers. Howson (1982) has written a biography (*A History of Mathematics Education in England*) of Elizabeth Williams who was Principal of Whitelands and Homerton, but we have little information about Williams's coevals and their successors. A whole career avenue for women has been swept away without any public debate, and without any 'rescue archaeology' on the lives of women who chose that career.

Joan Browne (1979) has written a history of the ATCDE from 1943 until it was absorbed into NATFHE. As the ATCDE was formed by amalgamating the Training College Association (founded 1891) and the Council of Principals (1913), her book includes data on women college principals this century. Women were in a majority in the Council of Principals, and between the wars there was an abortive move by a few men to form a separate association to escape a perceived female dominance. In the period from 1918 to 1939, lecturing in a college of education, though a respectable occupation for women, was not a highly paid one, for the salaries were the same as those for teaching in elementary school. Even the principals did not receive generous salaries, because until 1965 there was no agreed, national salary scale for them. As Browne (1979: 134) comments wryly, 'before that the salaries were based on gentlemen's agreements in each college. As the majority of the gentlemen on the principals' side were ladies, they did not do very well.'

It would be wrong to claim that lecturing in a teacher training college, or being principal of one, was a well-paid occupation, but it was a career, and gave women autonomy. In 1957 there were 108 teacher training colleges, nineteen for men, fifteen mixed, and seventy-four for women only. Since many of these had women principals, these were a source of status for women. After 1944 the criticisms of single-sex colleges grew in strength, so that gradually they became seen as anachronisms. In 1969 one retiring principal of a women's college told Browne (1979: 134) that her generation were 'the last of the lay abbesses'. They were, and a whole career path went with them.

From the end of the emergency training scheme until the mid-1970s, women outnumbered men in teacher training colleges in England and Wales (by 7,500 to 1,900 in 1976). After 1974 there was a dramatic change in higher education provision, which affected women particularly. The government decided that teachers should no longer be trained in specialist colleges, isolated from other students, and that a falling birth rate meant that there was a slackening demand for primary teachers immediately, and for secondary ones later. This meant that women's higher education opportunities were curtailed, and a career path for college lecturers almost vanished. The *Times Higher Education Supplement* (*THES*) of 19 August 1977 commented:

> The drastic reduction in places at the colleges of education which have traditionally provided education as well as training for both young and mature women is a setback to the slow progress which women have been making in the world of higher education .... Three times more women than men entered teacher education last year, more than half of them with one 'A' level. Many must now turn elsewhere for higher education.

The *THES* went on to argue that alternative arenas for women's higher education should be found, a call also made by Turner (1974) and Scribbins (1977), but nothing was done, and no public campaign resulted.

Thus in thirty years two career paths for women were lost, and nothing was done to replace them with alternatives in the new co-educational schools and multi-course tertiary colleges. Similar analyses can be made for other professions such as nursing, librarianship and social work, where reorganizations and bureaucratization have led to senior posts increasingly being held by men. Heath (1981: 120) pointed out that 'school-teaching, nursing and social work ... the helping professions provide a definite channel of upward mobility for career-orientated women'. As the senior posts in these occupations have become increasingly monopolized by males, women have been trapped in the lower-paid grades of these occupations with little chance of promotion. The sociology of education and professional socialization has not yet begun to focus on the consequences of this for these occupations, for social mobility, and for women's lives and careers.

Carol Dyhouse (1985) has shown that, while a few nineteenth-century feminists favoured co-education, others were anxious about its deleterious results for girls and women. The fears of that group have been amply justified. However, the surviving girls' schools in the period since 1945 have also betrayed the campaigning zeal of their foremothers, not least by allowing double conformity to become an end in itself, rather than a strategy. In this period, from 1948 to 1968, the elite sector lost confidence in itself, the majority of women in teaching were marrying, and the enthusiasm for co-education at school and in higher education swept away the female career structures for which the nineteenth-century feminists had fought. In the mass, state sector, there was one other trend that has been analysed by contemporary feminists. Once secondary education was compulsory, there was a growth in domestic science teaching: cookery, needlework, childcare. The origins of these subjects were in the era of social Darwinism (Dyhouse 1977) around 1900, but they were much expanded in the 1945–1968 period. Attar (1990) has written a devastating critique of the ideology and the practice of these subjects, designed to improve the health of the family and the harmony of the home, and to train women to service the domestic needs of men (Paechter 1998). Only with the coming of the national curriculum to England and Wales in 1988 did this 'subject' retreat from the school experience of most young women.

We have focused mainly on the secondary sector in this chapter. At the primary level there had been co-education in schools for many years in Britain, and so the everyday experience of teachers did not change as it did in the secondary schools. However there was a shift from the spinster career teacher of young children to a new pattern, where married women, and mothers, made up a substantial part of the work-force. McPherson (1972) in the USA and Nias (1989) and Evetts (1990) present data from the primary schools on this shift. There were promotion and career opportunities for women in the primary school, although, as Harry Wolcott (1973) showed, appointing panels often preferred a headmaster if they could find one. The career opportunities for the married woman with children in the UK in this period came frequently from the chronic shortage of teachers: when a school was desperate for staff, provision was made to create career spaces for mothers. As one headteacher told Evetts (1990: 98), 'I went back to teaching in 1963 [after a period as a full-time mother]. At that time, there was a tremendous shortage of teachers'. Similarly another headteacher explained;

'I hadn't planned to go back to teaching until my daughter was five. But she was three in fact when I went back' (Evetts, 1990: 110). In this case, the teacher stepped in when two staff members had been in a car crash, so she took her daughter with her to school, and taught her alongside the five-year-olds. When there is a national shortage of teachers, women can build a successful career in ways that vanish when the occupation is oversubscribed.

In this section we have concentrated on recounting the mixed history of women in teaching from 1948 to 1968. The legacy of that period lives on in the contemporary profession of teaching. In the next section we turn our attention to the broader picture, drawing on the sociological literature on the professions, as a further mechanism by which the contemporary teaching profession can be understood. There are at least three reasons for addressing this literature, and attendant concerns, in a feminist sociology of education text such as this one:

- It is important in a feminist text to critique the literature of sociology when it is deeply sexist while purporting to be objective. The literature on 'the professions' is a classic example of such a case.
- Understanding teaching should involve comparing teaching with other, similar occupations, in a feminist sociological framework.
- Despite a supposedly liberal ideology, the professions and semi-professions have managed to marginalize and exclude women. This exclusiveness casts doubts on how 'liberal' they really are.

The Sociology of the Professions, and of Teaching

The sociological literature on those occupations termed the learned professions (and on those termed the semi-professions, such as teaching) lacks any overall coherence or integration. There are several different traditions of research, and authors rarely utilize findings from other traditions. If a reader wishes to discover how sociologists of teaching have researched or commented on gender divisions within the field of study, it is necessary to scan several different bodies of literature from various traditions. In other words we are forced to do two things: to consider the implications of gender divisions for theories of the professions *and* to provide an account of women in professional jobs that does not limit itself to work from one theoretical school. These tasks are complicated by the necessity of linking the analysis to the sociology of education, which has allowed itself to become detached from the sociology of work and occupations.

The Functional and Trait Theorists

Those occupations commonly designated as professions were taken as particularly apt exemplars in functionalist theorizing (Parsons 1951). Talcott

Parsons's characterization of professional roles as achieved, universalistic, functionally specific, affectively neutral and collectively orientated (Parsons 1951) has been widely accepted by subsequent authors in this tradition. McPherson (1972), Lortie (1975), Lieberman (1956), Simpson and Simpson (1969) and Etzioni (1969) all provide analyses that adopt a functionalist or trait-theory perspective. Teaching is set against medicine or law and found to be 'deficient' – that is, not a proper profession. The main American tradition that challenged the functionalists' view of the professions was that of symbolic interactionism.

The Symbolic Interactionists

While the functionalists had tended to reproduce the professionals' own claims, suggesting such high-flow ideals as service and collectivity orientations, the interactionists focused on more mundane aspects of professional work. Writers in the Chicago vein studied how members of occupations (including the professions) operate pragmatically and survive amid conflicting pressures in the everyday performance of their work. The moral concerns of this latter school led them to celebrate the 'underdog' (Becker 1967), while debunking the rhetoric of superordinates. Whereas the functionalists tended to see professions as a special category of occupations, the symbolic interactionists saw them as essentially similar to other jobs. Consequent upon this desire to treat all types of occupation as potentially similar in sociologically interesting respects, Becker (1952a and b) and Geer (1966a and b) had both begun their research careers studying schoolteachers in urban Chicago, and moved on to studies of medical students and liberal arts undergraduates, and then turned their attention to occupational learning in different contexts.

There are few citations of the functionalist research in that of the symbolic interactionists and vice versa, and to an outsider it appears that each school has failed to notice the research of the other. While those two traditions in scholarship about the professions were carried on in mutual isolation they set the tone for research on both the working lives of qualified members of occupational groups and the aspiring students learning the role. The functionalists were overly reverent in their comments on the professions, and generally accepted the occupations' own self-evaluations with its rhetoric of service and collegiality (Gouldner 1962). The interactionists were more sceptical about such rhetoric, and focused on the everyday working lives of members of so-called professional occupations. The great strength of the Chicago School was their analyses of survival strategies in complex organizations, and members' perspectives on the organization of their work.

Other Authors and a Rapprochement

While most of the sociological work on the professions in the 1950s and 1960s was dominated by one or other of the two approaches outlined above, there were some voices to be heard claiming that neither group was moving the sociological enterprise forward. Johnson (1972) set out to show deficiencies in both approaches, and to refocus the debate onto issues of power, control and knowledge, while Freidson (1970a, 1970b, 1975, 1983) made the debate focus on the power that professional organizations have to ensure the autonomy of the occupation. Jamous and Peloille (1970) made an attempt to reorganize sociological thinking about occupations by focusing attention on each job's location in a two-dimensional space of indeterminacy and technicity. Indeterminacy is their term for the 'hidden curriculum' of job performance: all the tacit, implicit, unexamined ways of being a member of any occupational group – rules of thumb, genius, flair and other unspecifiable aspects of being a chef, nurse or street-sweeper. Technicity is the explicit, rule-governed, codified part of a job. Thus for a London taxi driver 'the knowledge' and ability to pass the driving test are the technical parts of the job; being able to deal with drunken, belligerent or bewildered passengers, other road users and other cabbies are the indeterminate. For a lawyer, the legal knowledge is the technical part of the job; dealing with clerks, colleagues and clients the indeterminate. (For a more detailed discussion of this work, see Atkinson et al. 1977.)

After 1968 a fourth approach to the analysis of professions also emerged, centred on feminism. Women such as Cynthia Epstein (1970) and Judith Lorber (1984) pioneered these approaches, subsequently developed by Anne Witz (1992). Using these feminist insights, new research was done on women in law, medicine, science, pharmacy, accountancy, town planning and other elite occupations (see Delamont 1989). Sandra Acker (1983, 1989, 1994) was the one of the first feminists to systematically employ these new perspectives in an analysis of teaching. Acker (1983) destroyed the credibility of the extant publications on the sociology of schoolteaching which, she demonstrated, was impregnated with unexamined sexism. Acker showed how classic functional and trait-theorist discussions of teaching, such as those of Lieberman (1956), Simpson and Simpson (1969) and Leggatt (1970), implied that a high proportion of women was responsible for teaching's failure to achieve the same social status as medicine, and, by implication, blamed teacher training courses for failing to inculcate women with proper professional standards.

When writers announced that teaching was not a profession, they were making a common-sense statement in pseudoscientific terms, and blaming the majority of its practitioners (women) for its lower status than law or medicine. In this climate, Amitai Etzioni (1969) coined the term 'semi-profession' to ghettoize teaching, social work, nursing and library science – all jobs where women were well represented and which have lower pay and status than male-dominated medicine and law. Arlene Daniels (1985) suggests that the term 'semi-profession' is a form of pathology, a disease called 'Etzioni-itis' which should be excised from our vocabulary. Certainly the label 'semi-profession' is unhelpful, and one that any feminist analysis will reject in favour of a more analytic and less static approach.

It is helpful to remember that the professions are characterized by a tension between their rhetorical public face and their individualistic private world of everyday practice. This separation, for analytic purposes, between 'public' and 'private' means we can begin to accommodate the data on gender divisions. The issues that need sociological and feminist attention are first, why women are clustered in the lowest-paid sectors of the occupation in powerless positions, and second, why their competent performance is so derided. Women have not managed to achieve equality either in numbers or in power and prestige within teaching. The work of Pierre Bourdieu (1984) and Jamous and Peloille (1970), especially the concepts of *habitus*, and the distinction between technical and indeterminate knowledge, are valuable in taking our understanding forward.

Paul Atkinson (1983) has argued that research on professional socialization, done by both major traditions, has neglected to apply the insights offered by Bourdieu's work. For Atkinson, symbolic violence, a cultural code, and the notion of *habitus* offer analytic potential for studying professional socialization, to enable research on that topic as a route out of stagnation. Delamont and Atkinson (1995) proposed it to revitalize research on teacher training. Of course, a profession, or its socialization process, or its training schools, is not characterized by one single *habitus*. However, as Atkinson (1983: 237) noted, 'one very common component of the habitus can be indicated. That is, the emphasis on "personal knowledge", "personal experience" and "personal judgement".' These components are recognizably Jamous and Peloille's (1970) indeterminacy, and are akin to Freidson's (1970a) 'clinical mentality'. As Atkinson (1983: 238) argued, 'The definition of "indeterminate" knowledge and its preservation is part and parcel of the politics of professional knowledge and professional power. It is a crucial claim in the quest for autonomy'.

Indeterminacy is not the habitus of any particular profession, for there is always tension between the indeterminate and the technocratic, and always disputes, within occupations and between them, about whose indeterminacy is relevant and valid for particular client groups (see Atkinson et al. 1977). For the purposes of understanding the position of women in teaching, however, that part of the habitus of the occupation that rests on indeterminacy is crucial. We focus on the notion of cultural capital and women's role in its reproduction, to illuminate aspects of the sociological literature on teaching. Incorporating women, via the structuralist ideas of Bourdieu, provides new angles on the topics of stratification and the professions. Bourdieu pointed out that:

The very rapid growth in girls' and women's education has been a significant factor in the devaluing of academic qualifications .... [W]omen now bring academic qualifications onto the labour market which previously were partly held in reserve (and were 'invested' only in the marriage market).

(Bourdieu 1984: 133–4)

Bourdieu's whole argument about the power of the habitus, and about symbolic violence, is that mastery of the habitus is treated by the initiates as a matter of natural talent, of personality, of the 'virtuality' of practitioners. That is, a central part of the essential performance skills of the occupation is *never* explicitly taught, but is believed to be inborn, natural and personal. Bourdieu used this to argue that the French secondary and higher education systems *de facto* examined qualities that were never explicitly taught, which middle- and upper middle-class children had from their families but working-class pupils did not, and thus he explained inequalities in educational outcomes. Atkinson (1983: 238) has suggested that 'the notorious propensity of (professional) occupational groups to self-recruit' may be explained in the same way. That is, practitioners of a profession and those in its training schools share a sort of 'mythical charter': that the sons (and daughters?) of practitioners 'have already assimilated much of the profession's oral tradition and habitus'.

Women and the Hidden Habitus

It is plausible to look for the marginal status that women have held in teaching as being due not to their lack of the technical skills needed for the job but to their perceived failure to behave in ways that reveal their mastery of the indeterminate – that is, their failure to share the habitus. Mary Rowe (1977) has called the subtle barriers that operate against women in the learned professions, and in science, Saturn's Rings. She argues that just as Saturn is partially obscured from us by its rings – whirling particles of dust and ice – so the real nature of much professional work is obscured from many marginal recruits (such as women and ethnic minorities). We prefer to use the powerful metaphor to suggest that the rings are obscuring the habitus, while leaving the purely technical skills of the job visible.

In schoolteaching, the majority of women have the technical knowledge and skills. However, in co-educational schools and teacher training institutions, the power-holders, elite men, share a set of values, beliefs and practices (a habitus) that is veiled from women and non-elite men by Saturn's Rings. This habitus is invisible, implicit, and taken for granted by the male elite. Inside each school, or teacher training institution, and then in the occupation as a whole, the argument goes, women are unaware of the indeterminate skills and knowledge shared by the elite. Women, in focusing on the classroom, and the everyday realities of classroom (private) practice, may be avoiding learning about the habitus of the ruling group in their particular school, teacher training institution and occupation segment.

This analytic framework can be used to explain the findings of Cunnison (1989), Wells (1985), Morgan et al. (1983), Hilsum and Start (1974) and Davidson (1985) on British women teachers and promotion, and the ethnographic materials on different, gendered, staff cliques such as Mac an Ghaill (1994), Ball (1987) and Connell (1985). Mairtin Mac an Ghaill's study revealed that the men controlling the school excluded their women colleagues, and the lower-status men, from the 'real' work, mission and processes of the school. The habitus of that particular school was obscured by Saturn's Rings from the majority of teachers, and each such school is a microcosm of the profession as a whole. This distinction between indeterminate and technical skills also helps explain the 'reluctance' of many women to seek promotion: it is not that women lack the technical skills to perform in promoted posts, it is that they have a distaste for the indeterminate aspects of the roles, in so far as they can see them through Saturn's Rings. The women leaders and managers interviewed by Gerver and Hart (1991) exemplify these views.

In England and Wales, there are now formal courses to train teachers to become school principals. If our analysis is correct, these will teach women the technical skills needed by headteachers, but are not designed to penetrate Saturn's Rings and reveal the habitus where the indeterminate knowledge resides. For women to enter elite sectors of the teaching profession, or what Hulmes (1986) called 'the leadership class' in education in substantial numbers, it is that habitus which has to become non-sexist, and ironically that is perhaps the least penetrable by feminism.

Conclusion

The years from 1948 saw the old, separate worlds of women and men in schools, teacher unions, teacher training and higher education swept away in favour of co-educational institutions. Women's career structures, and the careers of individual women, were severely damaged as a result, because in the new co-educational structures males took a disproportionate share of the top jobs, and the new structures took on male habituses. The dominant social science analyses of these emerging co-educational structures failed to address the gendered nature of their habituses and instead merely described the occupations and institutions in sexist terms. Since 1978, feminist analyses of the occupational structure, and of education, have enabled us to appreciate how damaging to women's careers the shift to co-educational institutions was. The past two decades have seen the beginnings of campaigns to improve the position of women in co-educational structures, and of feminist analyses of the consequences of them. Building on the pioneering work of Acker, and feminist analyses of the professions by authors such as Rowe (1977) and Witz (1992), it is possible to understand the disproportionate exclusion of women from the power centres of each co-educational institution, and from the teaching profession as a whole.

In the next chapter we consider the impact of feminism on the teaching research project. We discuss the relationships between feminist methodology and research strategies, examine the ways in which the lives and work of teachers have been researched, and consider the future research agenda.

Moving on ...

Elvira Luker is having difficulty on her first-year women's studies essay: 'What do you understand by the term "feminist methods"? Illustrate your answer with examples from at least TWO different social science disciplines'. She has read several articles, but is very confused. She understands that feminist research is concerned with women's issues, but finds it hard to think about feminism as a research method.

9   The Research Agenda

In the world of fast-paced intellectual exchange we deny at our peril that we are all within the high-speed, entrepreneurial world of academic fashion.

(Gordon 1995: 439)

Introduction

Our final substantive chapter engages with the epistemological and method-ological issues that are involved in studying teachers and the work of teaching from a feminist perspective and/or for feminist purposes. In doing so, the chapter has a number of specific aims, which provide an organiza-tional framework. First, we briefly describe the relationships between feminism and social research – paying particular attention to the feminist critiques of social research and to what feminist research might look like. Second, we provide an overview of research strategies available to the inves-tigator for gathering and analysing data on teachers and their everyday realities. Where possible we accompany these sketches with apposite exam-ples of the method in action, and accounts of its use by feminist scholars. Third, we examine the relationship between feminism, teaching and action research. Fourth, we pay some attention to contemporary debates and movements in social research, and how these may add to our understandings of teachers and their teaching. Finally we provide some pointers towards a research agenda for feminism and the teachers' work.

Feminism and Social Research

Feminist critiques of social science and social research have, quite appropri-ately, argued that there are gendered questions in the choice of research programme, research strategy and modes of analysis (Scott 1985). More specifically they have argued that the ideologies of gender have structured the social relations of research and the patterns of interaction during research. This can be seen as part of a complex set of arguments about how gender should be researched *and* which social research methods best serve a feminist agenda. Since the 1970s there has been ongoing philosophical debate, within and beyond the social sciences, about the nature of knowledge and 'scientific enquiry' (see Harding 1987, Neilsen 1990). In particular, the basis of such knowledge has been questioned, alongside calls for a re-examination of assumptions that have guided research and its social outcomes. This critique is particularly concerned with unpicking the established assumptions around the dichotomies of masculinity/femininity, male/female, objectivity/subjectivity, mind/body, reason/emotionality, and so on. The intellectual movement of the 1990s, captured under the auspices of postmodernism and post-structuralism, has added fuel to this debate, grounded as it is in an argument that there are no universal truths to be discovered, and that all knowledge grounded in human society is situated, partial, local, temporal and historically specific.

> The essence of the post-modern argument is that dualisms that can continue to dominate western thought are inadequate for understanding a world of multiple causes and effects, interacting in complex and non-linear ways, all of which are noted in a limitless array of historical and cultural specifications.
>
> (Lather 1991: 21)

These insights can be empowering for a feminist research agenda, throwing as they do the objective foundations for knowledge into doubt, and providing a forum from which feminists can legitimately abandon existing knowledges and create their own. The feminist critique of social research and the production of knowledge in turn places the researcher as positively present in the processes of empirical study. As Stanley and Wise (1990) argue, the researcher/research relationship is key to the research process and is about 'being there'. Emotion is a real research experience and our intellectual autobiography is constructed and reconstructed through social research (Coffey 1999). Liz Stanley (1990) has argued that social research can be recast as distinctly feminist – where researchers account for the conditions of knowledge production; where there is a focus on feminist research labour and a feminist labour process; where power is positioned as central to research writing, and where the relationship between epistemology and ontology is central. She argues that 'feminism is not merely a perspective, a way of seeing; nor even this plus an epistemology, a way of knowing; it is also an ontology, or a way of being in the world' (Stanley 1990: 14).

There is no consensus about the applicability of particular social research methods for feminist research praxis. Early commentators attempted to draw distinctions between research methods that are quantitative, 'hard' and 'masculine' and those that are qualitative, 'soft' and 'feminine'. However, this distinction artificially divides the strengths and weaknesses of different approaches, and does not engage sufficiently with the processes and praxis of research (Maynard 1994, 1996). Equally limiting were early attempts by feminists to cast feminist study in terms of being 'by', 'for' and 'about' women (Bowles and Duelli Klein 1983, Scott 1985). While these definitions have considerable merit they are problematic for those feminists who wish to investigate gender-power dynamics (Skelton 1998), which necessarily demand consideration of men and masculinities (Epstein et al. 1998, Mahony 1985) as well as women and femininities. Thinking simply in terms of by, for and about women can result in failure to take account of the gender-power dimensions of the research process and praxis.

While feminists have increasingly paid attention to issues of epistemology and method, Stanley and Wise's (1990) position that no one set of methods or techniques nor broad category or type of method should be seen as distinctly feminist is an increasingly agreed position. From this perspective feminist research praxis is not about particular methods or techniques but rather about the methodological framing, outcomes and reflections of research and the research process.

> We emphasise that there is no need for feminists to assign themselves to one 'end' or another of the dichotomy 'foundations v. relations', 'idealism v. materialism' and methodological individualism v. collectivism which have resurfaced in feminist discussions of methodology. We reject the disguised hegemonic claims of some forms of feminism and actively promote academic feminist purification.
>
> (Stanley and Wise 1990: 47)

More generally still, a feminist discourse of the nature and process of social research discounts the myth that research can ever be neutral or 'hygienic'. Feminist perspectives contribute to the demystification of social research, making problematic the stance of researcher and researched as unattached and objective instruments. Instead, research is recast as personal, emotional, sensitive, reflective and situated in existing cultural and structural contexts. We now turn to a brief sketch of social research methods which can be used to glean understandings of teachers and their everyday work realities.

Gathering and Analysing Data on the Work and Lives of Teachers

This section outlines the main social research methods that can be used to gather data on gender and teaching. It does not attempt to provide a systematic feminist critique of each method, as we felt that could be unproductive and disempowering. Our position is that all methods can be used for feminist goals, bearing in mind our discussion in the previous section. Good research on gender and education should engage with feminist perspectives, methodologies, theories and epistemologies as part of a research agenda.

Equally, gender should be treated as a dynamic to be investigated, and understood, rather than something that is known, familiar and to be taken for granted. In line with our general position (Coffey 1999, Delamont 1992b) we are arguing that researchers on teachers and teaching should actively consider all the possible methods available, not just the most fashionable or well-known one.

We shall deal with the following research strategies: individual interviews, (focus) group interviews, analysing written evidence, observation, surveys and (quasi-)experiments. We give a necessarily brief description of each, citations to sensible and usable methods, texts and examples of apposite research projects on gender (and teaching). Where possible we also point to autobiographical accounts on using that method for conducting research on gender.

Interviews with Individuals

There are three main types of data that researchers gather from single respondent interviews: life and oral histories, narratives, and current experiences and opinions.

Life history and oral history

Interviews, usually multiple interviews each lasting several hours, are the normal way of collecting oral history (that is, unwritten eyewitness accounts of the past) and life history data. The classic text on collecting oral history is by Thompson (1988), and Denzin (1989) also provides a good introduction. Oral and life history data have been used as a key way of understanding the lives and work of teachers. For example, there is an oral history of the Burnham system of adjudicating teachers' pay in England and Wales by Saran (1982); Goodson (1983) includes oral histories of curriculum change; and Evetts (1990) provides a collection of the career histories of women head teachers in primary and infant schools.

Feminists have collected and analysed life history data. Gluck and Patai (1991) offer a useful collection, containing pieces of oral history gathered by feminists. Peterson (1964) has written a classic piece of life history with women teachers in North America. More recently Sikes et al. (1985), Connell (1985) and Goodson (1983) have carried out life history work with men and women teachers in England, America and Australia. Life history work has also been used specifically to gather data on feminist teachers. Schulz (1998) uses this method with women teachers in Nepal, and Munro (1998) with women educators in North America. Sue Middleton's (1987, 1989) work with feminist teachers in New Zealand, and the recent collection edited by Weiler and Middleton (1999), illustrate the importance and value of such work. We still lack life histories systematically collected from staff in teacher training institutions, and little attempt has been made to use life history perspectives to document education systems as a whole. In the UK, for example, the work has been concentrated in England and there have been no systematic attempts to collect life histories of schoolteachers in Wales, Scotland and Northern Ireland.

Narratives

In the 1990s the collection and analysis of stories, especially teachers' stories, have become major research activities and are interweaved with the use of the life history method. Martin Cortazzi (1993) has written an excellent methods book on narrative, and his earlier book (Cortazzi 1991) is a useful example of the type of data produced when this method is used to engage with the lives and work of teachers. The emphasis here is with the preservation and exploration of teachers' own voices – and how teachers' voices can provide valuable insight into experiences and careers (Cortazzi 1991, 1993). The gathering and analysing of narratives is often done in the context of collecting life history data. Narrative analysis is a particular kind of research strategy, which centralizes the 'voices' of the researched. Biography and autobiography have been central tenets of this approach (Atkinson and Silverman 1997, Stanley 1992). Both life history and narrative are part of new genres of what Ivor Goodson (1995) calls 'personal knowledge'. However, while they do offer the potential of giving 'voice', stories and narratives do need to be interrogated and analysed in their social context (Witherall and Noddings, 1991). Life history and story gathering can be an opportunity for genuine collaboration between researcher and researched, and for the giving of voice to otherwise 'invisible' lives. As such they may provide an appropriate and acceptable means of studying teachers, especially women teachers. However, it is also important that in gathering their stories, we do not 'valorise the subjectivity of the powerless' (Goodson 1995). That is, we are concerned with documenting and understanding, but not romanticizing the individual (see Chapter 5 for a further discussion of this point).

Feminist researchers have utilized the narrative approach to 'give voice' to girls and women in education (see, for example, Fine 1993 and the collection edited by Witherall and Noddings 1991). Susan Chase (1995), in a collection of narratives gathered from American women school superintendents from 1986 to 1989, analyses these narratives to understand the relationships between teaching, gender and power. The narratives of three American women schoolteachers are the subject of Petra Munro's work (1998). The narrative accounts of these teachers are analysed by Munro in order to explore the gendered nature of the teaching profession, and how women teachers negotiate their sense of self and act as active agents with and against the dominant discourses of teaching.

It is worth acknowledging here that Becker's (1970) realization that the terrain of research involves not only differentiated voices but also stratified voices has a feminist connotation. That is, teachers' stories and histories cannot be decontextualized from story-lines derived from elsewhere *and* the dominant (patriarchal) messages they may implicitly carry.

Experiences and opinions

Many interviewers are trying to collect data on their respondents' current experiences and opinions. Some use a schedule, with pre-specified questions. Others have a more open-ended approach, choosing to focus the interview around a series of headings – which aims to elicit the respondent's views and experiences. The latter type is usually referred to as a qualitative or ethnographic interview. Useful methods texts are by Spradley (1979) and McCracken (1988). This kind of interview is, of course, one of the central ways in which researchers collect teachers' stories, which can then be analysed for their narrative value and characteristics (Cortazzi 1991, 1993).

Interviews that are used to collect data on teachers' current activities, experiences and opinions, and indeed data on the nature of the teacher's work *now*, may require fairly systematic (and perhaps schedule-based) questioning. Whether the interview here is pre-specified or a 'conversation with a purpose' (Burgess 1988), the emphasis is on eliciting respondents' world-views. These types of interviewing have also been subjected to critical feminist scrutiny (Finch 1984, Graham 1983).

Interviews are one of the primary means of collecting data on the contemporary lives and experiences of teachers, not least with women teachers. There are numerous examples of studies that have utilized an interviewing approach. See, for example, Taylor (1995), who interviewed female educational administrators in Canada, and Bloot and Browne (1996), who explored reasons for the under-representation of females at head of department level in PE in Australia by interviewing women physical educators. Bailey (1996) used interviews to explore the experiences of women teachers in a boys' school, and Ferfolja (1998) interviewed Australian lesbian teachers. Clarke (1996) also used in-depth interviewing (along with questionnaires) in her study of lesbian teachers and their identity management strategies.

Focus Groups and Group Interviews

Interviews can also be conducted with groups of respondents. Focus groups (see Morgan 1991, 1993) and group interviews are used to elicit group opinions, or to discover how some opinions are gained. Educational researchers have used group interviews, although more with pupils than teachers (see, for example, Haw 1998, Pugsley 1996). Group and focus group interviews with teachers are rare. Focus groups are particular forms of group interviews, where the researcher provides a group of respondents with a series of topics or, more often than not, a set of focusing materials or activities: photographs, documents, variables to prioritize and so forth. A focus group interview is not simply an alternation between researchers' questions and participants' responses. 'Instead, the reliance is on interaction within the group, based on topics supplied by the researcher, who typically takes the role of moderator' (Morgan 1991: 9–10).

Group and focus group interviews are usually taped and transcribed, and data are the resultant transcripts. Sometimes the group is assembled by the researcher for the purposes of the research, other times a pre-existing group is utilized. Sometimes the researcher works with a group over time, regularly collecting their talk; sometimes the study is a one-off. The focus group method is frequently used when the researcher wants to discover how opinions are formed, or views about something complex, not part of everyday immediate experience, or on particularly sensitive topics – where a more general (and distant) discussion may work better than individual interrogation. For example, Thomas (1999) utilized the focus group method to gain data from women talking about holiday romance and new sexual relationships abroad. The main aim of a focus group is to attempt to understand and document the processes by which views are shared, contrasted and developed.

A more general group interview is exactly what it sounds like: getting a group of people to respond to a series of questions. Educational researchers have utilized the group interview method, especially with pupils, because it saves time, and pupils often feel 'braver' in a group, and will egg each other on to tell stories of deviance or humour. For example, Woods (1986: 73) justified his decision to interview pupils in small groups by suggesting that 'they acted as checks, balances and prompts to each other, inaccuracies were corrected, incidents and reactions recalled and analysed'. The main difference from focus groups is that, in a group interview, the researcher works through an agenda of questions and solicits answers to them. As we noted above, group interviews with teachers are rarer than group interviews with pupils, but have been used, for example, to get at 'aims' for teaching in the primary school (see Ashton et al. 1975). The pressures of teachers' time are such that there may be real practical difficulties in establishing groups of teachers to be interviewed. Where group interviews with teachers have been carried out, they have proved useful ways of eliciting data (see, for example, Huber and Whelan 1999, Rainer and Guyton 1999). Less common than collecting talk, but equally valuable, is the collection of written materials, to which we now turn.

Written Evidence

There are a number of ways in which written materials can be used as social science data. Here we concentrate on three different kinds of written data: documents, diaries and open-ended/creative writing.

Documentary sources

Existing documents can and have been used to analyse and make sense of social settings. These can include historical and contemporary documents. Scott (1990) presents an introduction to social research using documentary sources, and Atkinson and Coffey (1997) provide a worked-through example of how organizational documents might be analysed. Scholars interested in gender have used documentary materials to recreate the lives of women and girls in education, which had been 'lost' from the mainstream accounts. Sheila Fletcher's (1980) analysis of the material held in the Public Record Office relating to the Endowed Schools Act of 1869, which enabled her to discover the evidence collected on girls' schools, is an exemplary study of this kind. Many of the studies we cite in Chapter 7 collect and analyse documentary sources to inform contemporary accounts of historical events (for example, Dyhouse 1995 on pioneer women in higher education). Documents can also inform our understandings of contemporary education, by providing an 'official' record of events, which can be used in a social science and feminist analysis. For example, educational texts and official documentation on curricula have been subjected to critical feminist scrutiny (see Chapter 3).

Diaries

Researchers have used diaries of two kinds. They have analysed diaries kept in the past for private consumption as a source of historical data (Plummer 1983), and they have asked people to keep diaries and submit them to the researcher. Anthony Coxon (1988), for example, asked gay men to keep diaries of their sexual encounters as part of a project on risk behaviour and HIV/AIDS. Educational examples include Colin Lacey (1970), who got the teenage boys at Hightown Grammar to keep diaries for him, and Hilary Burgess (1985), who asked staff at an English primary school to keep diaries as part of investigations into the primary mathematics curriculum. Many feminist scholars see diaries as a useful way of gathering data on women in the past and in the present.

Open-ended writing

There are examples of projects that use writing that has been 'commissioned' as part of the study itself. That is, researchers can ask respondents to write something – letters, stories, essays, autobiographies – which in turn form data that can be analysed. The ORACLE project (Delamont and Galton 1986) used essays written for the team by young secondary school pupils to get data on their early days in their new school, as had Bryan (1980). These essays revealed deep-seated ideas about masculinity and femininity held by nine- to twelve-year-olds. Delamont (1991) draws on stories specially written for her by sixth-form students in order to explore the transitions from primary to secondary school (also see Pugsley et al. 1996a and b). Kaye Haw's (1998) study of the education of Muslim girls in the UK included an analysis of stories written by school pupils about an academically successful Muslim girl.

Diaries and written narratives, both pre-existing 'natural' ones and those that are specifically research-driven, are valuable sources of social science data. In particular (and in common with spoken narratives) they contain storied qualities that can be analysed – for both content and structure. Social actors present, represent and contextualize personal knowledge and experiences through stories and narratives. Social actors use the conventional genre of the story to structure their experiences. Hence an analysis of written narratives can reveal collective and shared understandings and experience, alongside individual accounts of events and experiences (Coffey and Atkinson 1996).

Thus far we have discussed data collection methods that involve collecting *words*: either oral testimony or written materials. While these are invaluable methods for studying teachers, they cannot really tell us about *teaching*. While good researchers will always want to know about the teacher, her ideas, and her biography, the processes of interaction with pupils and students can only be collected 'second-hand' by such methods. We therefore move on to consider observational methods for doing research on teachers and teaching.

Data Collection in Classrooms

In this section we deal with methods of gathering data on the teachers' work by direct observation. Under this general heading we distinguish three separate methods of approach: ethnographic observation; the use of prespecified coding schedules; and making a permanent recording of classroom processes (through, for example, audio-visual methods). Delamont (1983, 1992b) provides a general introduction to observation of classrooms and schools. Croll (1986) deals with observations using a pre-specified coding schedule; Delamont (1992b) uses the more open-ended ethnographic approach, and Edwards and Westgate (1994) uses the collection of linguistic data in educational settings. We deal first with ethnographic research.

Ethnographic observation has been widely used to study the experiences of males and females in education, although gender issues did not feature in the pioneering work in the field (see, for example, Hargreaves 1967, Lacey 1970, Lambart 1977 and 1982, Spindler 1974, Wolcott 1967). Our own research has been predominantly in the ethnographic tradition (Coffey 1999, Delamont and Galton 1986, Hall et al. 1998 and 1999), but we have not rehearsed the arguments in its favour here (see Coffey et al. 1999). Instead we specifically focus on ethnographic studies that deal with issues around gender, teaching and feminism. Since the early days of ethnographic research on teachers and teaching, gender has been incorporated as one theme. Ethnographic work on educational experiences has produced studies of gender in nursery schools (Lloyd and Duveen 1992, Paley 1984), infant (King 1978, Serbin 1978), primary and elementary classrooms (Best 1983, Clarricoates 1987), secondary schools (Grant and Sleeter 1986, Mac an Ghaill 1994, Measor 1989), and further education classes (Cockburn 1987, Valli 1986). Ethnographic work on teachers specifically includes Beynon (1987) and Wolcott (1973). Projects on gender in higher education have also included ethnographic work (see, for example, US studies by Holland and Eisenhart 1990, Moffatt 1989). There has also been pioneering work undertaken on the relationships between race, gender, sexuality and educational experiences (Mirza 1992, Mac an Ghaill 1988 and 1994). The papers collected by Woods and Hammersley (1993) address the contentious issue of how ethnographers can collect reliable and valid data on inequalities of sex and race in everyday school life.

Large-scale projects using pre-specified coding schedules have also been used to study schools and classrooms (see, for example, Delamont and Galton 1986, Galton et al. 1999). Indeed, such approaches might be argued to be an ideal means of discovering and exploring systematic differences between, for example, male and female patterns of classroom talk or male and female teachers' contact with pupils and with each other. However, schedule-based, systematic observation has not been appropriated to any extent to study gender in education, nor has it been appropriated as a method by feminist researchers. The critiques of the positivist paradigm in classroom research (see Gage 1989 for a full account of the 'paradigm wars') have not, so far, come from feminists. However, in so far as systematic, precoded observational schedules and quasi-experimental research designs are grounded in 'scientific' psychology, they can be subjected to feminist critique for unexamined assumptions about gender. There are few feminist studies using pre-specified coding schedules (Whyte 1986 is a rare exception), and relatively few such studies have collected data on gender issues from any perspective. This has meant that a few very small studies (most notoriously that of Spender 1982) are frequently cited, even though they could not be considered reliable and valid by positivist, malestream standards.

Direct observation, especially ethnographic observation, has been subjected to recent feminist criticism (Clough 1992, Wolf 1992) and to debates over what might constitute feminist ethnographic praxis (Abu-Lughod 1990). Feminists have reflected upon the practice of conducting ethnographic fieldwork (see, for example, Abu-Lughod 1986, Skeggs 1994), and the usefulness of an ethnographic, interactional approach as a way of revealing women's standpoint (Farrell 1992, Langellier and Hall 1989,

Stanley and Wise 1990). Feminist scholars (in particular but not exclusively anthropologists) have engaged in an epistemological and methodological enterprise of establishing what a distinctive feminist ethnography is (or might be) (Jennaway 1990, Strathern 1987, Walter 1995), in response in part to feminist critiques of 'malestream' ethnography. The essence of the argument has not been the gender of the researcher, but rather the gendered social context of the research activity. Conventional ethnography has been criticized more generally for privileging certain voices at the expense of others. Within this context the knowledges and discourses that are gathered and represented have been criticized as being that of a powerful (and male) world. The accounts presented have been described as monologic rather than dialogic – thereby failing to capture multiple voices and perspectives.

Atkinson and Coffey (1995) provide a more detailed discussion of the critiques levelled at ethnographic data and their claim of realism (including a discussion of feminist critiques). For our purposes here, suffice it to say that, while observation offers an appropriate way of gathering data on teachers' everyday social worlds, as a method it should also be treated critically and problematically, and subjected to a critical feminist analysis. Research based on permanent recording with a gender agenda is also sparse, and there are no studies of feminist teachers using audio- or videotape. The research on gender issues using these methods is interesting for feminists, however. For example, Roger Shuy's (1986) analysis of how one male teacher responded to female and male pupils' responses to questions (females got neutral 'OK', males got a challenging 'defend that answer') shows how valuable such research can be for feminist explorations, and use in action research (see below). We now turn from data collection by observation to more positivist methods, starting with the survey.

Surveys

The survey, by a questionnaire, which is either completed by respondents in writing or worked through by an interviewer, is probably the commonest social research method overall, but one that is often eschewed by feminists. Oppenheim (1992) offers a good introduction to questionnaire design. Marsh (1982) on the survey is also accessible. Cohen and Manion (1994) provide clear guidelines on the conduct of surveys in educational research. Examples of gender-related surveys are by Kelly (1985a), who did a national survey of teachers' attitudes to gender issues, and Smithers and Zientek (1991), who surveyed 218 infant teachers about gender and the 1988 England and Wales Education Reform Act. Surveys and questionnaires are useful ways of gaining quantifiable data on attitudes and opinions, although they are less satisfactory ways of gaining detailed data on lives and experiences. It is no longer the case that they are seen as the antithesis of feminist research, although the more generally criticisms levelled at such methods –

'surface' rather than 'depth' data, issues of size and sampling, difficulties of providing more than the broad picture, descriptive rather than analytical – mean that we should treat such methods with caution.

Experiments and Quasi-experiments

Finally in this overview of methods we turn to the experiment. Experimental social research is not commonly used as a means of collecting data on schooling. Cohen and Manion define the experiment and the quasi-experiment: 'the essential feature of experimental research is that the investigator deliberately controls and manipulates the conditions which determine the events in which he [*sic*] is interested' (Cohen and Manion 1980: 188).

In educational research the quasi-experiment is more common than 'true experiments' (Cohen and Manion 1980: 163), primarily because it is not really possible to conduct experiments in school/educational settings. Sarah Tann's (1981) investigation of mixed and single-sex small groups performing educational tasks and Galton and Delafield's (1981) work on self-fulfilling prophecies are both quasi-experiments carried out in real schools, where gender is one key variable. Many of the practical enquiries carried out by feminists and others, such as asking children to draw 'men', 'scientists', 'people' and so on as a way of seeing if children recognize generic terms as gendered, can be thought of as quasi-experiments, especially where they overlap with action research (see Nilan 1995 on the production of men and women through the use of drama lessons and script production, and Matthews 1996 on drawing scientists).

Action Research and Teaching

Action research is described by Cohen and Manion (1980: 174) as 'a small scale intervention in the functioning of the real word and close examination of the effects of such intervention'. In other words, action research refers to a kind of research that sets in train some changes in a setting, and then seeks to monitor the progress and effects of such change (Carr and Kemmis 1986, Noffke and Stevenson 1995). Action research has been a small but significant part of the research enterprise on gender and education. Fundamentally it has involved teachers as researchers, analysts and the catalysts for change. Teachers-as-researchers, through an action research model, have been responsible for researching their own practice and for enacting change in schools. Action research projects can take a number of forms – and involve teachers to differing levels. Some aim to work *with* teachers. Others are more explicit in making teachers the researchers.

Projects aimed at taking forward feminist ideas about curriculum development have adopted an action research model. In the UK one of the best-known examples of this is GIST – Girls into Science and Technology –

which ran in the early 1980s (Whyte 1987). Academic researchers worked with the full range of teachers in ten Manchester schools, and implemented a set of innovations designed to encourage young women to persevere with 'male' craft and science subjects, after they became optional rather than compulsory curriculum subjects (then at age 14 years). The team brought adult women working as scientists and technicians into the schools to act as role models, raised the consciousness of the teachers about the gender dynamics of classrooms, and experimented with teaching maths and science to single-sex classes in co-educational schools. The reports on GIST (Kelly 1985b, Whyte 1986) highlighted that one of the main difficulties of the project were the teachers themselves. Choosing to attempt to work with the full range of teachers meant working with teachers (mostly men) who were unsympathetic to the aims of the project and who were explicitly anti-feminist. Other projects in the UK – such as the Girls and Technology Education (GATE) project and Girls and Occupational Choice (GAOC) opted for closer collaboration with teachers – relying on volunteer teachers (already sympathetic to the cause). However, these projects, too, were not without problems: 'teachers committed to an individual childcentred approach and to co-education were wary of using gender as a discriminator for differential behaviour towards children, and indeed of giving girls something which they were not giving to boys' (Chisholm and Holland 1987: 252).

Action research has become a mainstay of small-scale research on gender and education, and has been a source and site of collaboration between feminist academics, teachers and other educational workers. Work in secondary schools (Burchall and Millman 1989, Kelly 1985a and 1985b, McKinnon and Ahola-Sidaway 1995, Whyte 1986) has been matched by work in nursery and primary education (Browne and France 1986). Action research has been carried out with girls (Quicke and Winter 1995, Weiner 1985) and with boys (Askew and Ross 1988, Jackson and Salisbury 1996). Sexuality and sex education has also provided a particular focus for action research initiatives (Holly 1989, Jones and Mahony 1989). Teachers have been instrumental in the development and practical application of such research, and in some cases have become researchers themselves. May and Rudduck (1983), for example, report on a project in Norfolk, UK, which gave early-years teachers the opportunity to become independent researchers. Teachers were encouraged and helped to design and conduct their own investigations into the gender dynamics of their own schools. Ian Stronach and Margaret Maclure (1997) report on the 'teachers as researchers' project in the UK, which aimed to study teacher action research. The project included life history interviews with key actors of the British teacher-centred action research movement. They highlight that teachers who move into action research, often through a process of leaving teaching, face a number of oppositional dilemmas:

... between theory and practice; between the personal and the professional; between the organisational cultures of the social and the academy; between 'insider' and 'outsider' perspectives; between the sacred language of science, scholarship or research, and the mundane dialects of practice and everyday experience.

(Stronach and Maclure 1997: 116–7)

In Stronach and Maclure's terms, action research is a 'boundary dweller', pasted between research and teaching, theory and practice. It is perhaps because of this that it may be particularly well suited to a feminist approach to social research, and teaching. Action research has:

... drawn its power (and also, of course, its problems of legitimation within the institutional discourse of theory and research) from its challenge to the customary dispositions of 'privilege' in the unequal relations of dualism – between theory and practice, subjectivity and objectivity, academic and practitioner. It has developed a powerful critique of the academic discourse of positivist science and scholarship, and the tyrannies that theory and expertise have exacted upon the teacher as the Other.

(Stronach and Maclure 1997: 128–9)

Of course, the concept of the teacher-as-researcher is related to aspects of the teacher-as-reflective-practitioner (Gore and Zeichner 1991, James 1996, Schon 1983 and 1987, Valli 1992, Zeichner and Liston 1987). Teacher education has been concerned with engaging student teachers in exercises of reflection, and in the development of reflexive practice (Harrington et al. 1996, Stenhouse 1975, Wade and Yarborough 1996). Gaby Weiner (1994) draws on the notion of the reflective practitioner and teacher as (action) researcher to develop the idea of a feminist praxis in educational research. By encompassing Stanley's (1990) conceptualization of praxis – a commitment to change, a rejection of conventional dualisms of theory and practice, relating research to knowledge production rather than supply process – Weiner articulates a feminist critical praxis for educational (teacher? feminist?) research. This includes a number of features:

- deriving from experience and rooted in practice;
- continually subject to revision as a result of experience;
- reflexive and self-reflexive;
- widely accessible and open to change;
- grounded in the analysis of women's (and men's) multiple and different experiences and material values;
- explicitly political and value led;

- within the classroom; imbued with feminist organisational practices grounded in equality; non-hierarchy and democracy;
- within educational research, additionally rejecting conventional dualisms, such as theory/practice, mental/manual, epistemology/methodology.

(Weiner 1994: 130)

The 'Best' Method for Research on Gender

It has not been our intention here to favour one method or another. Exemplary research can and has been done on gender and education (and on teachers) using different methods, and combinations of methods. We would add that good research in general makes visible and problematizes gender and the dynamics of gender. It is vital to collect and report data on gender in the settings, and to pay equal attention to all the informants and voices in a setting. How social actors understand, view and 'do' gender needs to be a central part of all research endeavours. It is necessary to examine the relation between gender and power in the field setting; *and* all the time the researcher needs to make his or her *own* beliefs about gender (in all these ways) problematic.

(Re)presenting Research

Thus far we have not engaged significantly with the debates over the relationships between social research and postmodernism. Stronach and Maclure (1997) discuss the postmodern discourse and practice in educational research, and we do not intend to reiterate their arguments in detail here. In attempting to articulate the spaces offered by postmodernism and post-structuralism (Weiner 1998: 462), Stronach and Maclure present new ways of thinking about research design, analysis, and importantly representation – suggesting that educational research needs to address the issues and opportunities put forward by (post)feminism and postcolonialism, globalization, the reformulation of identities, and the challenges to mainstream conventional disciplines (such as literary studies, anthropology, philosophy and sociology).

> Political surrenders are familiar enough to us now and we need a kind of cultural revolution in educational research, not in favour of some kind of new orthodoxy, but in favour of experiment, creativity and risk. To those who confine themselves to the politics of nostalgia, we would say that mourning that loss (of certainty, 'science', 'enlightenment', 'ideas' or 'autonomy') is a necessary thing, especially if it constitutes the double loss of something that never existed. But it should not become a way of life. Life goes on and with it, perhaps, even, sometimes, if we are

creative enough, persistent enough, a sharper and less compliant educational research.

(Stronach and Maclure 1997: 152)

The relationships between postmodernism (post-structuralism, postfeminism) have been particularly well articulated and debated by those working within qualitative research. Yvonna Lincoln and Norman Denzin (1994), for example, in their apparently authoritative review identify a narrative periodization of the development of qualitative research – from positivist and modernist 'movements' – through multiplicity and crisis – to diversity and a series of tensions.

> Qualitative research embraces two tensions at the same time. On the one hand, it is drawn to a broad, interpretative, post-modern, feminist, and critical sensibility. On the other hand, it can also be drawn to more narrowly defined positivist, post-positivist, humanistic and naturalistic conceptions of human experience and its analysis.
>
> (Lincoln and Denzin 1994: 576)

Lincoln and Denzin characterize a future of qualitative research suffused with reflexive, experimental texts that are messy, subjective, open-ended, conflictual and feminist-influenced (Lincoln and Denzin 1994: 559). The narrative periodization offered by Lincoln and Denzin has been criticized as being overly rigid (Coffey 1999), and less than satisfactory for conceptualizing qualitative research in education (Delamont et al. 2000). However, the moves towards a more critical appreciation of the production of research texts and the implication of multiple voices and multiple selves in (and in the authoring of) research are important identifications to be made. More so than ever before we are aware of the 'craft skills' of writing and representing research. This is encapsulated in the burgeoning of texts on how to write and read research (Atkinson 1996, Hammersley 1991). A more self-conscious approach to writing has been encouraged (for example, in texts such as Ely et al. 1997), exploring and understanding how we compose meaning from our data and how we make our data meaningful to others. At the very least, writing and representing research are no longer taken-for-granted aspects of the research process. The articulation of the self in the products of research has also become a matter of critical reflection. Relationships between the research process, the writing process and the self have reconceptualized the emotional and personal dimensions of research (Coffey 1999), and drawn attention to issues of authorship and authenticity. 'Authors' are no longer all but 'invisible'. Conventional texts, as research texts, have been criticized for not doing justice to the multi- or polyvocality of social life and the polyvocality of social forms.

In practice, the impact of such articulations on the written products of social research has been peripheral rather than central, including within educational research (Delamont et al. 2000). That said, new representational forms have been proposed and experimented with, in order to reflect the general postmodernist agenda of how research is translated into representations and forms of knowledge production. This can be seen as being especially significant to the feminist concern with the production and representation of knowledges. Feminists have questioned conventional styles of writing and representing (Wolf 1992), and feminist epistemology has challenged conventional forms of scholarly narrative as masculinist (Behar and Gordon 1995). Attempts to transform the researcher's position of privilege and 'undo' the conventions of academic scholarship production have challenged the conventional textual formats of scholarly writing (as exemplified in the collection edited by Ellis and Bochner 1996, and described by Ely et al. 1997). Alternative genres have included scripts, poetry, performance texts, diaries and collaborative writing. Many draw on a dialogic approach to text (Allan 1994, Dwyer 1977, Holquist 1990), and they promote a self-conscious auto/biographical approach to writing. They exemplify the relationships between social research and the production and writing of selves and lives (Ely et al. 1997, Hastrup 1992, Stanley 1992).

Dialogic approaches to representation exploit the conventions of naturalistic theatre or conversation – to make real social events and interactions. Such an approach draws on the poetical and theatrical qualities of everyday social life. Ethno-dramas have been produced which aim to capture multiple voices of complex social situations. These have often been particularly sensitive situations or settings – (see Bluebond-Langner 1990, Ellis and Bochner 1992, Fox 1996, Mienczakowski 1996, Paget 1990 and 1993).

A variation of this theme is the use of poetic style and innovation as ways of (re)presenting. It is argued that poetry offers a mechanism of capturing the pauses, rhyme and rhythm of everyday life and conversation (Richardson 1994). Laurel Richardson (1992) used the words of Louisa May (a 'mountain' woman), derived from life history interview data, to (re)construct a poetic account of her life. She drew on the conventions of poetical writing to re-present the ethnopoetics of Louisa May's life and words. The resultant poetry is both striking and emotive, illustrating Richardson's argument that poetry provides a mode of evocative representation of qualitative data. Ely et al. (1997) share the poetry of their qualitative writing group and argue that poems provide ways of creating and sharing analyses and meanings. Poems, they suggest, can foreshadow, encapsulate and move a story forward, thus providing a breathing space or thinking space, a place to contradict and share emotions and process. In this sense poetry can be a mechanism for including rather than alienating readers.

Scripts, dialogues, poetry and similar genres have not been used extensively within educational research. McCoy's (1997) use of poetry as a way of exploring pre-service teachers' use of the discourses of cultural difference is a particularly striking and seductive way of presenting what would otherwise be potentially difficult arguments and ideas. Stronach and Maclure (1997) write some of their text as messy text – with reader/author dialogue, footnotes and text notes interwoven into the text – which is presented in different columns on the page. Middleton (1995) also experiments with her writing in a piece on feminist educational theory, writing in two columns to represent the academic and the personal voice. The *International Journal of Qualitative Studies in Education* has published a number of experimental educational texts. See, for example, the poetry of Torres (1997) and Retana (1998), and the narrative of Gray (1998).

Collaborative approaches to textual production and the writing of research is another distinctive and innovative way in which represention is challenged and reconfigured. Collaboration has been a feature of feminist and action research. Kaye Haw's work on educating Muslim girls (1998) is a good example of a feminist collaborative approach to the writing (and researching) task with educational research. The text is collaboratively authored by Haw (a white, non-Muslim researcher, Saeeda Shah (a Muslim, Pakistani woman, and head of a tertiary college in Pakistan) and Maria Hanifa (a woman Muslim teacher in one of the school settings of the research). The text contains conversations and dialogues, personal reflections, (auto)biographical notes, responses and alternative visions. Crucially it provides a view of research which (cautiously) celebrates polyvocality and the (auto)biographical. Creative approaches to the production of research texts can aid and promote a reflexive and self-conscious approach to textual production and the creation of knowledge. Some, like Sparkes (1995), argue that they create the opportunity for more realistic pictures of events, and serve to blur the power boundaries between researcher and researched. This is not, however, a universally agreed view, even by those who have engaged in and practised different modes of representation. Lather (1991), for example, has argued that alternative representative forms do not remove the issue of power from the production of research. Texts are still authored – and selected, collected, edited, presented, written, crafted and read. As such, alternative forms of writing may blur or question boundaries but do not remove the issues. Indeed the very artfulness of many alternative or experiential texts actually draws attention to the craft work of authorship. Ethno-drama, theatrical scripts and poetry serve to emphasize the creative potential and power of the author by overtly manipulating the appearance and ordering of words and text. By foregrounding the researcher as author, they could be conceptualized as a means of increasing, rather than diminishing, the distance between researcher and *Other*. Equally such textual practice exposes the research-as-author to new forms of critical scrutiny. In dealing with critiques about authority and authorship by presenting new forms of representation, such practices expose the researcher to 'getting it right' not only as a social researcher, and scriptor of social life, but also as a more or less successful poet, playwright or creative writer.

Conclusion – A Research Agenda

It is difficult and contentious to formulate a research agenda, especially so where exemplary work is already being undertaken and where the research task is potentially so huge. We hope that, in the course of the book, readers will have developed their own ideas for research questions, projects and debates on gender and teaching from a feminist perspective. Here we present what appear to us to be both urgent and ongoing tasks for the progressive understanding of feminism and the teacher's work.

Building and Maintaining the Database

We still lack a large, reliable database on classroom interaction patterns across all ages and in all subjects. It is still difficult systematically to compare girls' and boys', men's and women's experiences of classroom interaction in mixed and single-sex classrooms. The claims that girls routinely receive less attention and/or teacher attention of different kinds from boys are still difficult to substantiate, although we may feel we 'know' they are true. Furthermore we are still unclear of how variables such as the gender and sexuality of the teacher relate to these interactions. Similarly our data on teacher interactions are weak. Without this large and basic body of data we cannot really claim to know what the gendered experiences of schooling and teaching are.

More of the Same

What we hope this book has demonstrated is that there is a small but significant body of good research on gender, feminism and teaching. We now know more about the past and present lives of (women/feminist) teachers, and the everyday work of the teacher than ever before, and these analyses are increasingly informed by feminist perspectives and insights. *But* the picture is still far from complete. Many of our insights are still patchy, 'voices' are still absent or silent or lost, experiences still not fully documented. It is vital that the 'gender' project in the understanding of teaching and learning continues and increasingly becomes more mainstream (but not 'malestream').

Feminist Research on Masculinities

The 1990s have seen a growing research interest in masculinity, both generally and in relation to schooling. Much of this work has been informed by feminist perspectives and theoretical frameworks, methodologies and episte-mologies (Connell 1987 and 1995, Mac an Ghaill 1994, Sewell 1998), and undertaken by feminists (Epstein et al. 1998, Kenway 1995, Skelton 1996, 1998). Feminists have also been critical of elements of the work on masculinities, specifically arising from the so-called new men's studies. This movement has been criticized for omitting or distorting some elements of feminism, and of even not being profeminist at all (see Cannan and Griffin 1990, Griffin and Wetherell 1992). Skelton (1998) provides an analysis of studies of masculinities undertaken by men, and, while there are good exam-ples that complement existing feminist agendas, some, she still argues, are in danger of centralizing boys and male experiences and of relegating girls to the sideline. Feminists have engaged with work on masculinities (see Raphael Reed 1999), and we would argue that this work is vital to any understanding of feminism and the teachers' work.

> It is up to us as feminists to retain a watchful eye on the work on boys' underachievement/masculinities and schooling and critique as and when appropriate. Also it is important that we keep scrutinising our own agendas in terms of ensuring that all work on masculinities keeps in its sights the impact the findings have for the school lives and experiences of girls and women.
>
> (Skelton 1998: 224)

Teachers' Occupational Cultures and Action Research

There remains a need to design effective ways to incorporate feminist insights into teachers' occupational culture, so that schools change as a result of existing research (see Hatch 1999, who also argues that research on the work of the teacher should be used to inform teacher education and prepare student teachers for the everyday realities of teaching).

Barbara Lloyd's (1989) observations in the South East of England in reception classes at two schools and Hilton's (1991) data on playgroup workers showed teachers of young children in the UK reinforcing the very behaviours in girls that they dislike. Lisa Serbin's (1978) research showed nursery school teachers objecting to girls 'clinging' and keeping close to them. Yet, when observed, it became clear that girls could only get teachers' attention and response when physically close. Girls beyond touching distance were ignored, unlike boys, who received teacher attention wherever they were in the nursery. Other studies of teachers (see Acker 1994, Delamont 1990), and of recruits to the occupation (Sikes 1991, Coffey and Acker 1991) reveal an occupational group unaware of feminist perspectives, and ideas of gender as socially constructed, unconscious of the school's role in reinforcing conservative messages about sex roles, and/or unwilling or unable to respond to feminist initiatives.

These data, on feminism's seeming lack of impact on schoolteachers, show the urgency of the action research task on occupational culture. They can also sensitize researchers to investigate how far other intellectual currents and bodies of scholarly findings (such as postmodernism or the findings on the positive impact of parents reading aloud to children) have penetrated teachers' occupational culture. Despite the currency of feminist ideas in recent years, the apparent resistance to them in many educational settings highlights the resilience of occupational and institutional cultures.

(Re)presenting Teachers' Lives

The relative failure of educational research to engage with postmodern agendas, and especially new forms of representation, means that important avenues for feminist understandings and representations of teaching are not being exploited. We are not advocating here an avant-garde move towards experimentation for experimentation's sake; we are suggesting that more vigorous and critical engagement with the autobiographical, experimental, emotional and representational aspects of research should be part of any future agenda for research on feminism and the teacher's work – for the insights such aspects provide are crucial to rethinking the complexity of teachers' lives and work.

Years from now …

Carlotta Comperton swept her post off the floor and headed towards the kitchen. Once the kettle had been filled, and Edmund, her Siamese cat, had been duly stroked, she rifled through the bundle of mainly bills and circulars. She noted with delight that one of her former pupils, Davida Lessiter, had sent her a postcard from Vancouver, where she was now an associate professor of women's history. Carlotta also recognized the hand-writing on the envelope at the bottom of the pile. She hadn't seen her old friend Arlette Traherne since the educational policy forum at Westminster last year. But she always looked forward to her regular witty bulletins on university life. Carlotta finished making her mug of tea and went into her study. She flopped onto the sofa by the window and was quickly joined by a vocal Edmund. Slipping her shoes off, and tucking her feet underneath her, she carefully opened Arlette's letter. She smiled to herself at the headed notepaper: 'From the office of the Vice Chancellor, Professor Arlette Traherne', and immediately felt warmed by the familiar rounded scrawl that filled the page:

> My dearest Carlotta, as you can see, the notepaper is frightful, but I thought a note on it would amuse you. I heard your keynote address at the headteachers' conference was a huge success, so well done you!

Will I be able to prise you away from that school of yours for a summer visit to sunny Ledshire? A headteacher must be able to give herself some time off for good behaviour, surely. I am sure Elvira would love you to be here for her inaugural professorial lecture. And by the way did you know that Lois Elvery is coming back to Ledshire. She has just been made deputy at Prior's End ...

Conclusion

New intellectual movements, especially successful ones, do not go uncontested.

(Laslett and Thorne 1997: 19)

Our main aim has been to provide a feminist analysis of the everyday work and world of the classroom teacher. We hope we have been able to demonstrate the importance of such an analysis for understanding contemporary classroom practices and experiences, as well as for developing alternative pedagogies and educational futures. Our general conclusions are threefold. First, we wish to stress that many aspects of the teacher's work have not yet been subjected to a thoroughgoing feminist scrutiny. Such scrutiny will make research on teachers and teaching better, because it will challenge the taken-for-granted familiarity of much of the published research. This point does not undermine feminist scholarship and research that has already been achieved. Nor should it underemphasize the impact that feminism has already had on the work and world of the classroom. As we have argued, the relationships between feminism and teaching are long-standing and sustained, and we see no reason why that should not continue to be so. Indeed we would stress the centrality of feminism to contemporary classroom life, teaching praxis, and the lives of many teachers.

Second, we have stressed the importance of historical continuities in understanding contemporary classroom life. There are continuities between nineteenth-century feminist educational pioneers who successfully campaigned to establish teaching as a women's career, drawing on the theorists and intellectuals of first-wave feminism and the issues facing feminist teachers today. Feminist scholars and teachers should not lose site of the successes and innovations of these early pioneers, as they draw on contemporary feminisms and feminist theory to inform their research and teaching. The teacher's work and the teaching career should be thought of as part of a sustained feminist project.

Finally, we wish to stress the contradictions inherent in (new) intellectual movements such as postmodernism. As we have stressed throughout, we are not supporters of the claim that feminism is dead, outmoded or passé. Feminism, albeit in different forms, is alive and well as a thought process, a tool for critical analysis and as a lived reality. We recognize, however, that intellectual movements such as postmodernism can be both dangerous and liberating for feminist thinkers, just as Freudianism was dangerous for the first-wave feminists, primarily because it undermined their claim to respectability. The feminist historian needs to be alert to ways in which intellectual climates change, and how that interacts with generational changes and experiences. The feminist scholar needs to be alert to the ways in which changing intellectual climates can make her very existence as a scholar suddenly precarious. Whenever women intellectuals see their world differently from the elite men around them they are in danger of finding that a new theory has defined them out of existence. Paradigm shifts in dominant group ideology rarely benefit the muted subordinate group. Feminist scholars need to be alert to men changing the question.

References

Abraham, J. (1989) 'Teacher ideology and sex roles in curriculum texts', *British Journal of Sociology of Education* 10, 1: 33–52.

Abu-Lughod, L. (1986) *Veiled Sentiments: Honor and Poetry in a Bedouin Society*, Berkeley: University of California Press.

—— (1990) 'Can there be a feminist ethnography?', *Women and Performance: A Journal of Feminist Theory* 5, 1: 7–27.

Acker, S. (1983) 'Women and teaching: a semi-detached sociology of a semi-profession', in S. Walker and L. Barton (eds) *Gender, Class and Education*, Basingstoke: Falmer Press.

—— (1988) 'Teachers, gender and resistance', *British Journal of Sociology of Education* 9, 3: 307–22.

—— (ed.) (1989) *Teachers, Gender and Careers*, Lewes: Falmer Press.

—— (1990) 'Teachers' culture in an English primary school: continuity and change', *British Journal of Sociology of Education*, 11, 3: 257–73.

—— (1994) *Gendered Education: Sociological Reflections on Women, Teaching, and Feminism*, Buckingham: Open University Press.

Adams, K. and Emery, K. (1994) 'Classroom coming out stories: practical strategies for productive self-disclosure', in L. Garber (ed.) *Tilting the Tower: Lesbians/Teaching/Queer Subjects*, New York: Routledge.

Adams, R. (1938) *I'm Not Complaining*, reprinted 1983, London: Virago.

Adler, S., Laney, J. and Packer, M. (1993) *Managing Women: Feminism and Power in Educational Management*, Milton Keynes: Open University Press.

Alberti, J. (1997) 'A fantasy of belonging?', in L. Stanley (ed.) *Knowing Feminisms: On Academic Borders, Territories and Tribes*, London: Sage.

Allan, S. (1994) ' "When discourse is torn from reality": Bakhtin and the principle of chronologoplicity', *Time and Society* 3: 193–218.

Apple, M. (1983) 'Work, gender and teaching', *Teacher's College Record* 84, 3: 611–28.

—— (1985) *Education and Power*, New York: Routledge & Kegan Paul.

—— (1986) *Teachers and Texts: A Political Economy of Class and Gender Relations in Education*, New York: Routledge & Kegan Paul.

—— (1998) 'Education and the new hegemonic blocs: doing policy the "right" way', *International Studies in Sociology of Education* 8, 2: 181–202.

Arnot, M., David, M. and Weiner, G. (1996) *Educational Reforms and Gender Equality in Schools*, Manchester: Equal Opportunities Commission.

Arnot, M. and Weiler, K. (eds) (1993) *Feminism and Social Justice in Education: International Perspectives*, London: Falmer Press.

Ashton, P., Keen, P., Davies, F. and Holley, B.J. (1975) *The Aims of Primary Education*, London: Macmillan.

Askew, S. and Ross, C. (1988) *Boys Don't Cry: Boys and Sexism in Education*, Milton Keynes: Open University Press.

Atkinson, P.A. (1978) 'Fitness, feminism and schooling', in S. Delamont and L. Duffin (eds) *The Nineteenth-Century Woman: Her Cultural and Physical World*, London: Croom Helm.

—— (1983) 'The reproduction of professional community', in R. Dingwall and P. Lewis (eds) *The Sociology of Professions: Lawyers, Doctors and Others*, London: Macmillan.

—— (1984) 'Strong minds and weak bodies', *British Journal of the History of Sport* 2, 1: 62–71.

—— (1996) *Sociological Readings and Re-Readings*, Aldershot: Avebury.

Atkinson, P.A. and Coffey, A. (1995) 'Realism and its discontents: on the crisis of cultural representation in ethnographic texts', in B. Adam and S. Allan (eds) *Theorizing Culture: An Interdisciplinary Critique After Postmodernism*, London: UCL Press.

—— (1997) 'Analysing documentary reality', in D. Silverman (ed.) *Qualitative Analysis*, London: Sage.

Atkinson, P.A., Reid, M.E. and Sheldrake, P.F. (1977) 'Medical mystique', *Sociology of Work and Occupations* 4, 3: 243–80.

Atkinson, P.A. and Silverman, D. (1997) 'Kundera's *Immortality*: the interview society and the invention of the self', *Qualitative Inquiry* 3, 3: 304–25.

Attar, D. (1990) *Wasting Girls' Time: The History and Politics of Home Economics*, London: Virago.

Bailey, L. (1996) 'The feminisation of a school? Women teachers in a boys' school', *Gender and Education* 8, 2: 171–84.

Baker, L. (1976) *I'm Radcliffe, Fly Me! The Seven Sisters and the Failure of Women's Education* New York: Macmillan.

Ball, S.J. (1987) *The Micro-politics of the School: Towards a Theory of School Organization*, London: Methuen.

—— (1990) *Politics and Policy Making in Education: Explorations in Policy Sociology*, London: Routledge.

—— (1994) *Postmodernism and Education*, Buckingham: Open University Press.

Banks, O. (1981) *Faces of Feminism: A Study of Feminism as a Social Movement*, Oxford: Martin Robertson.

Barale, M.A. (1994) 'The romance of class and queers: academic erotic zones', in L. Garber (ed.) *Tilting the Tower: Lesbians/Teaching/Queer Subjects*, New York: Routledge.

Barker, E. (1979) 'In the beginning: battle of creationist science against evolution', in R. Wallis (ed.) *On the Margins of Science*, Keele: Sociological Review Monograph 27.

Bartlett, A. (1998) 'A passionate subject: representations of desire in feminist pedagogy', *Gender and Education* 10, 1: 85–92.

References

Baym, N. (1990) 'The feminist teacher of literature: feminist or teacher?', in S.L. Gabriel and I. Smithson (eds) *Gender in the Classroom: Power and Pedagogy*, Urbana and Chicago: University of Illinois Press.

Beck, E.T. (1994) 'Out as a lesbian, out as a Jew: and nothing untoward happened?', in L. Garber (ed.) *Tilting the Tower: Lesbians/Teaching/Queer Subjects*, New York: Routledge.

Beck, J. (1996) 'Citizenship education: problems and possibilities', *Curriculum Studies* 4, 3: 349–66.

Becker, H.S. (1952a) 'The career of the Chicago public schoolteacher', *American Journal of Sociology* 57: 470–7.

—— (1952b) 'Social-class variations in the teacher–pupil relationship', *Journal of Education Sociology* 25: 451–65.

—— (1967) 'Whose side are we on?', *Social Problems* 14: 239–47.

—— (1970) 'Problems of inference and proof in participant observation', in H.S. Becker (ed.) *Sociological Work: Method and Substance*, Chicago: Aldine.

Behar, R. and Gordon, D. (eds) (1995) *Women Writing Culture*, Berkeley: University of California Press.

Bell, C. and Chase, S. (1993) 'The underrepresentation of women in school leadership', in C. Marshall (ed.) *The New Politics of Race and Gender*, Washington, DC: Falmer Press.

Benhabib, S. (1995) 'Feminism and post-modernism: an uneasy alliance', in S. Benhabib, J. Butler, D. Cornell and N. Fraser (eds) *Feminist Contentions: A Philosophical Exchange*, New York: Routledge.

Bentley, M. and Watts, D. (1994) 'Humanizing and feminizing school science: reviving anthropomorphic and animistic thinking in constructivist science education', *International Journal of Science Education* 16, 1: 83–97.

Berg, A., Kowaleski, J., Le Guin, C., Weinauer, E. and Wolfe, E.A (1998) 'Breaking the silence: sexual preference in the composition classroom', in G.E. Cohee, E. Daumer, T.D. Kemp, P.M. Krebbs, S.A Lafky and S. Runzo (eds) *The Feminist Teacher Anthology*, New York: Teachers College Press.

Bernstein, B. (1971) 'On the classification and framing of educational knowledge,' in M.F.D. Young (ed.) *Knowledge and Control: New Directions for the Sociology of Education*, London: Macmillan.

Best, R. (1983) *We've All Got Scars: What Boys and Girls Learn in Elementary School*, Bloomington: Indiana University Press.

Beynon, J. (1987) 'Miss Floral mends her ways', in L. Tickle (ed.) *The Arts in Education: Some Research Studies*, London: Croom Helm.

—— (1989) 'A school for men', in S. Walker and L. Barton (eds) *Politics and the Processes of Schooling*, Milton Keynes: Open University Press.

Blackmore, J. (1996) 'Doing emotional "labour" in the education labour market: stories from the field of women in management', *Discourse* 17: 337–50.

—— (1999) *Troubling Women: Feminism, Leadership and Educational Change*, Buckingham: Open University Press.

Blinick, B. (1994) 'Out in the curriculum, out in the classroom: teaching history and organizing for change', in L. Garber (ed.) *Tilting the Tower: Lesbians/Teaching/Queer Subjects*, New York: Routledge.

Bloot, R. and Browne, J. (1996) 'Reasons for the underrepresentation of females at head of department level in physical education in government schools in Western Australia', *Gender and Education* 8, 1: 81–101.

Bluebond-Langner, M. (1990) *The Private Worlds of Dying Children*, Princeton, NJ: Princeton University Press.

Booth, M. (1927) 'The present day education of girls', *The Nineteenth Century and After* 102: 259–69.

—— (1932) *Youth and Sex*, London: Allen & Unwin.

Bossert, S. (1982) 'Understanding sex differences in children's classroom experiences', in W. Doyle and T.L. Good (eds) *Focus on Teaching*, Chicago: University of Chicago Press.

Boulton, P. and Coldron, J. (1993) 'Equal opportunities, teacher education and Europe', in I. Siraj-Blatchford (ed.) *'Race', Gender and the Education of Teachers*, Milton Keynes: Open University Press.

—— (1998) 'Why women teachers say "stuff it" to promotion', *Gender and Education* 10, 2: 149–62.

Bourdieu, P. (1984) *Distinction: A Social Critique of the Judgement of Taste*, trans. Richard Nice, London: Routledge & Kegan Paul/Cambridge, Mass.: Harvard University Press (original French edn 1979, *La Distinction: Critique sociale du jugement*, Paris: Les Editions de Minuit).

—— (1993) *The Field of Cultural Production: Essays on Art and Literature*, Cambridge: Polity Press.

Boutilier, N. (1994) 'Reading, writing and Rita Mae Brown: lesbian literature in high school', in L. Garber (ed.) *Tilting the Tower: Lesbians/Teaching/Queer Subjects*, New York: Routledge.

Bowles, G. and Duelli Klein, R. (eds) (1983) *Theories of Women's Studies*, London: Routledge & Kegan Paul.

Brah, A. and Minhas, R. (1985) 'Structural racism or cultural difference: schooling for Asian girls', in G. Weiner (ed.) *Just a Bunch of Girls: Feminist Approaches to Schooling*, Milton Keynes: Open University Press.

Brodribb, S. (1992) *Nothing Mat(t)ers: A Feminist Critique of Postmodernism*, Melbourne: Spinifex Press.

Brophy, J. (1985) 'Interactions of male and female students with male and female teachers', in L.C. Wilkinson and C.B. Marrett (eds) *Gender Influences in Classroom Interaction*, Orlando, Fla.: Academic Press.

Brown, L. (1999) 'Beyond the degree: men and women at the decision making levels in British higher education', *Gender and Education* 11, 1: 5–26.

Browne, J.D. (ed.) (1979) *Teachers of Teachers: A History of the Association of Teachers in Colleges and Departments of Education*, London: Hodder & Stoughton.

Browne, N. and France, P. (1986) *Untying the Apron Strings*, Milton Keynes: Open University Press.

Bryan, K.A. (1980) 'Pupil perceptions of transfer', in A. Hargreaves and L. Tickle (eds) *Middle Schools: Origins, Ideology and Practice*, London: Harper & Row.

Bullough, R.V.J. (1997) 'Becoming a teacher: self and the social location of teacher education', in B.J. Biddle, T.L. Good and I.F. Goodson (eds) *International Handbook of Teachers and Teaching*, Dordrecht: Kluwer.

References

Burchall, H. and Millman, V. (eds) (1989) *Changing Perspectives on Gender: New Initiatives in Secondary Education*, Milton Keynes: Open University Press.

Burgess, H. (1985) 'Case study and curriculum research: some issues for teacher researchers', in R.G. Burgess (ed.) *Issues in Educational Research: Qualitative Methods*, London: Falmer Press.

—— (1989) 'A sort of career: women in primary schools', in C. Skelton (ed.) *Whatever Happens to Little Women? Gender and Primary Schooling*, Milton Keynes: Open University Press.

Burgess, R.G. (1986) *Sociology, Education and Schools: An Introduction to the Sociology of Education*, London: Batsford.

—— (1988) 'Conversations with a purpose: the ethnographic interview in educational research', in R.G. Burgess (ed.) *Studies in Qualitative Methodology*, Vol. 1: *Conducting Qualitative Research*, Greenwich, Conn.: JAI Press.

Burstall, S. (1907) *English High Schools for Girls*, London: Longmans Green.

—— (1911) *The Story of the Manchester High School for Girls*, Manchester: Manchester University Press.

—— (1933) *Retrospect and Prospect*, London: Longman.

Burstyn, J. (1980) *Victorian Education and the Ideal of Womanhood*, London: Croom Helm.

Buswell, C. (1981) 'Sexism in school routines and classroom practices', *Durham and Newcastle Research Review* 9, 46: 195–200.

Butler, E. (1959) *Paper Boats*, London: Longman.

Caine, B., Grosz, E. and de Lepervanche, M. (1988) *Crossing Boundaries: Feminism and the Critique of Knowledges*, Sydney: Allen & Unwin.

Cairns, J. and Inglis, B. (1989) 'A content analysis of ten popular history textbooks for primary schools with particular emphasis on the role of women', *Educational Review* 41, 3: 221–6.

Cameron, D. (1995) 'Rethinking language and gender studies: some issues for the 1990s', in S. Mills (ed.) *Language and Gender: Interdisciplinary Perspectives*, London: Longman.

Cannan, J. and Griffin, C. (1990) 'The new men's studies: part of the problem or part of the solution?' in J. Hearn and D. Morgan (eds) *Men, Masculinity and Social Theory*, London: Unwin Hyman.

Carr, W. and Kemmis, S. (1986) *Becoming Critical: Education, Knowledge and Action Research*, London: Falmer Press.

Carrington, B. and Short, G. (1987) 'Breakthrough to political literacy: political education, antiracist teaching and the primary school', *Journal of Education Policy* 3: 1–13.

Carrington, B. and Wood, E. (1983) 'Body-talk: images of sport in a multi-ethnic school', *Multi-racial Education* 11, 2: 29–38.

Carter, A. (ed.) (1990) *The Virago Book of Fairy Tales*, London: Virago.

Casey, K. (1993) *I Answer with My Life: Life Histories of Women Teachers Working for Social Change*, New York: Routledge.

Chase, S.E. (1995) *Ambiguous Empowerment: The Work Narratives of Women School Superintendents*, Amherst: University of Massachusetts Press.

Chisholm, L. and Holland, J. (1987) 'Anti-sexist action research in schools: the Girls and Occupational Choice project', in G. Weiner and M. Arnot (eds) *Gender under Scrutiny*, London: Hutchinson.

Clarke, G. (1996) 'Conforming and contesting with (a) difference: how lesbian students and teachers manage their identities', *International Studies in Sociology of Education* 6, 2: 191–210.

Clarke, M.G. (1937) 'Feminine challenge in education', in C. Arscott (ed.) *The Headmistress Speaks*, London: Kegan Paul, Trench, Trubner & Co.

Clarricoates, K. (1987) 'Child culture at school', in A. Pollard (ed.) *Children and Their Primary Schools*, London: Falmer Press.

Clough, P.T. (1992) *The End(s) of Ethnography: From Realism to Social Criticism*, Newbury Park, Calif.: Sage.

—— (1994) *Feminist Thought: Desire, Power, and Academic Discourse*, Oxford: Blackwell.

Coates, J. and Cameron, D. (eds) (1989) *Women in their Speech Communities: New Perspectives on Language and Sex*, London: Longman.

Cockburn, C. (1987) *Two Track Training*, London: Macmillan.

Coffey, A. (1992) 'Initial teacher education: the rhetoric of equal opportunities', *Journal of Education Policy* 7, 1: 109–13.

—— (1999) *The Ethnographic Self: Fieldwork and the Representation of Identity*, London: Sage.

Coffey, A. and Acker, S. (1991) ' "Girlies on the war-path": addressing gender in initial teacher education', *Gender and Education* 3, 3: 249–61.

Coffey, A. and Atkinson, P. (1996) *Making Sense of Qualitative Data*, Thousand Oaks, Calif.: Sage.

Coffey, A., Atkinson, P.A. and Delamont, S. (1999) 'Ethnography: past, post and future(s)', *Journal of Contemporary Ethnography* 13, 5: 460–71.

Cohee, G.E., Daumen, E., Kemp, T.D., Krebs, P.M., Lafky, S.A. and Runzo, S. (eds) (1998) *The Feminist Teacher Anthology*, New York: Teachers College Press.

Cohen, L. and Manion, L. (1980) *Research Methods in Education*, London: Croom Helm.

—— (1994) *Research Methods in Education* (4th Edition) London: Routledge.

Cohen, M. (1998) 'A habit of healthy idleness', in D. Epstein, J. Elwood, V. Hey and J. Maw (eds) *Failing Boys? Issues in Gender and Achievement*, Buckingham: Open University Press.

Collins, H. (1985) *Changing Order: Replication and Induction in Scientific Practice*, London: Sage.

Coloroso, B. (1982) *Discipline: Winning at Teaching Without Beating Your Kids*, Boulder, Colo.: Media for Kids.

Commeyras, M. and Alvermann, D.E. (1996) 'Reading about women in world history textbooks from one feminist perspective', *Gender and Education* 8, 1: 31–48.

Connell, R.W. (1985) *Teacher's Work*, Sydney: Allen & Unwin.

—— (1987) *Gender and Power*, Cambridge: Polity Press.

—— (1992) 'Citizenship, social justice and the curriculum', *International Studies in Sociology of Education* 2, 2: 133–46.

—— (1995) *Masculinities*, Cambridge: Polity Press.

Connell, R.W., Ashenden, D.J., Kessler, S. and Dowsett, G.W. (1982) *Making the Difference*, Sydney: Allen & Unwin.

Connelly, F.M. and Clandinin, D.J. (1988) *Teachers as Curriculum Planners: Narratives of Experience*, New York: Teachers College Press.

References

—— (1995) 'Narrative and education', *Teachers and Teaching* 1, 1: 73–86.

Copelman, D.M. (1996) *London's Women Teachers: Gender, Class, and Feminism*, London: Routledge.

Cortazzi, M. (1991) *Primary Teaching: How It Is*, London: David Fulton.

—— (1993) *Narrative Analysis*, London: Falmer Press.

Coulter, R.P. (1995) 'Struggling with sexism: experiences of feminist first year teachers', *Gender and Education* 7, 1: 33–50.

Coxon, A.P.M. (1988) 'Something sensational', *The Sociological Review* 36, 2: 353–67.

Croll, P. (1986) *Systematic Classroom Observation*, London: Falmer Press.

Cross, A. (1972) *The Theban Mysteries*, London: Gollancz.

Cross, B.M. (1965) *The Educated Woman in America*, New York: Teachers College Press.

Crozier, J. and Anstiss, J. (1995) 'Out of the spotlight: girls' experience of disruption', in M. Lloyd Smith and J. Dwyfor Davies (eds) *On the Margins: The Educational Experience of 'Problem' Pupils*, Stoke-on-Trent: Trentham Books.

Cunnison, S. (1985) *Making it in a Man's World,* Occasional Paper No 1, Hull: University of Hull Department of Sociology and Social Anthropology.

—— (1989) 'Gender joking in the staffroom', in S. Acker (ed.) *Teachers, Gender and Careers*, London: Falmer Press.

—— (1994) 'Women teachers: career identity and perceptions of family constraints – changes over a recent decade', *Research Papers in Education* 9, 1: 81–106.

Dale, R.R. (1969) *Mixed or Single-Sex School?* London: Routledge & Kegan Paul.

Daly, P. (1996) 'The effects of single sex and coeducational secondary schooling on girls' achievement', *Research Papers in Education* 11, 3: 289–306.

Dane, C. (1917) *Regiment of Women*, London: Heineman.

Daniels, A. Kaplan (1985) *Comments at the Conference on Women and Work: Integrating Qualitative Methods*, Racine, Wis.: Wingspread Conference Center.

Darmanin, M. (1995) 'Classroom practices and class pedagogies', in J. Salisbury and S. Delamont (eds) *Qualitative Studies in Education*, Aldershot: Avebury.

David, M. (1993) *Parents, Gender and Education Reform*, Cambridge: Polity Press.

Davidson, H. (1985) 'Unfriendly myths about women teachers', in J. Whyte, R. Deem, L. Kant and M. Cruickshank (eds) *Girl-Friendly Schooling*, London: Methuen.

Davies, L. (1990) *Equity and Efficiency? School Management in an International Context*, New York: Falmer Press.

—— (1992) 'School power cultures under economic constraint', *Educational Review* 43, 2: 127–36.

De Lyon, H. and Migniuolo, F.W. (eds) (1989) *Women Teachers*, Milton Keynes: Open University Press.

Deegan, M.J. (1988) *Jane Addams and the Men of the Chicago School 1892–1918*, New Brunswick, NJ: Transaction Books.

Deem, R. (ed.) (1984) *Co-Education Reconsidered*, London: Methuen.

Dei, G.J.S., Mazzuca, J., McIsaac, E. and Zine, J. (1998) *Reconstructing 'Drop-out': A Critical Ethnography of the Dynamics of Black Students' Disengagement from School*, Toronto: Toronto University Press.

Delamont, S. (1980) *The Sociology of Women*, London: Methuen.

—— (1983) *Interaction in the Classroom*, London: Routledge & Kegan Paul.

—— (1986) 'Discussion: a view from a quadruple outsider', *Teaching and Teacher Education* 2, 4: 329–32.

—— (1989) *Knowledgeable Women: Structuralism and the Reproduction of Elites*, London: Routledge.

—— (1990) *Sex Roles and the School*, London: Methuen.

—— (1991) 'The hit list and other horror stories', *Sociological Review* 39, 2: 238–59.

—— (1992a) 'Old fogies and intellectual women', *Women's History Review* 1, 1: 39–61.

—— (1992b) *Fieldwork in Educational Settings: Methods, Pitfalls and Perspectives*, London: Falmer Press.

—— (1993a) 'The beech-covered hillside', in G. Walford (ed.) *The Private Schooling of Girls: Past and Present*, London: Woburn Press.

—— (1993b) 'Distant dangers and forgotten standards', *Women's History Review* 2, 2: 233–52.

—— (1998) 'You need the leotard: revisiting the first PE lesson', *Sport, Education and Society* 3, 1: 5–17.

—— (1999) 'Gender and the discourse of derision' *Research Papers in Education* 14, 1: 3–21.

Delamont, S. and Atkinson, P.A. (1990) 'Professions and powerlessness', *The Sociological Review* 38, 1: 90–110.

—— (1995) *Fighting Familiarity: Essays on Education and Ethnography*, Cresskill, NJ: Hampton Press.

Delamont, S., Atkinson, P.A. and Coffey, A. (2000) 'The Twilight Years?', *International Journal of Qualitative Studies in Education* (forthcoming).

Delamont, S. and Galton, M. (1986) *Inside the Secondary Classroom*, London: Routledge & Kegan Paul.

Denscombe, M. (1985) *Classroom Control: A Sociological Perspective*, London: Allen & Unwin.

Denzin, N.K. (1989) *Interpretive Biography*, Qualitative Research Methods, vol. 17, Newbury Park, Calif.: Sage.

DES (1989) *Initial Teacher Training: Approval of Courses, Circular No. 24/89*, Department of Education and Science (Circular No. 59/89 Welsh Office), London: HMSO.

DfEE (1998) *Statistics of Education: Teachers, England and Wales 1998*, Department for Education and Employment, London: HMSO.

Dixon, C. (1997) 'Pete's tool: identity and sex play in the design and technology classroom', *Gender and Education* 9, 1: 89–104.

Draper, J. (1991) 'Encounters with sex and gender: some issues arising out of the transition from a single to a mixed sex school', paper presented at St Hilda's Conference on Education and Qualitative Research, University of Warwick.

Dudley, J. (with Nee Benham, M.K.P.A.) (1997) 'The story of an African-American teacher–scholar: one woman's narrative', *International Journal of Qualitative Studies in Education* 10, 1: 63–83.

Dwyer, K. (1977) 'On the dialogue of fieldwork', *Dialectical Anthropology* 2: 143–51.

Dyhouse, C. (1977) 'Good wives and little mothers', *Oxford Review of Education* 3, 1: 21–35.

—— (1985) 'Feminism and the debate over co-education', in J. Purvis (ed.) *The Education of Girls and Women*, Leicester: History of Education Society.

References

—— (1995) *No Distinction of Sex? Women in British Universities, 1870–1939* London: UCL Press.

EC (1990) *Conclusion of the Council and Ministers of Education on the Enhanced Treatment of Equality of Educational Opportunities for Girls and Boys* 90/C162/05, Brussels: European Commission.

Edwards, A. (1995) 'Teacher education: partnerships in pedagogy?', *Teaching and Teacher Education* 11, 6: 595–610.

Edwards, A.E. and Westgate, D. (1994) *Investigating Classroom Talk* (2nd edition), London: Falmer Press.

Edwards, T. (1990) 'Schools of Education: their work and their future', in J.B. Thomas (ed.) *British Universities and Teacher Education: A Century of Change*, Lewes: Falmer Press.

Eggleston, S.J. (1974) 'Sex and the single schools', *Times Educational Supplement* 10 June.

Ehrlich, S. and King, R. (1992) 'Gender-based language reform and the social construction of meaning', *Discourse and Society* 3, 2: 151–7.

Ellis, C. and Bochner, A.P. (1992) 'Telling and performing personal stories: the constraints of choice in abortion', in C. Ellis and M.G. Flaherty (eds) *Investigating Subjectivity: Research on Lived Experience*, Newbury Park, Calif.: Sage.

—— (eds) (1996) *Composing Ethnography: Alternative Forms of Qualitative Writing*, Walnut Creek, Calif.: Altamira Press.

Ely, M., Vinz, R., Downing, M and Anzul, M. (1997) *On Writing Qualitative Research: Living by Words*, London: Falmer Press.

EOC (1989) *Initial Teacher Training in England and Wales* (Formal Investigative Report), Manchester: Equal Opportunities Commission.

Epstein, C.F. (1970) *Woman's Place: Options and Limits in Professional Careers*, Berkeley: University of California Press.

Epstein, D. (ed.) (1994) *Challenging Lesbian and Gay Inequalities in Education*, Buckingham: Open University Press.

Epstein, D., Elwood, J., Hey, V. and Maw, J. (eds) (1998) *Failing Boys? Issues in Gender and Achievement*, Buckingham: Open University Press.

Esland, G. (1971) 'Teaching and learning as the organisation of knowledge', in M.F.D. Young (ed.) *Knowledge and Control: New Directions for the Sociology of Education*, London: Macmillan.

Etzioni, A. (ed.) (1969) *The Semi-Professions and their Organization*, Englewood Cliffs, NJ: Prentice-Hall.

Evans, M. (1993) 'Reading lives: how the personal might be social', *Sociology* 27, 1: 5–14.

—— (1997) 'Negotiating the frontier: women and resistance in the contemporary academy', in L. Stanley (ed.) *Knowing Feminisms: On Academic Borders, Territories and Tribes*, London: Sage.

Evans, T.D. (1988) *A Gender Agenda: A Sociological Study of Teachers, Parents and Pupils in Their Primary Schools*, Sydney: Allen & Unwin.

Evetts, J. (1990) *Women in Primary Teaching: Career Contexts and Strategies*, London: Unwin Hyman.

Farrell, S.A. (1992) 'Feminism and sociology introduction: the search for a feminist/womanist methodology in sociology', in S. Rosenberg Zalk and

J. Gordon-Kelter (eds) *Revolutions in Knowledge: Feminism in the Social Sciences*, Boulder, Colo.: Westview Press.

Fass, P.S. (1977) *The Damned and the Beautiful: American Youth in the 1920s*, New York: Oxford University Press.

Fenwick, D.T. (1998) 'Managing space, energy and self: junior high teachers experiences of classroom management', *Teaching and Teacher Education*, 14, 6: 619–32.

Ferfolja, T. (1998) 'Australian lesbian teachers: a reflection of homophobic harrassment of high school teachers in New South Wales government schools', *Gender and Education* 10, 4: 401–16.

Fetterley, J. (1978) *The Resisting Reader: A Feminist Approach to American Fiction*, Bloomington: Indiana Press.

Finch, E. (1947) *Carey Thomas of Bryn Mawr*, New York: Harper.

Finch, J. (1984) ' "It's great to have someone to talk to": the ethics and politics of interviewing women', in C. Bell and H. Roberts (eds) *Social Researching*, London: Routledge & Kegan Paul.

Fine, G.A. (1988) 'Good children and dirty play', *Play and Culture* 1: 43–56.

Fine, M. (1993) 'Sexuality, schooling and adolescent females', in L. Weis and M. Fine (eds) *Beyond Silenced Voices: Class, Race and Gender in United States Schools*, Albany: State University of New York Press.

Fisher, J. (1994) 'Unequal races: gender and assessment', in D. Graddol, J. Maybin and B. Stierer (eds) *Researching Language and Literacy in Social Context*, Clevedon: Multilingual Matters.

Flanders, N.A. (1970) *Analysing Teaching Behaviour*, New York: Addison-Wesley.

Flax, J. (1990) 'Postmodernism and gender relations in feminist theory', in L.J. Nicholson (ed.) *Feminism/Postmodernism*, London: Routledge.

—— (1993) 'The end of innocence', in J. Butler and J.W. Scott (eds) *Feminists Theorise the Political*, New York: Routledge.

Fletcher, S. (1980) *Feminists and Bureaucrats*, Cambridge: Cambridge University Press.

—— (1984) *Women First: The Female Tradition in English Physical Education 1880–1980*, London: Athlone Press.

Flynn, E.A. and Schweickart, P.P. (eds) (1986) *Gender and Reading*, Baltimore, Md.: Johns Hopkins University Press.

Foley, D. (1989) *Learning Capitalist Culture: Deep in the Heart of Tejas*, Philadelphia: University of Philadelphia Press.

Fordham, S. (1996) *Blacked Out: Dilemmas of Race, Identity, and Success at Capital High*, Chicago: University of Chicago Press.

Foucault, M. (1977) *Discipline and Punish: The Birth of the Prison*, Harmondsworth: Penguin.

Fox, K.V. (1996) 'Silent voices: a subversive reading of child sexual abuse', in C. Ellis and A.P. Bochner (eds) *Composing Ethnography: Alternative Forms of Qualitative Writing*, Walnut Creek, Calif.: Altamira Press.

Fox-Genovese, E. (1986) 'The claims of a common culture: gender, race, class and the canon', *Salmagundi* 72 (Fall): 134–51.

Frankfort, R. (1977) *Collegiate Women: Domesticity and Career in Turn-of-the-Century America*, New York: New York University Press.

Franzosa, S. (1992) 'Authoring the educated self: educational autobiography and resistance', *Educational Theory* 42: 160–72.

References

Freidson, E. (1970a) *Professional Dominance*, New York: Atherton Press.

—— (1970b) *Profession of Medicine: A Study of the Sociology of Applied Knowledge*, New York: Dodd, Mead & Co.

—— (1975) *Doctoring Together: A Study of Professional Social Control*, New York: Elsevier.

—— (1983) 'The theory of professions', in R. Dingwall and P. Lewis (eds) *Sociology of the Professions: Lawyers, Doctors and Others*, London: Macmillan.

French, J. and French. P. (1984) 'Gender imbalances in the primary classroom: an interactional account', *Educational Research* 26, 2: 127–36.

—— (1993) 'Gender imbalances in the primary classroom: an interactional account', in P. Woods and M. Hammersley (eds) *Gender and Ethnicity in Schools*, London: Routledge.

Furlong, J., Whitty, G., Miles, S., Barton, L. and Barrett, E. (1996) 'From integration to partnership: changing structures in ITE', in R. McBride (ed.) *Teacher Education Policy: Some Issues Arising from Research and Practice*, London: Falmer Press.

Furlong, V.J., Hirst, P.H., Pocklington, K. and Miles, S. (1988) *Initial Teacher Training and the Role of the School*, Milton Keynes: Open University Press.

Gage, N.L. (1989) 'The paradigm wars and their aftermath', *Educational Researcher* 18, 7: 4–10.

Galton, M. and Delafield, A. (1981) 'Expectancy effects in primary classrooms', in B. Simon and J. Willcocks (eds) *Research and Practice in the Primary Classroom*, London: Routledge & Kegan Paul.

Galton, M., Hargreaves, L., Comber, C., Wall, D. and Pell, T. (1999) 'Changing patterns of teacher interaction in primary classrooms 1976–96', *British Educational Research Journal* 25, 1: 23–37.

Galton, M., Simon, B. and Croll, P. (1980) *Progress and Performance in the Primary Classroom*, London: Routledge.

Geer, B. (1966a) 'Notes on occupational commitment', *School Review* 74: 31–47.

—— (1966b) 'Occupational commitment and the teaching profession', *School Review* 77, 1: 31–47.

George, R. and Maguire, M. (1998) 'Older women training to teach', *Gender and Education* 10, 4: 417–31.

Gerver, E. and Hart, L. (1991) *Strategic Women*, Aberdeen: Aberdeen University Press.

Gibson, M. A. (1998) *Accommodation Without Assimilation: Sikh Immigrants in an American High School*, Ithaca, NY: Cornell University Press.

Gill, D. (1990) Response on behalf of Hackney Teachers to National Curriculum History Working Group Final Report, Submission to DES.

Gilligan, C. (1982) *In a Different Voice: Psychological Theory and Women's Development*, Cambridge, Mass.: Harvard University Press.

Gilligan, C. and Attanucci, J. (1988) 'Two moral orientations: gender differences and similarities', *Merrill-Palmer Quarterly* 34, 3: 223–37.

Gilligan, C., Lyons, N.P. and Hanmer, T.J. (eds) (1990) *Making Connections: The Relational Worlds of Adolescent Girls at Emma Willard School*, Cambridge, Mass.: Harvard University Press.

Ginsburg, M. (1987) 'Reproduction, contradiction and conceptions of profession-alism: the case of preservice teachers', in T. Popkewitz (ed.) *Critical Studies in Teacher Education*, Lewes: Falmer Press.

Giroux, H.A. (1988) 'Critical theory and the politics of culture and voice: rethinking the discourse of educational research', in R.R. Shermann and R.B. Webb (eds) *Qualitative Research in Education: Focus and Methods*, Lewes: Falmer Press.

Gissing, G. (1893) *The Odd Women*, reprinted 1980, London: Virago.

Gluck, S.B. and Patai, D. (eds) (1991) *Women's Words: The Feminist Practice of Oral History*, London: Routledge.

Golding, E. and Chen, M. (1993) 'The feminization of the principalship in Israel', in C. Marshall (ed.) *The New Politics of Race and Gender. The 1992 Yearbook of the Politics of Education Association*, Washington, DC: Falmer Press.

Goodlad, J. (1991) *Teachers for our Nation's Schools*, San Francisco: Jossey Bass.

Goodson, I. F. (1981) 'Life history and the study of sociology', *Interchange* 11, 4: 62–76.

—— (1983) *School Subjects and Curriculum Change*, London: Croom Helm.

—— (1988) *The Making of the Curriculum: Collected Essays*, New York: Falmer Press.

—— (ed.) (1992) *Studying Teachers' Lives*, New York: Teachers College Press.

—— (1995) 'The story so far: personal knowledge and the political', *International Journal of Qualitative Studies of Education* 8: 89–98.

—— (1997) 'The life and work of teachers', in B.J. Biddle, T.L. Good, I.F. Goodson (eds) *International Handbook of Teachers and Teaching*, Dordrecht: Kluwer.

Gordon, D. (1995) 'Conclusion', in R. Behar and D. Gordon (eds) *Women Writing Culture*, Berkeley: California University Press.

Gordon, T. (1992) 'Citizens and Others: gender, democracy and education', *International Studies in Sociology of Education* 2, 1: 43–56.

Gore, J.M. and Zeichner, K.M. (1991) 'Action research and reflective teaching in preservice teacher education: a case study from the United States', *Teaching and Teacher Education* 7: 119–36.

Gosden, P. (1990) 'The James report and recent history,' in J.B. Thomas (ed.) *British Universities and Teacher Education: A Century of Change*, Lewes: Falmer Press.

Gouldner, A. (1962) 'Anti-minotaur', *Social Problems* 9: 199–212.

Graddol, D. and Swann, J. (1989) *Gender Voices*, Oxford: Blackwell.

Graham, H. (1983) 'Do her answers fit his questions? Women and the survey method', in E. Gamarnikow, D. Morgan, J. Purvis and D. Taylorson (eds) *The Public and the Private*, London: Heineman.

Grant, C. and Sleeter, C. (1986) *After the School Bell Rings*, London: Falmer Press.

Grant, G. (1988) *The World We Created at Hamilton High*, Cambridge, Mass.: Harvard University Press.

Gray, J. (1998) 'Telling data: from "A Tale of Inclusion"', *International Journal of Qualitative Studies in Education* 11, 4: 579–81.

Gray, J., Hopkins, D., Reynolds, D., Wilcox, B., Farrell, S. and Jesson, D. (1999) *Improving Schools*, Buckingham: Open University Press.

Gregg, J. (1995) 'Discipline, control and the school mathematics tradition', *Teaching and Teacher Education*, 11, 6: 579–94.

Griffin, C. and Wetherell, M. (1992) 'Feminist psychology and the study of men and masculinity: part II: politics and practices', *Feminism and Psychology* 2: 133–68.

Griffin, P. (1991) 'From hiding out to coming out! Empowering lesbian and gay educators', *Journal of Homosexuality* 2: 167–95.

Guttentag, M. and Bray, H. (eds) (1976) *Undoing Sex Stereotypes: Research and Resources for Educators*, New York: McGraw-Hill.

Hall, G. Stanley (1904) *Adolescence*, 2 vols, New York: Appleton.

Hall, T., Coffey, A. and Williamson, H. (1999) 'Self, space and place: youth identities and citizenship,' *British Journal of Sociology of Education* 20, 4 (forthcoming).

Hall, T., Williamson, H. and Coffey, A. (1998) 'Conceptualizing citizenship: young people and the transition to adulthood', *Journal of Education Policy* 13: 301–15.

Haller, J. and Haller, R. (1974) *The Physician and Sexuality in Victorian America*, Urbana: University of Illinois Press.

Halsaa, B., Nordkvelle, Y. and Sletten, A.K. (1995) 'Gender and curriculum reform in the college: experiences of a Norwegian college', in H. Ruotonen, L. Boyson, K. Krogh-Jespersen and E. Lahelma (eds) *Content and Gender: Transforming the Curriculum in Teacher Education*, Sheffield: PAVIC Publications/Association for Teacher Education in Europe.

Hammersley, M. (1991) *Reading Ethnographic Research: A Critical Guide*, London: Longman.

—— (1993) 'An evaluation of a study of gender imbalance in primary classrooms', in P. Woods and M. Hammersley (eds) *Gender and Ethnicity in Schools*, London: Routledge.

Haraway, D. (1989) *Primate Visions: Gender, Race and Nature in the World of Modern Science*, London: Routledge.

Harding, S. (1986) *The Science Question in Feminism*, Milton Keynes: Open University Press.

—— (ed.) (1987) *Feminism and Methodology: Social Science Issues*, Milton Keynes: Open University Press.

—— (1991) *Whose Science? Whose Knowledge? Thinking from Women's Lives*, Milton Keynes: Open University Press.

—— (1993) 'Introduction', in S. Harding (ed.) *The 'racial' economy of science*, Bloomington: Indiana University Press.

Harding, S. and Hintikka, M.B. (eds) (1983) *Discovering Reality: Feminist Perspectives on Epistemology, Metaphysics, Methodology and Philosophy of Science*, Dordrecht: Reidel.

Hargreaves, D. (1967) *Social Relations in a Secondary School*, London: Routledge & Kegan Paul.

Harrington, H.L., Quinn-Leering, K. and Hodson, L. (1996) 'Written case analysis and critical reflection', *Teaching and Teacher Education* 12, 1: 25–38.

Harrison, L. (1975) 'Cro-Magnon Woman – in eclipse', *Science Teacher* 42, 4: 9–11.

Hastrup, K. (1992) 'Writing ethnography: state of the art', in J. Okely and H. Callaway (eds) *Anthropology and Autobiography*, London: Routledge.

Hatch, J.A. (1999) 'What preservice teachers can learn from studies of teachers' work', *Teaching and Teacher Education* 15, 3: 229–42.

Haw, K., with Shah, S. and Hanifa, M. (1998) *Educating Muslim Girls: Shifting Discourses*, Buckingham: Open University Press.

Hawkey, K. (1996) 'Image and the pressure to conform in learning to teach', *Teaching and Teacher Education* 12, 1: 99–108.

Haywood, C. and Mac an Ghaill, M. (1996) 'Schooling masculinities', in M. Mac an Ghaill (ed.) *Understanding Masculinities*, Buckingham: Open University Press.

Heath, A. (1981) *Social Mobility*, London: Fontana.

Heilbrun, C. (1988) *Writing a Woman's Life*, New York: W.W. Norton.

Hendry, E. (1987) *Exams for the Boys*, London: Fawcett Society.

Henwood, F. (1996) 'WISE choices? Understanding occupational decision-making in a climate of equal opportunities for women in science and technology', *Gender and Education* 8, 2: 199–214.

Herbert, C. (1985) *Talking of Silence: The Sexual Harassment of Schoolgirls*, London: Falmer Press.

Herman, S. (1976) 'American marriage manuals: a feminist analysis', in M. Kelly (ed.) *Woman's Being, Woman's Place*, Boston: G.K. Hall.

Hilsum, S. and Start, K.B. (1974) *Promotion and Careers in Teaching*, Slough: National Foundation for Education Research.

Hilton, G.L.S. (1991) 'Boys will be boys – won't they?', *Gender and Education* 3, 3: 311–14.

HMSO (1994) *The Rising Tide: A Report on Women in Science, Engineering and Technology*, London: HMSO.

Hodkinson, H. and Hodkinson, P. (1999) 'Teaching to learn, learning to teach? School-based non-teaching activity in an initial teacher education and training partnership scheme', *Teaching and Teacher Education* 15, 3: 273–86.

Hoff, J. (1994) 'Gender as a postmodern category of paralysis', *Women's History Review* 3, 2: 149–68.

Hoffman, N. (1981) *Woman's 'True' Profession: Voices from the History of Teaching*. Old Westbury, NY: The Feminist Press.

Holland, D.C. and Eisenhart, M. (1990) *Educated in Romance: Women, Achievement, and College Culture*, Chicago: Chicago University Press.

Holland, J. (1988) 'Girls and occupational choice', in A. Pollard, J. Purvis and G. Walford (eds) *Education, Training and the New Vocationalism*, Milton Keynes: Open University Press.

Holly, L. (ed.) (1989) *Girls and Sexuality: Teaching and Learning*, Milton Keynes: Open University Press.

Holquist, M. (1990) *Dialogism: Bakhtin and his World*, London: Routledge.

Holtby, W. (1936) *South Riding*, reprinted 1974, Glasgow: Fontana.

Howson, G. (1982) *A History of Mathematics Education in England*, Cambridge: Cambridge University Press.

Hoyle, E. and Megarry, J. (eds) (1980) *World Yearbook of Education 1980: Professional Development of Teachers*, London: Kogan Page.

Huber, J. and Whelan, K. (1999) 'A marginal story as a place of possibility', *Teaching and Teacher Education* 15, 4: 381–96.

Huberman, M., with Grounauer, M. and Marti, J. (1993) *The Lives of Teachers*, New York: Teachers College Press.

Huberman, M., Thompson, C.L. and Weiland, S. (1997) 'Perspectives on the teaching career', in B.J. Biddle, T.L. Good and I.F. Goodson (eds) *International Handbook of Teachers and Teaching*, Dordrecht: Kluwer.

Hulmes, W. (1986) *The Leadership Class in Scottish Education*, Edinburgh: John Donald.

References

Humm, M (1992) 'Introduction', in M. Humm (ed.) *Feminisms: A Reader*, New York: Harvester Wheatsheaf.

Hunt, F. (ed.) (1987) *Lessons for Life: The Schooling of Girls and Women, 1850–1950*, Oxford: Basil Blackwell.

Jackson, D. and Salisbury, J. (1996) 'Why should secondary schools take working with boys seriously?', *Gender and Education* 8, 1: 103–16.

Jackson, P.W. (1968) *Life in Classrooms*, New York: Holt, Rinehart & Winston (2nd edn, 1990, New York: Teachers College Press).

Jackson, S. (1996) 'Heterosexuality as a problem for feminist theory', in L. Adkins and V. Merchant (eds) *Sexualizing the Social: Power and the Organization of Sexuality*, London: Macmillan.

James, J. (1998) 'Gender, race and radicalism', in G.E. Cohee, E. Daumer, T.D. Kemp, P.M. Krebbs, S.A Lafky and S. Runzo (eds) *The Feminist Teacher Anthology*, New York: Teachers College Press.

James, P. (1996) 'Learning to reflect: a story of empowerment', *Teaching and Teacher Education* 12, 1: 81–97.

Jamous, H. and Peloille, B. (1970) 'Professions or self-perpetuating system?', in J.A. Jackson (ed) *Professions and Professionalisation*, Cambridge: Cambridge University Press.

Jennaway, M. (1990) 'Paradigms, postmodern epistemologies and paradox: the place of feminism in anthropology', *Anthropological Forum* 6, 2: 167–89.

Johnson, T.J. (1972) *Professions and Power*, London: Macmillan.

Jones, C. (1985) 'Sexual tyranny in mixed schools', in G. Weiner (ed.) *Just a Bunch of Girls: Feminist Approaches to Schooling*, Milton Keynes: Open University Press.

Jones, C. and Mahony, P. (eds) (1989) *Learning our Lines: Sexuality and Social Control in Education*, London: The Women's Press.

Jørgensen, A. (1995) 'Developing teaching methods in mathematics: equal opportunities perspective', in H. Ruotonen, L. Boyson, K. Krogh-Jespersen and E. Lahelma (eds) *Content and Gender: Transforming the Curriculum in Teacher Education*, Sheffield: PAVIC Publications/Association for Teacher Education in Europe.

Joyce, M (1987) 'Being a feminist teacher', in M. Lawn and G. Grace (eds) *Teachers: The Culture and Politics of Work*, London: Falmer Press.

Kainan, A. (1994) *The Staff Room: Observing the Professional Culture of Teachers*, Aldershot: Ashgate.

Kaufman, P.W. (1984) *Women Teachers on the Frontier*, New Haven, Conn.: Yale University Press.

Kean, H. (1990) *Deeds Not Words: The Lives of Suffragette Teachers*, London: Pluto.

Kehily, M.J. (1995) 'Self narration, autobiography and identity construction', *Gender and Education* 7, 1: 23–32.

Keller, E.F. (1985) *Reflections on Gender and Science*, New Haven, Conn.: Yale University Press.

Kelly, A. (1985a) 'Traditionalists and trendies', *British Educational Research Journal* 11, 2: 91–104.

—— (1985b) 'Changing schools and changing society: some reflections on the Girls into Science and Technology project', in M. Arnot (ed.) *Race and Gender: Equal Opportunities Policies in Education*, Oxford: Pergamon.

—— (1988) 'Gender differences in teacher–pupil interactions: a meta-analytic review' *Research in Education* 39: 1–23.

Kenealy, A. (1899) 'Woman as an athlete', *The Nineteenth Century* 45, 635–45.

—— (1920) *Feminism and Sex-Extinction*, London: Fisher-Unwin.

Kenway, J. (1995) 'Masculinities in schools: under seige, on the defensive and under reconstruction?', *Discourse* 16: 59–79.

—— (1996) 'Reasserting masculinity in Australian schools', *Women's Studies International Forum* 19, 4: 447–66.

Kessler, S., Ashenden, D.J., Connell, R.W. and Dowsett, G.W. (1985) 'Gender relations in secondary schooling', *Sociology of Education* 58: 34–48.

Khayatt, M.D. (1992) *Lesbian Teachers: An Invisible Presence*, Albany: State University of New York Press.

—— (1997) 'Sex and the teacher: Should we come out in class?', *Harvard Educational Review* 6, 7: 126–43.

King, R. (1978) *All Things Bright and Beautiful? A Sociological Study of Infants' Classrooms*, Wiley: Chichester.

Kitch, S.L. (1994) 'Straight but not narrow: a gynetic approach to the teaching of lesbian literature,' in L. Garber (ed.) *Tilting the Tower: Lesbians/Teaching/Queer Subjects*, New York: Routledge.

Klages, M. (1994) 'The ins and outs of a lesbian academic', in L. Garber (ed.) *Tilting the Tower: Lesbians/Teaching/Queer Subjects*, New York: Routledge.

Koerner, M.E. (1992) 'Teachers' images: reflections of themselves', in W.H. Schubert and W.C. Ayers (eds) *Teacher Lore: Learning from Our Own Experience*, New York: Longman.

Kontogiannopoulou-Polydorides, G. (1991) 'Greece', in M. Wilson (ed.) *Girls and Young Women in Education: A European Perspective*, Oxford: Pergamon.

Lacey, C. (1970) *Hightown Grammar: The School as a Social System*, Manchester: Manchester University Press.

—— (1977) *The Socialisation of Teachers*, London: Methuen.

Lakoff, R. (1975) *Language and Women's Place*, New York: Colophon Books.

Lambart, A. (1977) 'The sisterhood', in M. Hammersley and P. Woods (eds) *The Process of Schooling*, London: Routledge & Kegan Paul.

—— (1982) 'Expulsion in context', in R. Frankenberg (ed.) *Custom and Conflict in British Society*, Manchester: Manchester University Press.

Langellier, K. and Hall, D. (1989) 'Interviewing women: a phenomenological approach to feminist communication research', in K. Caiter and C. Spitzack (eds) *Doing Research on Women's Communication: Perspectives on Theory and Method*, Norwood, NJ: Ablex.

Laslett, B. and Thorne, B. (eds) (1997) *Feminist Sociology: Life Histories of a Movement*, New Brunswick, NJ: Rutgers University Press.

Lather, P. (1991) *Getting Smart: Feminist Research With/In the Postmodern*, London: Routledge.

Lawrence-Lightfoot, S. (1983) *The Good High School: Portraits of Character and Culture*, New York: Anchor Books.

Leggatt, T. (1970) 'Teaching as a profession', in J.A. Jackson (ed.) *Professions and Professionalisation*, Cambridge: Cambridge University Press.

Lemons, J.S. (1973) *The Woman Citizen: Social Feminism in the 1920s*, Urbana: University of Illinois Press.

References

Leonard, P. (1998) 'Gendering change? Management, masculinity and the dynamics of incorporation', *Gender and Education* 10, 1: 71–84.

Lewis, M. (1990) 'Interrupting patriarchy: politics, resistance and transformation in the feminist classroom', *Harvard Educational Review* 60, 4: 467–88.

Lie, S. and Malik, L (eds) (1994) *World Yearbook of Education 1994: The Gender Gap in Higher Education*, London: Kogan Page.

Lieberman, M. (1956) *Education as a Profession*, Englewood Cliffs, NJ: Prentice-Hall.

Lincoln, Y.S. and Denzin, N.K. (1994) 'The fifth moment', in N.K. Denzin and Y.S. Lincoln (eds) *Handbook of Qualitative Research,*Thousand Oaks, Calif.: Sage.

Lloyd, B. (1989) 'Rules of the gender game', *New Scientist* 2 December, 66–70.

Lloyd, B. and Duveen, G. (1992) *Gender Identities and Education: The Impact of Starting School*, New York: Harvester Wheatsheaf.

Lloyd, S. McIntosh (1979) *A Singular School: Abbot Academy, 1828–1973*, Hanover, NH: University of New England Press.

Lobban, G. (1974) 'Presentation of sex roles in British reading schemes', *Forum* 16, 2: 57–60.

—— (1975) 'Sex roles in reading schemes', *Educational Review* 27, 3: 202–10.

Lorber, J. (1984) *Women in Medicine*, London: Tavistock.

Lortie, D.C. (1975) *Schoolteacher: A Sociological Study*, Chicago: Chicago University Press.

Lynch, K. (1991) 'Republic of Ireland', in M. Wilson (ed.) *Girls and Young Women in Education: A European Perspective*, Oxford: Pergamon.

Mac an Ghaill, M. (1988) *Young, Gifted and Black: Student–Teacher Relations in the Schooling of Black Youth*, Milton Keynes: Open University Press.

—— (1994) *The Making of Men: Masculinities, Sexualities and Schooling*, Buckingham: Open University Press.

—— (1996) 'Deconstructing heterosexuals within school arenas', *Curriculum Studies* 4, 2: 195–213.

Maccia, E.S., Coleman, M.A. and Estep, M. (eds) (1975) *Women and Education*, Springfield, Ill.: Charles C. Thomas.

McCoy, K. (1997) 'White noise – the sound of epidemic: reading/writing a climate of intelligibility around the "crisis" of difference', *International Journal of Qualitative Studies in Education* 10, 3: 333–48.

McCracken, G.D. (1988) *The Long Interview*, Beverley Hills, Calif.: Sage.

McKellar, B. (1989) 'Only the fittist of the fittist will survive; black women and education', in S. Acker (ed.) *Teachers, Gender and Careers*, Lewes: Falmer Press.

McKinnon, M. and Ahola-Sidaway, J. (1995) 'Working with the boys: a North American perspective on non-traditional work initiatives for adolescent females in secondary schools', *Gender and Education* 7, 3: 327–40.

McLaughlin, D. and Tierney, W.G. (1993) *Naming Silenced Lives: Personal Narratives and Processes of Educational Change*, New York: Routledge.

McLaughlin, H.J. (1991) 'Reconciling caring and control: authority in classroom relationships', *Journal of Teacher Education* 42, 3: 189–95.

McPherson, G. (1972) *Small Town Teacher*, Cambridge, Mass.: Harvard University Press.

McWilliams Tullberg, R. (1998) *Women at Cambridge*, 2nd edn, Cambridge: Cambridge University Press.

Maclure, M. (1993) 'Arguing for your self: identity as an organising principle in teacher's jobs and lives', *British Educational Research Journal* 19: 311–22.

Maguire, M. (1995) 'Dilemmas in teaching teachers: the tutor's perspective, *Teachers and Teaching* 1, 1: 119–132.

Mahony, P. (1985) *Schools for the Boys*, London: Hutchinson.

—— (1989) 'Sexual violence and mixed schools', in C. Jones and P. Mahony (eds) *Learning our Lines: Sexuality and Social Control in Education*, London: The Women's Press.

—— (1995) 'Teaching how to change and changing how to teach: limits and possibilities in teacher education', in H. Ruotonen, L. Boysen, K. Krogh-Jespersen and E. Lahelma (eds) *Content and Gender: Transforming the Curriculum in Teacher Education*, Sheffield: PAVIC/Association for Teacher Education in Europe.

—— (1997) 'Talking heads: a feminist perspective on public sector reform in teacher education', *Discourse* 18, 1: 87–102.

Mahony, P. and Hexhall, I. (1997) 'Sounds of silence: the social justice agenda of the teacher training agency', *International Studies in Sociology of Education* 7, 2: 137–56.

Marsh, C. (1982) *The Survey Method*, London: Allen & Unwin.

Martin, J.R. (1985) *Reclaiming a Conversation: The Ideal of the Educated Woman*, New Haven: Yale University Press.

Martino, W. (1995) 'Deconstructing masculinity in the English classroom: a site for reconstituted gendered subjectivity', *Gender and Education* 7, 2: 205–20.

Masson, M. and Simonton, D. (eds) (1996) *Women and Higher Education: Past, Present and Future*, Aberdeen: Aberdeen University Press.

Matthews, B. (1996) 'Drawing scientists', *Gender and Education* 8, 2: 231–44.

May, N. and Rudduck, J. (1983) *Sex Stereotyping and the Early Years of Schooling*, Centre for Applied Research in Education, Norwich: University of East Anglia.

Maynard, M. (1994) 'Methods, practice and epistemology', in M. Maynard and J. Purvis (eds) *Researching Women's Lives from a Feminist Perspective*, London: Taylor & Francis.

—— (1996) *Feminist Social Research: Pragmatics, Politics and Power*, London: UCL.

Measor, L. (1984) 'Gender and the sciences: pupils' gender based conceptions of school subjects', in M. Hammersley and A. Hargreaves (eds) *Curriculum Practice*, Lewes: Falmer Press.

—— (1989) 'Are you coming to see some dirty films today?', in L. Holly (ed.) *Girls and Sexuality: Teaching and Learning*, Milton Keynes: Open University Press.

Measor, L. and Sikes, P. (1992) *Gender and Schools*, London: Cassell.

Medley, D.M. and Mitzel, H.E. (1963) 'Measuring classroom behaviour by systematic observation', in N.L. Gage (ed.) *Handbook of Research on Teaching*, Chicago: Rand McNally.

Mercer, G. (1997) 'Feminist pedagogy to the letter: a musing on contradictions', in L. Stanley (ed.) *Knowing Feminisms: On Academic Borders, Territories and Tribes*, London: Sage.

Metz, M. (1978) *Classrooms and Corridors: The Crisis of Authority in Desegregated Secondary Schools*, Berkeley: University of California Press.

Middleton, S. (1987) 'Schooling and radicalism: life histories of New Zealand feminist teachers', *British Journal of Sociology of Education* 8, 2: 169–89.

References

—— (1989) 'Educating feminists', in S. Acker (ed.) *Teachers, Gender and Careers*, London: Falmer Press Press.

—— (1993) *Educating Feminists: Life Histories and Pedagogy*, New York: Teachers College Press.

—— (1995) 'Doing feminist educational theory: a post-modernist perspective', *Gender and Education* 7, 1: 87–100.

Mienczakowski, J.E. (1996) 'The ethnographic act: the construction of consensual theatre', in C. Ellis and A.P. Bochner (eds) *Composing Ethnography: Alternative Forms of Qualitative Writing*, Walnut Creek, Calif.: Altamira Press.

Mirza, H.S. (1992) *Young, Black and Female*, London: Routledge.

—— (ed.) (1997) *British Black Feminism: A Reader*, London: Routledge.

Moffat, N. (1989) *Coming of Age in New Jersey: College and American Culture*, New Brunswick, NJ: Rutgers University Press.

Moles, R. (1995) 'Exploration of equal opportunity issues through second level geography teaching in the Republic of Ireland', in H. Ruotonen, L. Boysen, K. Krogh-Jespersen and E. Lahelma (eds) *Content and Gender: Transforming the Curriculum in Teacher Education*, Sheffield: PAVIC/Association of Teacher Education in Europe.

Morgan, C., Hall, V. and McKay, H. (1983) *The Selection of Secondary School Head-teachers*, Milton Keynes: Open University Press.

Morgan, D. (1991) *Focus Groups as Qualitative Research*, Newbury Park, Calif.: Sage.

—— (ed.) (1993) *Successful Focus Groups: Advancing the State of the Art*, Newbury Park, Calif.: Sage.

Munro, P. (1998) *Subject to Fiction: Women Teachers' Life History Narratives and the Cultural Politics of Resistance*, Buckingham: Open University Press.

Nance, D. and Fawns, R. (1993) 'Teachers' working knowledge and training: the Australian agenda for reform of teacher education', *Journal of Education for Teaching* 19, 2: 159–73.

Neilsen, J.M. (ed.) (1990) *Feminist Research Methods*, Boulder, Colo.: Westview Press.

Nias, J. (1989) *Primary Teachers Talking: A Study of Teaching as Work*, London: Routledge.

Nieb, C.D. (1994) 'Collaborating with Clio: teaching lesbian history', in L. Garber (ed.) *Tilting the Tower: Lesbians/Teaching/Queer Subjects*, New York: Routledge.

Nilan, P. (1995) 'Making up men', *Gender and Education* 7, 2: 175–88.

Nilson, A.P. (1975) 'Women in children's literature', in E.S. Maccia, M.A. Coleman and M. Estep (eds) *Women and Education*, Springfield, Ill.: Charles C. Thomas.

Nixon, J., Martin, J., McKeown, P. and Ranson, S. (1997) 'Towards a learning profession', *British Journal of Sociology of Education* 18, 1: 5–28.

Noddings, N. (1984) *Caring: A Feminist Approach to Ethics and Moral Education*, Berkeley and Los Angeles: University of California Press.

—— (1992) *The Challenge to Care in Schools: An Alternative Approach to Education*, New York: Teachers College Press.

Noffke, S.E. and Stevenson, R.B. (eds) (1995) *Educational Action Research: Becoming Practically Critical*, New York: Teachers College Press.

Northam, J. (1982) *Girls and Boys in Primary Maths*, London: Books in Education.

NUT (1981) *Promotion and the Women Teacher*, Manchester: Equal Opportunities Commission/National Union of Teachers.

Okely, J. (1978) 'Privileged, schooled and finished', in S. Ardener (ed.) *Defining Females*, London: Croom Helm.

Oppenheim, A.N. (1992) *Questionnaire Design, Interviewing and Attitude Measurement*, London: Punter.

Oram, A. (1987) 'Sex antagonism in the teaching profession: equal pay and the marriage bar 1910–39', in M. Arnot and G. Weiner (eds) *Gender and the Politics of Schooling*, London: Hutchinson.

O'Shaughnessy, F. (1979) 'The ground of our being', in Anon (ed.) *The King's High School Warwick 1879–1979*, Warwick: Privately Printed.

Ozga, J. and Lawn, M. (1988) 'School work: interpreting the labour process of teaching', *British Journal of Sociology of Education* 9: 323–36.

Paechter, C. (1998) *Educating the Other: Gender, Power and Schooling*, London: Falmer Press.

Paget, M.A. (1990) 'Performing the text', *Journal of Contemporary Ethnography* 19: 136–55.

—— (1993) *A Complex Sorrow: Reflections on Cancer and an Abbreviated Life*, Philadelphia: Temple University Press.

Paley, V.G. (1984) *Boys and Girls: Superheroes in the Doll Corner*, Chicago: Chicago University Press.

Parker, A. (1996) 'The construction of masculinity within boys' physical education', *Gender and Education* 8, 2: 141–58.

Parsons, T. (1951) *The Social System*, London: Routledge & Kegan Paul.

Partington, G. (1976) *Women Teachers in the Twentieth Century*, Slough: National Foundation for Education Research.

Personal Narratives Group (1989) *Interpreting Women's Lives: Feminist Theory and Personal Narratives*, Bloomington: Indiana University Press.

Peshkin, A. (1978) *Growing Up American: Schooling and the Survival of Community*, Chicago: University of Chicago Press.

—— (1985) *God's Choice: The Total World of a Fundamentalist Christian School*, Chicago: University of Chicago Press.

Peterson, W.A. (1964) 'Age, sex and the teachers' role', in B.J. Biddle and W. Ellena (eds) *Contemporary Research on Teacher Effectiveness*, New York: Holt, Rinehart & Winston.

Plummer, K. (1983) *Documents of Life: An Introduction to the Problems and Literature of a Humanistic Method*, London: Allen & Unwin.

Pratt, J. (1985) 'The attitudes of teachers', in J. Whyte, R. Deem, L. Kant and M. Cruickshank (eds) *Girl-Friendly Schooling*, London: Methuen.

Prentice, A. and Theobald, M. (eds) (1991) *Women Who Taught: Perspectives on the History of Women and Teaching*, Toronto: University of Toronto Press.

Proweller, A. (1998) *Constructing Female Identities: Meaning Making in an Upper Middle Class Youth Culture*, Albany: State University of New York Press.

Pugsley, L. (1996) 'Focus groups, young people and sex education', in J. Pilcher and A. Coffey (eds) *Gender and Qualitative Research*, Aldershot: Ashgate.

Pugsley, L., Coffey, A. and Delamont, S. (1996a) 'I don't eat peas anyway', in I. Shaw and I. Butler (eds) *A Case of Neglect*, Aldershot: Avebury.

—— (1996b) 'Daps, dykes, five mile hikes', *Sport, Education and Society* 1, 2: 133–46.

Purvis, J. (1989) *Hard Lessons: The Lives and Education of Working-Class Women in Nineteenth-Century England*, Cambridge: Polity Press.

References

QCA (1998) *Report of the Advisory Group on Education for Citizenship and the Teaching of Democracy in Schools*, London: Qualifications and Curriculum Authority.

Quantz, R. (1985) 'The complex visions of female teachers and the failure of unionisation in the 1930s', *History of Education Quarterly* 25: 439–58.

—— (1992) 'Interpretive method in historical research', in R. Altenbaugh (ed.) *The Teacher's Voice*, London: Falmer Press.

Quicke, J. and Winter, C. (1995) 'Best friends: a case study of girls' reactions to an interaction designed to foster collaborative group work', *Gender and Education* 7, 3: 259–82.

Rainer, J. and Guyton, E. (1990) 'Democratic practices in teacher education and the elementary classroom', *Teacher and Teacher Education* 15: 121–32.

—— (1999) 'Democratic practices in teacher education and the elementary classroom', *Teaching and Teacher Education* 15: 121–32.

Raphael Reed, L. (1999) 'Troubling boys and disturbing discourses on masculinity and schooling: a feminist exploration of current debates and interventions concerning boys in school', *Gender and Education* 11, 1: 93–110.

Retana, N. (1998) 'The Hopwood doctorate', *International Journal of Qualitative Studies in Education* 11, 1: 3–4.

Richardson, D. (ed.) (1996) *Theorizing Heterosexuality*, Buckingham: Open University Press.

Richardson, L. (1992) 'The consequences of poetic representation: writing the other, rewriting the self', in C. Ellis and M.G. Flaherty (eds) *Investigating Subjectivity: Research on Lived Experience*, Newbury Park, Calif.: Sage.

—— (1994) 'Writing: a method of inquiry', in N.K. Denzin and Y.S. Lincoln (eds) *Handbook of Qualitative Research*, Thousand Oaks, Calif.: Sage.

Riddell, S. (1989) 'It's nothing to do with me: teachers' views and gender divisions in the curriculum', in S. Acker (ed.) *Teachers, Gender and Careers*, Lewes: Falmer Press.

—— (1992) *Gender and the Politics of the Curriculum*, London: Routledge.

Riseborough, G. (1988) 'Pupils, recipe knowledge, curriculum knowledge and the cultural production of class, ethnicity and patriarchy: a critique of one teacher's practices,' *British Journal of Sociology of Education* 9, 1: 39–54.

Robinson, K.H. (1992) 'Classroom discipline: power, resistance and gender', *Gender and Education* 4, 3: 273–87.

Roman, L. (1992) 'The political significance of other ways of narrating ethnography', in M.D. Le Compte, W.L. Millroy and J. Preissle (eds) *The Handbook of Qualitative Research in Education*, San Diego: Academic Press.

Rosenberg, R. (1982) *Beyond Separate Spheres*, New Haven, Conn.: Yale University Press.

Rosser S.V. (1998) 'Warming up the classroom climate for women', in G.E. Cohee, E. Daumer, T.D. Kemp, P.M. Krebs, S.A. Lafky and S. Runzo (eds) *The Feminist Teacher Anthology*, New York: Teachers College Press.

Rousmaniere, K. (1997) *City Teachers: Teaching and School Reform in Historical Perspective*, New York: Teachers College Press.

Rowbotham, S. (1989) *The Past Is Before Us: Feminism in Action Since the 1960s*, London: Pandora.

Rowe, M. (1977) 'The Saturn's rings phenomenon', in P. Bourne (ed.) *Proceedings of the Conference on Women's Leadership and Authority in the Health Professions*, Santa Cruz: University of California.

Russett, C.E. (1990) *Sexual Science: The Victorian Construction of Womanhood*, Cambridge, Mass.: Harvard University Press.

Rust, F. O'Connell (1999) 'Professional conversations: new teachers explore teaching through conversation, story and narrative', *Teaching and Teacher Education* 15, 4: 367–80.

Sachs, J. and Blackmore, J. (1998) 'You never show you can't cope: women in school leadership roles managing their emotions', *Gender and Education* 10, 3: 265–80.

Sadker, D. and Sadker, M. (1985a) 'The treatment of sex equality in teacher education', in S.S. Klein (ed.) *Handbook for Achieving Sex Equality through Education*, Baltimore, Md.: Johns Hopkins University Press.

—— (1985b) 'Sexism in the schoolroom of the 80s', *Psychology Today* (March): 54–7.

Salisbury, J. (1996) *Educational Reforms and Gender Equality in Welsh Schools*, Cardiff: Equal Opportunities Commission.

Sanders, S. (1995) 'Teachers' understandings of subject: a cause for research?, in J. Salisbury and S. Delamont (eds) *Qualitative Studies in Education*, Aldershot: Avebury.

Saran, R. (1982) 'The politics of bargaining relationships', *Educational Management and Administration* 10, 2: 39–43.

Sayers, D.L. (1935) *Gaudy Night*, London: Gollancz.

Schon, D. (1983) *The Reflexive Practitioner: How Professionals Think in Action*, New York: Basic Books.

—— (1987) *Educating the Reflective Practitioner*, San Francisco: Jossey-Bass.

Schulz, L.Z. (1998) 'Being and becoming a woman teacher: journey through Nepal: the path taken', *Gender and Education* 10, 2: 163–84.

Scott, J. (1990) *A Matter of Record: Documentary Sources in Social Research*, Cambridge: Polity Press.

Scott, P. (1989) 'Challenging heterosexism in the curriculum: roles for teachers, governors and parents', in C. Jones and P. Mahony (eds) *Learning Our Lines: Sexuality and Social Control in Education*, London: The Women's Press.

Scott, S. (1985) 'Feminist research and qualitative methods', in R.G. Burgess (ed.) *Issues in Educational Research: Qualitative Methods*, London: Falmer Press.

Scribbins, K. (1977) 'Women in education', *Journal of Further and Higher Education* 1, 3: 17–39.

Serbin, L.A. (1978) 'Teachers, peers and play preferences', in B. Sprung (ed.) *Perspectives in Non-Sexist Early Childhood Education*, New York Teachers College Press.

Sewell, T. (1998) 'Loose cannons: exploding the myth of the "black macho" lad', in D. Epstein, J. Elwood, V. Hey, and J. Maw (eds) *Failing Boys?*, Buckingham: Open University Press.

Shah, S. (1989) 'Effective permeation of race and gender issues in teacher education courses', *Gender and Education* 1, 3: 109–18.

Shakeshaft, C. (1989) *Women in Educational Administration*, Newbury Park, Calif.: Sage.

Sharpe, S. (1976) *Just Like a Girl*, Harmondsworth: Penguin.

References

Shaw, J. (1976) 'Finishing school', in D.L. Barker and S. Allen (eds) *Sexual Divisions and Society*, London: Tavistock.

—— (1980) 'Education and the individual', in R. Deem (ed.) *Schooling for Women's Work*, London: Routledge & Kegan Paul.

Shen, J. and Hsieh, C.L. (1999) 'Improving the professional status of teaching: perspectives of future teachers, current teachers and education professors', *Teaching and Teacher Education* 15, 3: 315–24.

Shuy, R. (1986) 'Secretary Bennett's teaching,' *Teaching and Teacher Education* 2, 4: 315–24.

Sikes, P. (1991) 'Nature took its course: student teachers and gender awareness', *Gender and Education* 3, 2: 145–63.

—— (ed.) (1997) *Parents who Teach: Stories from Home and from School*, London: Cassell.

Sikes, P., Measor, L. and Woods, P. (1985) *Teacher Careers: Crises and Continuities*, Milton Keynes: Open University Press.

Simpson, R.L. and Simpson, I.H. (1969) 'Women and bureaucracy in the semi-professions', in A. Etzioni (ed.) *The Semi-Professions and their Organization*, Englewood Cliffs, NJ: Prentice-Hall.

Skeggs, B. (1994) 'Situating the production of feminist ethnography', in M. Maynard and J. Purvis (eds) *Researching Women's Lives from a Feminist Perspective*, London: Taylor & Francis.

Skelton, C. (1989) 'And so the wheel turns: gender and initial teacher education', in C. Skelton (ed.) *Whatever Happens to Little Women? Gender and Primary Schooling* Milton Keynes: Open University Press.

—— (1996) 'Learning to be tough: the fostering of maleness in one primary school', *Gender and Education* 8, 2: 185–97.

—— (1998) 'Feminism and research into masculinities and schooling', *Gender and Education* 10, 2: 217–28.

Skelton, C. and Hanson, J. (1989) 'Schooling the teachers: gender and initial teacher education', in S. Acker (ed.) *Teachers, Gender and Careers*, Lewes: Falmer Press.

Sklar, K.K. (1973) *Catherine Beecher*, New Haven: Yale University Press.

Smith, S. (1993) 'Who's talking/Who's talking back? The subject of personal narrative', *Signs* 18, 2: 329–407.

Smithers, A. and Zientek, P. (1991) *Gender, Primary Schools and the National Curriculum*, Manchester: Manchester University School of Education.

Smylie, M.A. (1997) 'Research on teacher leadership: assessing the state of the art,' in B.J. Biddle, T.L. Good and I.F. Goodson (eds) *International Handbook of Teachers and Teaching*, Dordrecht: Kluwer.

Snitow, A. (1990) 'A gender diary', in M. Hirsch and E. Fox Keller (eds) *Conflicts in feminism*, London: Routledge.

Soloman, J. (1993) *Teaching Science, Technology and Society*, Milton Keynes: Open University Press.

Sparkes, A.C. (1994) 'Self, silence and invisibility as a beginning teacher: a life history of a lesbian experience', *British Journal of the Sociology of Education* 15, 1: 93–118.

—— (1995) 'Writing people: reflections on the dual crises of representation and legitimation in qualitative inquiry', *Quest* 47, 2: 158–95.

Sparkes, A.C., Templin, T.J. and Schempp, P.G. (1990) 'The problematic nature of a career in a marginal subject: some implications for teacher education', *Journal of Education for Teaching* 16: 3–28.

Spencer, D.A. (1997) 'Teaching as women's work', in Biddle, B.J., Good, T.L. and Goodson, I.F. (eds) *International Handbook of Teachers and Teaching*, Dordrecht: Kluwer.

Spender, D. (1982) *Invisible Women: The Schooling Scandal*, London: Writers and Readers Publishing Cooperative.

—— (1985) *Man-Made Language*, London: Routledge & Kegan Paul.

Spindler, G. (1974) 'Schooling in Schonhausen', in G. Spindler (ed.) *Education and Cultural Process*', New York: Holt, Rinehart and Winston.

Spradley, J.P. (1979) *The Ethnographic Interview*, New York: Holt, Rinehart & Winston.

Squirrell, G. (1989) 'In passing ... teachers and sexual orientation', in S. Acker (ed.) *Teachers, Gender and Careers*, Lewes: Falmer Press.

Stacey, J., Bereaud, S. and Daniels, J. (eds) (1974) *And Jill Came Tumbling After: Sexism in American Education*, New York: Dell.

Stanley, L. (1990) 'Feminist praxis and the academic mode of production: an editorial introduction', in L. Stanley (ed.) *Feminist Praxis*, London: Routledge.

—— (1992) '*The Auto/biographical I: Theory and Practice of Feminist Auto/biography*, Manchester: Manchester University Press.

—— (1993) 'On auto/biography in sociology', *Sociology* 27, 1: 41–52.

—— (1997) 'Introduction: on academic borders, territories, tribes and knowledges', in L. Stanley (ed.) *Knowing Feminisms: On Academic Borders, Territories and Tribes*, London: Sage.

Stanley, L. and Morgan, D. (1993) 'Editorial introduction', *Sociology* 27, 1: 1–4.

Stanley, L. and Wise, S. (1990) 'Method, methodology and epistemology in feminist research processes,' in L. Stanley (ed.) *Feminist Praxis*, London: Routledge.

—— (1993) *Breaking Out Again: Feminist Ontology and Epistemology*, London: Routledge.

Stanworth, M. (1981) *Gender and Schooling: A Study of Sexual Divisions in the Classroom*, London: Hutchinson.

Steedman, C. (1990) *Childhood, Culture and Class in Britain: Margaret McMillan, 1860–1931*, New Brunswick, NJ: Rutgers University Press.

Stenhouse, L. (1975) *An Introduction to Curriculum Research and Development*, London: Heinemann.

Stone, L. (1993) 'Contingency: The "constancy of teaching"', *Teachers College Record* 94, 4: 815–35.

Strathern, M. (1987) 'An awkward relationship: the case of feminism and anthropology', *Signs* 12, 2: 276–91.

Stronach, I. and Maclure, M. (1997) *Educational Research Undone: The Postmodern Embrace*, Buckingham: Open University Press.

Sutherland, M. (1985) 'Whatever happened about co-education?', *British Journal of Educational Studies* 18, 2: 155–63.

Swann, J. and Graddol, D. (1994) 'Gender inequalities in classroom talk', in D. Graddol, J. Maybin and B. Stierer (eds) *Researching Language and Literacy in Social Context*, Clevedon: Multilingual Matters.

References

Swidler, A. (1978) *Organization Without Authority: Dilemmas of Social Control in Free Schools*, Cambridge, Mass.: Harvard University Press.

Tann, S. (1981) 'Grouping and group work', in B. Simon and J. Willcocks (eds) *Research and Practice in the Primary Classroom*, London: Routledge & Kegan Paul.

Tannen, D. (1991) *You Just Don't Understand: Women and Men in Conversation*, London: Virago.

Tartwijk, J. Van, Brekelmans, M., Wubbels, T., Fisher, D.L. and Fraser, B.J. (1998) 'Students' perceptions of teacher's interpersonal style: the front of the classroom as the teacher's stage', *Teaching and Teacher Education* 14, 6: 607–18.

Taylor, A. (1995) 'Glass ceilings and stone walls: employment equity for women in Ontario school boards', *Gender and Education* 7, 2: 123–42.

Tey, J. (1947) *Miss Pym Disposes*, London: Peter Davies.

Thomas, H. (1979) *History, Capitalism and Freedom*, London: Centre for Policy Studies.

Thomas, M. (1999) *Foreign Affaires*, Unpublished Ph.D. Thesis, University of Wales, Cardiff.

Thompson, B. (1989) 'Teacher attitudes: complacency and conflict', in C. Skelton (ed.) *Whatever Happens to Little Women?* Milton Keynes: Open University Press.

Thompson, P. (1988) *The Voice of the Past: Oral History*, London: Oxford University Press.

Thorne, B. (1992) 'Boys and girls together... but mostly apart', in J. Wrigley (ed.) *Education and Gender Equality*, London: Falmer Press.

—— (1993) *Gender Play: Girls and Boys in School*, Buckingham: Open University Press.

Thorne, B., Kramarae, C. and Henley, N. (1983) *Language, Gender and Society*, Rowley, Mass.: Newberry House.

Torres, C. (1997) 'In memory of Louise Spindler', *International Journal of Qualitative Studies in Education* 10, 4: 499.

Torrington, O. and Weightman, J. (1989) *The Reality of School Management*, Oxford: Blackwell.

TTA (1996a) *National Curriculum for Initial Teacher Training*, London: Teacher Training Agency.

—— (1996b) *A Strategic Plan for Teacher Supply and Recruitment*, London: Teacher Training Agency.

Tuckey, C. (1992) 'Who is a scientist? Children's drawings reveal all', *Education 3–13* 20: 30–2.

Turner, B. (1974) *Equality for Some*, London: Ward Lock.

Turner, E., Riddell, S. and Brown, S. (1995) *Gender Equality in Scottish Schools: The Impact of Recent Educational Reforms*, Glasgow: Equal Opportunities Commission.

Tyack, D. (1974) *The One Best System: A History of American Urban Education*, Cambridge, Mass.: Harvard University Press.

Valli, L. (1986) *Becoming Clerical Workers*, New York: Routledge & Kegan Paul.

—— (ed.) (1992) *Reflective Teaching Education: Cases and Critiques*, Albany: State University of New York Press.

Van Every, J. (1996) 'Sinking into his arms … arms in his sink: heterosexuality and feminism revisited,' in L. Adkins and V. Merchant (eds) *Sexualizing the Social: Power and the Organization of Sexuality*, London: Macmillan.

Vicinus, M. (1985) *Independent Women: Work and Community for Single Women, 1850–1920*, London: Virago.

Vincent, C. (1996) *Parents and Teachers: Power and Participation*, London: Falmer Press.

Wade, R.C. and Yarborough, D.B. (1996) 'Portfolios: a tool for reflective thinking in teacher education', *Teaching and Teacher Education* 12, 1: 63–79.

Walford, G. (1980) 'Sex bias in physics textbooks', *School Science Review* 62 (December): 220–7.

—— (1983) 'Girls in boys' public schools', *British Journal of Sociology of Education* 4, 1: 39–54.

Walford, G. and Miller, H. (1991) *City Technology Colleges*, Milton Keynes: Open University Press.

Walker, M. (1983) 'Control and consciousness in the college', *British Educational Research Journal* 9, 2: 129–40.

Walkerdine, V. (1988) *The Mastery of Reason: Cognitive Development and the Production of Rationality*, London and New York: Routledge.

—— (and the Girls and Mathematics Unit) (1989) *Counting Girls Out*, London: Virago.

—— (1990) *Schoolgirl Fictions*, London: Verso.

Walter, L. (1995) 'Feminism anthropology?' *Gender and Society* 9, 3: 272–88.

Warren, K.J. (1998) 'Recounting the future: the feminist challenge to the malestream curriculum', in G.E. Cohee, E. Daumer, T.D. Kemp, P.M. Krebs, S.A. Lafky and S. Runzo (eds) *The Feminist Teacher Anthology*, New York: Teachers College Press.

Webb, K. and Blond, J. (1995) 'Teacher knowledge: the relationship between caring and knowledge', *Teaching and Teacher Education* 11, 6: 611–25.

Weiler, K. (1988) *Women Teaching for Change*, New York: Bergin & Garvey.

—— (1991) 'Friere and feminist pedagogy of difference', *Harvard Educational Review*, 61, 4: 449–74.

Weiler, K. and Middleton, S. (eds) (1999) *Telling Women's Lives: Narrative Inquiries in the History of Women's Education*, Buckingham: Open University Press.

Weiner, G. (ed.) (1985) *Just a Bunch of Girls: Feminist Approaches to Schooling*, Milton Keynes; Open University Press.

—— (1989) 'Professional self-knowledge versus social justice: a critical analysis of the teacher-researcher movement', *British Educational Research Journal* 15, 1: 41–51.

—— (1993) 'Shell-shock or sisterhood: English School history and feminist practice', in M. Arnot and K. Weiler (eds) *Feminism and Social Justice in Education*, London: Falmer Press.

—— (1994) *Feminisms in Education: An Introduction*, Milton Keynes: Open University Press.

—— (1998) 'Review of I. Stronach and M. Maclure (1997) *Educational Research Undone*, Buckingham: Open University Press', *Gender and Education* 10, 4: 461–2.

Wells, J.H. (1985) 'Humberside goes neuter', in J. Whyte, R. Deem, L. Kant and M. Cruickshank, M (eds) *Girl-Friendly Schooling*, London: Methuen.

References

Whitehead, J., Menter, I. and Stainton, R. (1996) 'The reform of initial teacher training: the fragility of the new school-based approach and questions of quality', *Research Papers in Education* 11, 3: 307–22.

Whitty, G., Barton, L. and Pollard, A. (1987) 'Ideology and control in teacher education', in T. Popkewitz (ed.) *Critical Studies in Teacher Education*, Lewes: Falmer Press.

Whyte, J. (1986) *Girls into Science and Technology: The Story of a Project*, London: Routledge & Kegan Paul.

Whyte, J.B. (1987) 'Issues and dilemmas in action research', in G. Walford (ed.) *Doing Sociology of Education*, London: Falmer Press.

Whyte, J., Deem, R., Kant, L. and Cruickshank, M. (eds) (1988) *Girl-Friendly Schooling*, London: Methuen.

Widdowson, F. (1983) *Going Up into the Next Class: Women and Elementary Teacher Training 1840–1914*, London: Hutchinson.

Wilkinson, L.C. and Marrett, C.B. (eds) (1985) *Gender Influences in Classroom Interaction*, Orlando, Flo.: Academic Press.

Williamson, H. (1997) 'Youth work and citizenship', in J. Bynner, L. Chisholm and A. Furlong (eds) *Youth Citizenship and Social Change in a European Context*, Aldershot: Ashgate.

Wilson, E. (1980) *Only Half-Way to Paradise*, London: Tavistock.

Wilton, T. (1995) *Lesbian Studies: Setting an Agenda*, London: Routledge.

Witherall, K. and Noddings, N. (eds) (1991) *Narrative and Dialogue in Education*, New York: Teachers College Press.

Witz, A. (1992) *Professions and Patriarchy*, London: Routledge.

Wober, M. (1971) *English Girls' Boarding Schools*, London: Allen Lane.

Wolcott, H.F. (1967) *A Kwakiutl Village and School*, New York: Holt, Rinehart & Winston.

—— (1973) *The Man in the Principal's Office: An Ethnography*, New York: Holt Rinehart & Winston.

Wolf, M. (1992) *A Thrice Told Tale: Feminism, Postmodernism, and Ethnographic Responsibility*, Stanford, Calif.: Stanford University Press.

Wood, E. and Geddis, A.N. (1999) 'Self-conscious narrative and teacher education: representing practice in professional course work', *Teaching and Teacher Education* 15, 1: 107–120.

Woods, P. (1986) *Inside Schools: Ethnography in Educational Research*, London: Routledge & Kegan Paul.

—— (1990) *Teacher Skills and Strategies*, London: Routledge.

Woods, P. and Hammersley, M. (eds) (1993) *Gender and Ethnicity in Schools: Ethnographic Accounts*, London: Routledge.

Woody, T. (1929) *A History of Women's Education in the United States* (2 vols), reprinted 1966, New York: Octagon Books.

Wright, J. (1998) 'Lesbian instructor comes out: the personal is pedagogy', in G. E. Cohee, E. Daumer, T.D. Kemp, P.M. Krebs, S.A. Lafky and S. Runzo (eds) *The Feminist Teacher Anthology*, New York: Teachers College Press.

Wrigley, J. (ed.) (1992) *Education and Gender Equality*, London: Falmer Press.

Young, M.F.D. (1971) *Knowledge and Control: New Directions for the Sociology of Education*, London: Macmillan.

Zeichner, K.M. and Liston, D.P. (1987) 'Teaching students to reflect', *Harvard Educational Review* 57: 23–48.

Zimmern, A. (1898) *The Renaissance of Girls' Education in England*, London: Innes.

Index